Catherine Parr

Catherine Parr

ELIZABETH
NORTON

AMBERLEY

First published 2010

Amberley Publishing Plc
Cirencester Road, Chalford,
Stroud, Gloucestershire, GL6 8PE

www.amberley-books.com

Copyright © Elizabeth Norton, 2010

The right of Elizabeth Norton to be identified
as the Author of this work has been asserted in
accordance with the Copyrights, Designs and
Patents Act 1988.

ISBN 978 1 84868 582 6

British Library Cataloguing in Publication Data.
A catalogue record for this book is available
from the British Library.

Typeset in 10pt on 12pt Sabon.
Typesetting and Origination by FonthillMedia.
Printed in the UK.

CONTENTS

THE PARRS OF KENDAL:
1512 – 1523

The woman who would become the sixth, and last, queen of Henry VIII, was born into a prominent, but not royal, family and, during her childhood and early adulthood, Catherine Parr can never have dreamt of the future that lay in store for her. Until the last year of her life, she endured a life of duty, making three arranged marriages in order to ensure her family's position and her own status. She was the most reluctant of all Henry VIII's queens, but she was also one of the greatest and the roots of her good sense and ability to survive lay in her childhood.

Catherine Parr was the daughter of Sir Thomas Parr of Kendal and his wife, Matilda, or Maud, Green of Green's Norton in Northamptonshire. The Parrs' family seat was Kendal in Cumbria, in the north-west of England, and the castle still dominates the town with extensive views over the north and south-west. A survey of the castle was made in 1572 and it is possible to envisage what the castle would have been like in Catherine's time from this:

> The castle of Kendal is situate on the knowl of an hill, within the park there, and on the east side of the town, with a fair and beautiful prospect. The outer walls are embattled 40 feet square,

and within the same no building left, saving only to the north side is situate the front of the gate-house, the hall, with an ascent of stairs to the same, with a buttery and pantry at the end thereof; one great chamber and two or three lesser chambers, and rooms of ease adjoining the same, being all in decay, both in glass and slate, and in all other separation needful. Under the hall are two or three small rooms or cellars. In the south side is situate a dove cot in good repair.

In the early thirteenth century the castle belonged to Gilbert Fitz-Reinfred who married Helwise de Lancaster. The castle then passed to their son, William de Lancaster and, on his death, to his nephew Peter le Brus. When Peter's son died without issue the castle passed to his eldest sister, Margaret le Brus. Margaret's granddaughter, Elizabeth de Ross inherited the castle and lands associated with it and, in the late fourteenth century, married William de Parr, the first Parr to be associated with Kendal. On William's death in 1405 the castle and lands passed to his son, John Parr, who died only three years later. The lands and castle then continued to pass from father to son up to Catherine's time.

Catherine's ancestors had been associated with Kendal since the earliest records and, in the town and surrounding area, they were second only to the king. The Parrs rose steadily over the centuries and in 1396, for example, William de Parr was able to increase the family wealth through his purchase of a licence to buy corn in Ireland and ship it to England. William died wealthy in 1404 and the inquest taken at his death records that his lands in Kendal were worth £40 a year, a comfortable sum for the early fifteenth century. The family's lands were worth a high enough sum in 1413 for a kinsman, Thomas Tunstall, to purchase the wardship of the eight-year-old heir, Thomas de Parr, from the king for 200 marks in order to marry him to his daughter. Thomas de Parr died in 1464 leaving lands worth 100 marks a year to his son, Catherine's grandfather, William Parr.

While the Parrs had steadily increased their status and wealth over the years, it was Catherine's grandfather, William, who brought the family to national prominence. William Parr was a close associate of King Edward IV, and, in 1475, accompanied the king on his campaign in France. Edward IV also made his friend a knight of the Garter and controller of his household and it is doubtless through the king's influence that William was able to make an advantageous marriage with Elizabeth, daughter and co-heiress of Lord Fitzhugh. This was a particularly prestigious match and it was through Elizabeth that Catherine could claim royal blood as a descendant of Edward III. William did not long survive his marriage, dying in 1483 and leaving his widow to raise two young sons, Thomas, who was Catherine's father and the heir to the family, and William. Elizabeth Fitzhugh further secured the fortunes of the family in the difficult years at the end of the Wars of the Roses by marrying the Lancastrian, Sir Nicholas Vaux of Harrowden in Northamptonshire soon after she was widowed. Vaux was a fond stepfather for his wife's two sons and his support for the Lancastrian cause, coupled with Elizabeth Fitzhugh's connections with Margaret Beaufort, the mother of Henry VII, secured the family's survival on the accession of the first Tudor king in 1485.

Elizabeth Fitzhugh died in 1507 and Sir Nicholas Vaux set about looking for opportunities for himself and his elder stepson. The two men's interest fell on the young sisters, Anne and Matilda, or Maud, Green, the heiresses of a neighbouring landowner, Sir

Thomas Green of Green's Norton. In 1507 Thomas Parr was twenty-nine years old and his stepfather considerably older but both married the teenage sisters, with Vaux taking Anne, the elder sister, and Thomas the younger, Maud. Sir Thomas Green had died in 1506 leaving his daughters wealthy. Both marriages were happy and the two couples remained close to each other with the Parrs residing in Northamptonshire when they were not at court.

The Parr's eldest child, a son, did not long survive his birth but, in 1512, Maud gave birth to her second child, a girl whom she named Catherine, after the queen, Catherine of Aragon. The date of Catherine's birth is nowhere recorded and the place itself is hotly debated. Traditionally, it has always been supposed that Catherine was born at Kendal Castle. Thomas Parr's royal duties did take him to the north of England from time to time but, by 1512, he had long since ceased to see Kendal as his home and both he and Maud favoured their house in Blackfriars and Maud's own estates in Northamptonshire. Catherine was almost certainly born in one of these two locations rather than the semi-derelict Kendal Castle and it is unlikely that she ever had cause to visit her ancestral home. Catherine's birth was followed by that of a younger brother, William, in 1513 and a sister, Anne, in 1515. Maud was pregnant at the time of her husband's death although no records for this child exist and it must have died either before birth or soon afterwards.

Catherine's early childhood was mainly spent at her parents' house at Blackfriars as it was crucial for both her parents that they remained close to London. Thomas Parr did not find particular favour with Henry VII, but on the accession of Henry's son, Henry VIII in 1509 he became a fixture at the court. This increasing prominence can be seen first in Thomas's appointment as one of the

Squires of the Body at the funeral of Henry VII. Three months later Thomas performed the same office at the coronation of the new king and, as a significant honour, the day before the coronation he was dubbed a Knight of the Bath. Thomas Parr was in high favour with the new king from the very beginning of the reign and it is telling that Sir Thomas Boleyn, the father of Anne Boleyn, was also a Squire of the Body at both occasions and dubbed a Knight of the Bath, but that his name featured less prominently in the lists than the more favoured Thomas Parr. This occurred again in June 1513 when both Thomas Parr and his stepfather attended the king on his campaigns in France. Both men were listed higher in accounts of the campaign than Sir Thomas Boleyn and Sir John Seymour, the father of Henry's third wife, Jane Seymour. Thomas was of identical rank to the other two men but the Parrs, and Thomas's maternal family, the Fitzhughs, were well established and Catherine's family had closer ties to the court and king than some of Henry's other English wives.

Both Catherine's parents and the Vauxs lived well beyond their means and, by the death of Henry VII in 1509, they had incurred enormous debts owing to the Crown. The reason for these debts is nowhere recorded and they may have included arrears due on the wardships of Anne and Maud Green, something indicated by the inclusion of the two sisters as debtors to the Crown. They were vast sums and it would have been nearly impossible for either family to pay them off. This was recognized by the king and, in recognition of his friendship for both Thomas and Vaux, in October 1509 he cancelled the first of the debts, recording that he had agreed to release 9,000 marks owing to the Crown.

Henry VIII recognized that the debts incurred by the nobility and gentry to his father were excessive and his forgiveness of the debts owed by the Vauxs and the Parrs were part of a wider policy of conciliation with his nobility. In a note of his policy in 1509 it was recorded that:

> Hereafter ensue divers recognizances and other weighty matters drawn by our special commandment out of divers books signed with the hand of our dearest father, to rest of remembrance in this present book, to the intent it may appear to us hereafter how favourable and benevolent sovereign lord we have been unto divers our nobles and other our subjects, in discharge and pardoning of many and sundry of the same weighty causes, whereby they stand the more especially bounden unto us, and therefore truly and faithfully to serve us according to their duties, when and as oft as the case necessarily shall require; and to the end, also, that the remainant of these matters and causes following, being not discharged, be put in respite and suspense till our mind and pleasure be further known in that behalf.

The following year Thomas Parr and his stepfather were released from a further debt of 6,550 marks owed to the king, the remainder of an original sum of 7,000 marks. In March 1513 a further, and final, debt of 9,000 marks was pardoned, of which only 2,450 had been paid.

During the years of Catherine's early childhood, both her parents remained in high favour, with the couple receiving in November 1510, for example, the grant of a manor from the king. They received a grant of a number of other castles and manors in both Northampton and Oxfordshire in March 1516. In January 1512 Thomas's prestige was further improved with the death of his cousin, Lord Fitzhugh of Ravensworth. Thomas received half of the extensive Fitzhugh estates and the king also considered granting the title of Lord Fitzhugh to Catherine's father although he was dissuaded by the concern that:

> Lord Dacre is the son and heir of the elder sister, one of the heirs of Lord Fitzhugh, dec. To give the name to the heir of the younger daughter would be a dishonour to him. The pre-eminence growing, by law, to the elder daughter's heirs for presentment and advowsons, & c. by that name and dignity given to the heirs of the younger should be lost and men think that Sir Thomas Parre descended of the elder sister.

Thomas Parr never did receive his peerage, but he remained in favour and, in April 1516, was chosen to travel to Newcastle to meet Henry's sister, Margaret, Queen of Scotland, and escort her south. He remained prominent in her retinue and led her through Cheapside for her official reception in London, taking her to her lodgings at Baynard's Castle. Honours continued to be steadily passed to Thomas Parr and he was appointed as a sheriff of Warwickshire and Leicestershire for several years in a row. He was also proposed as a knight of the Garter although this was ultimately denied him.

Catherine's family was on the rise and it was a great shock when, in November 1517, Thomas died of the plague. He had time to prepare his Will on 7 November, recording that Maud was to receive the income from some of his manors for life. Thomas also left the sum of £800 'which sum I will to be equally divided between my daughters Kateryn and Anne towards their marriage', before bequeathing the remainder of his estates to William, his heir. Catherine was around five years old at the time of her father's death and is unlikely to have had many memories of him, though the death had a profound effect on her childhood and her life.

As a wealthy widow, Maud Parr was expected to remarry in order to ensure that her young family had a male protector. Maud however, was an independent and spirited woman and completely dismissed this route, instead choosing to pursue her own court career, just as she had done during her marriage. Maud was held in high regard by Henry VIII's first wife, Catherine of Aragon, and, in her widowhood, she secured a prestigious and lucrative position at court as one of the queen's ladies. In October 1519 Maud was recorded as one of a privileged group of ladies granted a permanent room at court. She was listed again as a member of the court the following month and the next year was chosen to accompany the queen to Calais to attend the most spectacular event of Henry's reign, the Field of the Cloth of Gold. Maud was also friendly with the king and, in 1530, made him a gift of a coat of Kendal cloth. Maud was still listed as having had lodgings at court in January 1526 and, with only five other ladies, including the king's own sister, was given the honour and privilege of a permanent suite of rooms. Maud was rarely at home during the early years of her widowhood although she maintained her own separate establishment in which her children resided.

It has been suggested by a number of historians that Catherine, given her privileged position as the daughter of one of the queen's closest friends, might have been selected to share the education of Catherine of Aragon's daughter, Princess Mary. There is no evidence for this and, given the four year age gap between the two girls, it is unlikely that Catherine was ever considered a suitable schoolmate for the younger princess. In any event, there is evidence that Maud herself oversaw the education of her children. According to a kinsman of the Parrs, Lord Dacre, writing to his son-in-law, Lord Scrope, the younger peer was well advised to consider sending his son to live in Maud's household 'for I assure you he might lerne wt her as well as yn any place that I knowe, as well nature, as Frenche and other language, whiche me semes were a commodious thinge'. No specific details survive of the education given to Catherine and her younger siblings. This has led to a great deal of speculation over just how extensive it was. In a letter to Catherine in 1546, Prince Edward commented:

Although all your letters are sweet to me, yet these last were pleasing beyond the rest, most noble queen and most kind mother, for which I return you exceeding thanks. But truly by these I perceive that you have give your attention to the Roman characters, so that my preceptor could not be persuaded but that your secretary wrote them, till he observed your name written equally well. I also was much surprised, I hear too, that your highness is progressing in the Latin tongue and in the Belles Lettres. Wherefore I feel no little joy, for letters are lasting, but other things that seem so perish.

Edward's letter seems to suggest that Catherine's education had been lacking and that she had been taught neither Latin nor fine handwriting. This is further suggested in a letter by Catherine herself, written in English in response to a Latin missive sent by the University of Cambridge. In her letter, Catherine reprimanded the university for writing in Latin saying 'and as they be Latynely written, (which ys so signified unto me by those that be lernyd in the Latyne tongue,) so I know you could have utteryd your desires and opinions familiarly in our vulgar tonge, aptyst for my intelligence'. Again, this has been taken to suggest that Catherine was ignorant of Latin. Edward's letter however might just as well refer to a translation project that Catherine was working on than a study of the language itself and Catherine's own letter may show false modesty. There is evidence to suggest that Catherine received a good education, not least the fact that Lord Dacre believed that an education with Maud would be advantageous for his grandson.

Catherine learned French during her childhood and, as queen, she spoke fluently with ambassadors in this language. A letter from Princess Elizabeth to Catherine in 1544, seeking Catherine's assessment of a translation work produced by the princess from French to English, also demonstrates the queen's known familiarity with the language. According to Elizabeth:

> And although I know that, as for my part which I have wrought in it (as well spiritual as manual), there is nothing done as it should be, nor else worthy to come in your grace's hands, but rather all imperfect and inconvenient, yet do I trust also that, howbeit it is like a work which is but new begun and shapen, that the file of your excellent wit and godly learning, in the reading of it (if so it vouchsafe for your highness to do), shall rub out, polish, and mend (or else cause to mend), the words (or rather the order of my writing), the which I know, in many places, to be rude, and nothing done as it should be. But I hope that, after to have been in your grace's hands, there shall be nothing in it worthy of reprehension.

There is evidence from Catherine's own writings that she read and understood Latin and it appears that she also knew some Greek and Italian, as well as having an interest in Spanish. Maud devoted herself to her children's futures.

While Catherine was the eldest child, William, as the son, was the focus of his mother's hopes. In the summer of 1525 the king's six-year-old illegitimate son, Henry Fitzroy, Duke of Richmond, was given his own household and set out in some style on the long journey north to Sheriff Hutton where his establishment was to be based. Catherine's uncle, Thomas Parr's younger brother, Sir William Parr of Horton, was given the highly desirable post of Chamberlain to young Richmond and it was due to his influence that, on 26 July 1525, Richmond spent a night at Maud's household to break his journey to the north. The Parrs made a good impression and, when the procession left to move north, young William joined the train to become a member of the Duke's household.

In 1525, when William left to join the Duke of Richmond, Catherine was aged around thirteen. She was of medium height, with her coffin measuring only five foot four inches from top to bottom. She was no particular beauty and, in later life, Henry VIII's famously ill-favoured wife, Anne of Cleves, was able to comment without contradiction that she was much more beautiful than Catherine. In spite of this Catherine, with her auburn hair and pale skin was pretty enough and she was later described as having 'a lively and pleasing appearance'. There is some evidence that she had a high opinion of herself and one story claims that:

Shee was told by an astrologer that did calculate her nativitie, that she was borne to sett in the highest of Imperiall majestie: which became moste true. She had all the eminent stars and planets in her house: this did worke such a loftie conceite in her that her mother could nevver make her serve or doe any small worke, saying her hands were ordained to touch crownes and sceptres, not needles and thymbles.

The future foreseen for Catherine is too close to what she actually became for the story to be believable. It is certain that Maud hoped that her daughter would have a bright future as the wife of a great nobleman. Even before William left the household in 1525, Maud had begun to consider Catherine's future.

2

MISTRESS BURGH OF GAINSBOROUGH OLD HALL: 1523 – SPRING 1533

Catherine's ambitious mother expended considerable energies in ensuring that her children married well. In spite of this, the arrangements for Catherine's first marriage were not easily concluded.

Maud first turned her attentions to her elder daughter's marriage in 1523, when Catherine was eleven. Maud already had a potential husband in mind for Catherine and, during a meeting with her kinsman, Lord Dacre, at Greenwich she broached the subject of a marriage between Catherine and Lord Dacre's grandson, the teenaged heir of Lord Scrope of Bolton. Catherine's intended husband, Henry Scrope, came from a good family and it was an excellent match for Catherine. Armed with Lord Dacre's agreement, Maud wrote to Lord Scrope, confident that he would also approve the match. It was therefore a great shock when she received his response, as she wrote to complain to Lord Dacre himself. According to Maud:

Most honourable and my very good lord, I heartly rec'mend me vnto you. Where it pleased you att your last being here to take payn in the mater in consideracion of marriage between the Lord

Scrop's son and my doughtor Kateryn, for the whiche I hertly thank you; at which time I thought the matter in good furtherance. Howe bee yt, I perceive that my said Lord Scrop is nott agrreable to that consideracyon, as more plainly may appere vnto you by certeyn articles sent to me from my seyd lord; the coppy of which articles I send you herein inclosyd. My lord's pleasour is to have a full answere from me before La'mas next coming, wherefore it may please you to bee so good to have this matter in your remembraunce, for I perceive well this matter is not lyke to take effecte except it be by your helpe.

Lord Scrope made it plain to Maud that he was not happy with the marriage, surprising her with a list of articles that she would have to agree to if negotiations were to progress. This list survives and demonstrates the unreasonable nature of Lord Scrope's requirements in which he demanded a considerable dowry to be paid directly to himself. Maud was outraged and complained to Lord Dacre that the amount was too high and that the jointure offered by Lord Scrope for Catherine in the event that she was widowed was too small. She was also nonplussed when, unusually, Lord Scrope insisted that, in the event of Catherine's death before the marriage was solemnized or consummated, he would repay none of her dowry. She complained:

ther can be no p'fyte marriage vntill my lord's son com to the age of xiiii, and my doughter to the age of xii, before whiche tyme if the marriage shuld take none effect, or be dissolved either by deth, wardshipp, disagreement, or otherwise, whiche may bee before thatt tyme, notwithstondine marriage solemysed, repayment must need be hadd of the hole, or ells I might fortune to pay my money for nothinge.

Lord Dacre was embarrassed at Lord Scrope's abandonment of the terms that he had already agreed with Maud and wrote to inform her that:

> I do think, seing my Lord Scrope cannot be contente wt the communicac'ons that was had at my last being wt you, whiche was thought reasonable to me, and as I perceve semblably to his counsel, that this matter cannot be brought to no p'fite end w'out mutuall communication to be had with my said lord, aither by my self, my son, or my brother. Wherfore, as sone as conveniently any of us may be spared this matter shal be laboured, trusting verily that I shall bringe it to a good pointe, and as I shal do therein ye shal be advertised at length.

He added further that it was within his power to help arrange the marriage as 'I have the promise of my said lord, and of my doughter, his wif, that they shal not marie their son w'out my consent, which they shall not have to no p'son but vnto youe'. He confided that Lord Scrope was desperately short of money and that he had hoped to sell his son to the highest bidder. Lord Dacre counselled patience assuring Maud that 'I shall doo in this matter, or in any other that is or may be aither pleasure, profitte, or suyrtie, to you or my said cousin, yor daughter, that hath in my power.'

Lord Scrope was considerably less favourable to the marriage and he resented his father-in-law's interference. Certainly, he treated Maud rudely and, as she confided in a letter to Lord Dacre of 12 August, he told her servant that 'he wold no longer drive tyme in that matter with me, but he would be at large and take his best advantage as with the lord treasurer, whiche had made moc'ons to be in communicac'on with him'. Informed of this by Maud, Lord

Dacre immediately wrote to his son-in-law in an attempt to turn him towards the match with Catherine. According to Lord Dacre:

> My lorde, your son and heire, is the gretest jewell that ye can have, seeing that he must present your own p'son after your deth, vnto whome I pray God lend long years. And yf ye be disposyd to marie, him, or he be com to full age, when he may have som [blank] hym self, I cannot see, w'ont that ye wold marry him to one heire of land, which wolbe right costly, that ye can mary hym to so good a stok as my lady Parr, for divers considerations, first, in remembering the wisdom of my seid lady, and the god wise stok of the Grenes whereof she is comen, and also of the wise stok of the Pars of Kendale, for al whiche men doo looke when they do mary their child, to the wisedome of the blood of that they do marry wt. I speke not of the possibilities of my lady Parr's daughter, who has but one child between her, and viiic [800] marcs land to inherit therof. Such possibilities doth oftyntymes fall, and I speke it because of the possibilitie that befelle vnto myself by my marriage, and therefor, in myn opinion, the same is to be regarded.

After pointing out the many advantages to the marriage, Lord Dacre turned to Lord Scrope's demands, advising his son-in-law to be guided by what was commonly agreed for such a marriage.

Lord Scrope refused to move on his demands, in spite of his father-in-law's pressure, and there was a clear power struggle between the two men with Lord Dacre adamant that the marriage would go ahead and Lord Scrope equally adamant that it would not. Catherine was caught in the middle of this and, by March, nearly a year after the negotiations had begun, Maud had finally had enough, writing to Lord Dacre to inform him that, on the advice of her late husband's kinsman and executor, Cuthbert Tunstall, Bishop of London, and other friends, she had decided to seek a husband for Catherine elsewhere. Maud, intent on keeping Lord Dacre's friendship assured him that, for her own part, there was no marriage for Catherine that 'I wold have beyn so glad shuld have goon forward as this, or ells I wold not have made so large offers for the forderaunce of the same as I have'. Lord Dacre was however far from happy and he wrote back to Maud, complaining of his surprise and sadness at the decision to which she had come. Catherine may, in any event, have been well out of the match and young Henry Scrope did not long survive his aborted marriage negotiations, just as Maud feared in the wrangling over the dowry and jointure.

With no immediate replacement as a husband for Catherine, Maud turned her attentions towards William. Maud had made an ambitious choice for Catherine but, for her only son, she was prepared to reach far above what could be expected for his marriage. By 1526 it was clear that the Earl of Essex, who was both elderly and in ill health, would have no sons and that his only child, Anne Bourchier, would inherit his vast estates. Anne Bourchier's husband would also have been the most likely candidate to receive the earldom of Essex after his father-in-law's death and, as such, she was the most sought after heiress in England. Emboldened by her close relationship with the royal family and her own ambition, Maud was determined to secure Anne Bourchier for her son and, with an enormous outlay of capital that plunged her into debt and impoverished her, she was successful, with the marriage between the thirteen-year-old William and ten-year-old Anne being solemnized in February 1527. William was immediately taken into his father-in-law's household and the marriage was the fulfilment of Maud's dearest hopes, unaware as she was just how ill-matched the couple were and the disaster the marriage would become.

Although Maud had originally had grand hopes for Catherine in the Scrope marriage, by 1527 or 1528 she was forced to lower her standards considerably. With the debts incurred for William's marriage, Maud had little more to offer than the £400 left to Catherine in her father's Will and this was not enough to attract a high-profile suitor. She once again turned to family connections and, by early 1529 at the latest a marriage had been arranged and solemnized between Catherine and Edward Burgh, or Borough, the eldest son of Sir Thomas Burgh of Gainsborough Old Hall in Lincolnshire. Catherine's thoughts on the marriage are not recorded but Lincolnshire must have seemed impossibly distant as she set out for her new home.

For centuries there has been confusion over just who Catherine's husband actually was, with a number of historians claiming that, far from marrying Edward Burgh the younger, Catherine was forced to become a child bride for his elderly grandfather, Edward, Lord Burgh. Edward, Lord Burgh, had inherited his peerage from his father, the first Lord Burgh in 1496 when he was thirty-two years old. He married the heiress Anne Cobham in 1477 and the couple enjoyed a long and fruitful marriage before Anne's death in June 1526. In 1510 Lord Burgh was found to be a lunatic and 'distracted in memorie'. Insanity was unfortunately frequent in the Burgh family and, by the time of Catherine's arrival at Gainsborough in the late 1520s, the elderly Lord Burgh had spent a considerable amount of time under the guardianship of his eldest son, Sir Thomas Burgh. While Edward, Lord Burgh, has been commonly identified as Catherine's first husband it is impossible for this to be the case. Maud was a fond mother and there is no possibility that she would have consented to sending her teenaged daughter to be the wife of a diagnosed lunatic, well advanced in years and with a mature family of his own, even for the sake of a title for Catherine. Lord Burgh's family also had no reason to permit the match and, by the late 1520s, he was the father of adult children and his line was secure. The introduction of an unnecessary second wife would have been entirely illogical and, given the poor state of his health by the late 1520s, merely an expense when the inevitable happened and Catherine was left a widow. The confusion lies in the fact that Edward Burgh, Catherine's young husband, was given the same name as his grandfather and is a shadowy figure himself, but there can be no doubt that it was the younger man that Catherine married and not the elder. She is unlikely to have had much contact with her husband's grandfather who died in late 1528, either before or soon after her arrival in Lincolnshire.

Catherine travelled north to Lincolnshire soon after the marriage negotiations were completed in 1527 or 1528. The Burgh's family seat was Gainsborough Old Hall, an attractive and prominent building that still stands. The Hall was built in the fifteenth century by Catherine's husband's great-grandfather and a visit today shows it decorated in the style that it would have had at the end of the fifteenth century, only a few years before Catherine took up residence there. It must have seemed uncomfortably crowded with three generations of the family living in the same building and, from the first, Catherine was well aware that the dominant force in the family was her father-in-law, Sir Thomas Burgh.

Little is known about Catherine's husband, Edward Burgh. By the time of his marriage to Catherine he was in his twenties although there is no evidence that he had established a separate residence from his parents when his bride arrived. It has been suggested that he was in poor health, and his early death could point to this. However, there is evidence that his father had begun to prepare him for his future as head of the family, for example, in December 1530 surrendering the office of steward of the manor of Kirton Lyndsey and securing a new grant in the joint names of himself and his son. Clearly Edward was considered by his father to be fit and able enough to take a role in local affairs and, in December 1532, shortly before his death, he was also made a commissioner of the peace with his father for the Lindsey area in Lincolnshire. Coming as it did shortly before his death, this grant suggests that Edward's death was due to a short and sudden illness rather than any long-standing condition. There is no evidence that Catherine and Edward did not live together as man and wife and the absence of any child or recorded pregnancy in Catherine is likely to be attributable to her notoriously low fertility rather than to any inadequacy on Edward Burgh's part. Maud Parr would also have made enquiries before arranging the match to ensure that Edward was healthy and likely to live.

Both Edward and Catherine were dominated by his father, Sir Thomas Burgh. Sir Thomas, who assumed the title of Lord Burgh on his father's death, was a powerful personality, even going so far as to throw another daughter-in-law out of his house some time after Catherine left the household. By the time that Catherine arrived at Gainsborough, Thomas was aged around forty and he was already a prominent figure in local politics. In both 1517 and 1518 he was appointed as one of the three sheriffs of Lincolnshire, an appointment that was repeated in 1524. Thomas's wife, as mistress of the house, was given the governance of Catherine on her arrival at Gainsborough and the older woman set about teaching Catherine the skills that she needed to run her own household in due course. However, it was always Sir Thomas Burgh who was in overall control at the Hall.

As well as local interests, Sir Thomas spent time at the court in London. Like Catherine's own father, he had been appointed as one of the Squires for the Body at the funeral of Henry VII in 1509 and the two men may well have been acquainted. He was obviously in some favour with the king and was appointed as one of the gentlemen sent to ensure the safety of Berwick during the war with Scotland in 1513. Sir Thomas was a well-known adherent to the religious reform movement, which supported the break with Rome. His support for the reform can be seen in his behaviour during the Pilgrimage of Grace, a conservative uprising. The uprising against Henry VIII broke out on 1 October 1536 at Louth in Lincolnshire amid rumours of further changes to be made to the traditional Church. Unaware of this unrest, on 3 October according to a letter written by Sir Thomas himself to the king:

Sir William Askew, and other your grace's commissioners of your subsidy appointed to sit at Caster this Tuesday, requiring me, Sir Robert Tyrwhytt, and others, to be with them; suddenly came there a great multitude of people from Loweth, and was within a mile of us. Thereupon the inhabilants made us a direct answer that they would pay no more silver, and caused the bells to be rung a larome. There was no remedy but to return to our horses, and the people so fast pursued that they have taken Sir Robert Tyrwytt, Sir William Askew, Thomas Portyngton, Sir Thomas Messendyn, Thomas Mourne, with other gentlemen, I hear the commonalty increase to them and I fear will do more, because they have taken the gentlemen who have the governance in these parts under your highness.

Burgh was able to escape only 'by reason of a good horse'. The rebels wanted noblemen as their captains but Burgh was anxious to resist them, even when he received a message from the rebels informing him that he must either become their captain 'or else they would pull him out of his house at Gaynsburrowe'. Rather than submit, Burgh fled his house in spite of threats that it would be burned down if he was found to be absent. Catherine had long since left Sir Thomas's household and family by the Pilgrimage of Grace, but his determination to escape the rebels when many of the gentry and nobility agreed, albeit under duress, to become leaders of the rebellion, is testament to his fierce religious principals. These were already clear by the time of Catherine's arrival at Gainsborough.

Sir Thomas Burgh's religious beliefs brought him into contact with Henry VIII's second wife, Anne Boleyn, who also had a great interest in reform and, at her marriage to the king in early 1533, he was appointed as her Lord Chamberlain, appearing prominently at great occasions such as the queen's coronation and the baptism of Princess Elizabeth. He was also an avid partisan of the reforming queen and took it upon himself to receive, and punish, reports of slander and disloyalty against her. One such report that reached him was in October 1533 when:

> Robert Borett, late of London, did rail upon the queen and my lord of Canterbury. These words he has confessed before Sir John Waynwright, vicar of Norton, Oliver Makineson, and others. He said, in the presence of Waynwright and John Cowke, that the queen was a churl's daughter, and also that she was a whore.

In May 1533, he was also personally rebuked by the king for appropriating the barge of Henry's first wife, Catherine of Aragon, for the new queen, stripping it of the old queen's banners and mutilating the arms of Spain. Sir Thomas Burgh was a powerful character and, as the first supporter of the religious reform that Catherine came into close contact with, he had a powerful effect on her own religious beliefs.

Maud Parr was entirely conservative in her religious faith and Catherine was raised as a Catholic, as was everyone of her generation. At some point during her early life, Catherine turned towards the religious reform and, while there is no evidence of when this occurred, the likelihood is that it was due to the influence of Sir Thomas Burgh during Catherine's time at Gainsborough. While Lincolnshire was, for the most part, religiously conservative, there was a reform movement working in the county and a neighbour, Anne Askew, who lived thirty miles from Gainsborough, later became a prominent reformer, having certainly acquired her beliefs in Lincolnshire.

In later life, Catherine provided her own account of her conversion to the reformed faith. Unfortunately, she gives no details to allow her conversion to be safely linked to any one period in her life but, in the absence of any later reformist influence as strong-willed as Sir Thomas Burgh's, at least until she became queen, it is likely that it refers to the period of her first marriage, when Catherine was young, impressionable and homesick. According to Catherine:

When I consider, in the bethinking of mine evil and wretched former life, mine obstinate, stony and intractable heart, to have so much exceeded in evilness, that it hath not only neglected, yea, contemned, and despised God's holy precepts and commandments; but, also embraced, received, and esteemed, vain, foolish, and feigned trifles, I am partly, by the hate I owe to sin, which hath reigned in me, and partly, by the love I owe to all Christians, whom I am content to edify, even, with the example of mine own shame, forced, and constrained, with my heart and words, to confess and declare to the world, how ingrate, negligent, unkind and stubborn, I have been to God my Creator, and how beneficial, merciful, and gentle, he hath been always to me his creature, being such a miserable and wretched sinner.

Catherine's conversion was an intensely powerful and personal experience and it is easy to see how she, as a girl, forced to move away from her own home and join a family far removed from her own, could have come to absorb the new religious teaching that she encountered there. Catherine soon bewailed her former beliefs, declaring later that she 'loved darkness better than light, yea, darkness seemed to me light. I embraced ignorance, as perfect knowledge, and knowledge seemed to me superfluous and vain'. Catherine lamented her earlier reliance on superstition and idolatry, claiming:

I could not think, but that I walked in the perfect and right way, having more regard to the number of walkers, than to the order of the walking; believing also, most assuredly, with company, to have walked to heaven, whereas, I am sure, they would have brought me down to hell.

For Catherine, her time at Gainsborough was a time of religious revelation and she never wavered in her new beliefs.

There is no evidence that Catherine was unhappy during her time at Gainsborough and she used the time of her first marriage to develop as a person. If Catherine's devotion to the religious reform was to be long-lasting however, this was more than could be said for her first marriage. Edward Burgh was still alive and apparently in good health in December 1532 when he is last recorded in the records. By the following spring, he was dead. Edward's death severed Catherine's links with the Burgh family and, with only a small pension to support herself, she was left to make her own way.

3

LADY LATIMER OF SNAPE CASTLE: SPRING 1533 – SEPTEMBER 1536

Arranging Catherine's marriage to Edward Burgh was the last major action that Maud Parr, in her devotion to her children, carried out. While Catherine was still living with her first husband, she received the shocking news that her mother had died early in December 1531. This was a major blow to Catherine and, in early 1533, she was very aware that she no longer had a home to return to.

By early 1533 both Catherine's brother and sister, William and Anne, were busy establishing themselves in the world. As the son-in-law of the Earl of Essex, William presented a figure of some prominence at court and, as the years went by, he was more frequently there, enjoying the entertainments and opportunities on offer. In June 1536, for example, just over three years after Catherine was widowed, he attended the marriage in the king's chapel at Westminster of Lord William Howard, the son of the late Duke of Norfolk. This marriage was a grand occasion and, after the service, William, along with a number of other young gentlemen of the court, jousted at the tilt, to the delight of the onlookers. By 1533 William Parr was fast making a name for himself at court.

Anne Parr also secured a place for herself with the queen, presumably using her mother's influence and she also quickly became prominent among the queen's ladies, serving all of Henry's last five wives. In 1538, for example, she is recorded as having received a gift of a French hood from another young lady living near the court and, by mid 1537, there were rumours that she was imminently to marry, again indicating that she was a figure of enough standing to attract gossip. It is likely that Catherine initially looked to her brother and sister in 1533 in the hope of securing a similar court position for herself. If she did, she was to be disappointed as, by April 1533, Anne Boleyn already had a full complement of ladies, appearing as queen for the first time publicly at Easter accompanied by a great train of ladies to reflect her new position. Catherine had to look elsewhere for somewhere to stay while she considered her future.

No direct evidence for Catherine's whereabouts during her first widowhood survives. A family legend among the Strickland family of Sizergh Castle in Cumbria claims that Catherine spent her time as a guest of the family there. Sizergh Castle was close to the Parr's ancestral home of Kendal and the two families were related, with Katherine de Strickland, a daughter of the Sizergh family, marrying John de Ros back in the fourteenth century. It was their daughter, Elizabeth, who married William de Parr and passed Kendal into the Parr family and the two families maintained their links over the succeeding generations. By 1533 the castle was occupied by Catherine Neville, the widow both of Sir Walter Strickland and Henry Burgh, the uncle of Catherine's first husband. Catherine herself was distantly related to Catherine Neville and the Burgh family connection was a further link. It is therefore plausible to assume that Catherine Neville, on being informed of young Edward Burgh's death, extended an invitation to his young widow to come and spend some time with her at Sizergh. For Catherine, this was the opportunity she needed to end her time as an unwanted burden on her first husband's family.

Sizergh Castle still stands today. Again, it must be stressed, that Catherine cannot be placed with certainty at Sizergh during 1533 but it is a likely location for her. According to legend, Catherine spent her time at Sizergh carrying out traditional female pursuits such as embroidery and two fine works of embroidery are said to have been made by her during this period. One, a counterpane, was worked in white satin with an elaborate design of a central medallion surrounded by wreaths of flowers, as well as a crowned eagle and monstrous beasts, all worked in fine, and expensive colours, including purple, crimson and gold. It seems improbable that Catherine, during the short time that she was at Sizergh, if she was there at all, could have completed this fine and elaborate work herself but it is not unreasonable to suggest that she may have assisted in the work during her stay because, as well as the fine education she received with her mother, she would also have been taught traditional female pursuits such as needlework.

Another reason for giving credence to the legend that Catherine spent her first widowhood at Sizergh Castle is that it placed her in exactly the right position to arrange her second marriage to John Neville, Baron Latimer, of Snape Castle in Yorkshire. Latimer had a London house at the Charterhouse but he spent most of his time on his family lands in Yorkshire, ensuring that he was conveniently close to Catherine at Sizergh Castle. With the death of her first husband, Catherine knew that her future lay in a rapid second marriage. Latimer, as a kinsman of Catherine Neville, would have been welcome to visit the castle in order to view Catherine for himself. He was also an associate of Catherine's kinsman, Cuthbert Tunstall, formerly Bishop of London and, by 1533, Bishop of

Durham, who had acted as one of her father's executors and felt a sense of responsibility towards both Maud Parr and her children. In 1530, for example, Tunstall received a commission from the king asking him to lead the Council of the North, a body in which Latimer's father, Richard Neville, Lord Latimer, was also a member. Cuthbert Tunstall may first have suggested the match to both Catherine and Latimer as a suitable one and, following a visit from the peer to Catherine at Sizergh, both parties were quickly in agreement.

The date of Catherine's second marriage, to John Neville, Lord Latimer, does not survive, but it was certainly before the end of 1533 and within only a few months of her first husband's death. In the sixteenth century such a rapid remarriage was not in any way uncommon and Catherine, who was both an orphan and virtually penniless, leapt at the opportunity of the second marriage offered to her. For Catherine, a marriage to Lord Latimer was a step up socially from her first marriage. The first Lord Latimer, George Neville, had received his title in 1432. George Neville was a younger son of the Earl of Westmorland by Joan Beaufort, a granddaughter of Edward III. He was also an uncle of the famous Warwick the Kingmaker and the Latimer family moved in the highest circles. In 1469, Richard Neville, the grandson of the first Lord Latimer succeeded to the title and he continued to increase the family's prestige, taking part in numerous royal occasions, such as attending the ceremony at Westminster Abbey in 1515 when the king's chief minister, Thomas Wolsey, received his cardinal's hat. He was deemed to be of sufficient status to sign an official appeal, along with a number of other leading noblemen, requesting that the Pope grant Henry VIII his divorce from Catherine of Aragon. The second Lord Latimer was succeeded by his eldest son, John Neville, in 1530.

Catherine's second husband was born on 17 November 1493 and was thirty-six when he succeeded his father. This was a fairly advanced age in which to inherit a peerage in the sixteenth century and Latimer had already demonstrated his competence in local affairs, serving as a member of Parliament for Yorkshire in 1529. By the time of his marriage to Catherine, Latimer had been married and widowed twice before, first to Dorothy de Vere, sister of the Earl of Oxford, who had borne him two children; John and Margaret, and secondly to Elizabeth Musgrave who died childless. By 1533 Latimer was looking for a new wife and a woman to be a mother to his children. For Catherine, Latimer's wealth and status was appealing and promised a life away from dependence on her family. She also quickly became fond of Latimer although there were a number of issues surrounding members of his family which must have caused her some disquiet before she consented to marry him.

Like the Burgh family, there was a history of hereditary insanity in the Latimer family which was a concern to Catherine who had been aware of the shadow cast over Gainsborough Old Hall by her first husband's grandfather, even if he may have died before her arrival there. The first Lord Latimer, George Neville, had been declared a lunatic in 1451 and custody of his property was given to his brother to administer. While there was no hint of any insanity in Catherine's second husband, his son John grew up to be a violent and troubled man, something that would have been obvious to Catherine as she attempted to befriend her stepson. More worryingly Latimer, who was one of fifteen children, had a large number of turbulent brothers to support and Catherine, as the mistress of the household, was often expected to deal with them.

In December 1530, for example, two of Latimer's brother, George and Christopher Neville, took legal action against their eldest brother, claiming that he had promised them the goods and chattels of their deceased father. This seems unlikely, particularly given the fact that George and Christopher were but two of Latimer's many siblings, but this was not the least of his concerns, or Catherine's, with them. Catherine cannot but have been aware of a scandal that erupted in Latimer's family in December 1532, only months before she first met him. While the legal action taken by George and Christopher Neville against their brother in 1530 had been tiresome, in 1532, the behaviour of another Neville brother, William, was distinctly treasonous. The first accusation against William Neville was brought by a gentleman named Thomas Wood. According to Wood, in speaking to William one day, he was surprised when his friend mentioned that he was going to become Earl of Warwick. William, a younger son, had absolutely no right to the extinct title, which had last been held by the grandson of his grandfather's cousin, Warwick the Kingmaker. Wood therefore asked him how he knew this and William replied, perfectly seriously:

> That one Jones of Oxford had by his cunning raised four king devils, which brought the said Jones into a tower, and showed him there the picture of the said William Nevyll standing in a robe of velvet and a coronall on his head, and said it was he that should be earl of Warwick.

Jones of Oxford was a famous wizard and necromancer and Wood advised his friend not to trust what he was told, warning him that 'devils would lie.' William Neville received a heavy dose of his family's instability and was firmly convinced by what he was told by those he consulted. While, to begin with, William's conduct appeared to be nothing more than the delusions of a narcissistic man, they quickly became more dangerous and Wood was horrified when William told him that:

> The king would shortly over sea, and should never return, and that he knew by divers prophecies he should not reign the full term of 24 years; also that before this Christmas the king of Scots should make three battles in England, and should come in by Worcester and obtain; and that he would be at one of these battles himself, for he had one who would show him when time should best be, and who should obtain, to whom he would learn and be retained.

Prophesying the king's death was treason and Elizabeth Barton, the famous nun of Kent, would go to her death for a similar offence soon afterwards. William however, who was so wrapped up in his own delusions of grandeur, does not appear to have appreciated this, instead asking Wood on another occasion who he thought he should promote to be his officers and council when he became Earl of Warwick. When Wood refused to be drawn on this, William listed who he had chosen, showing that he had put a great deal of thought into the matter. William then went on to compound his offence, answering Wood, when questioned on how he intended to come by the earldom, that he would not receive it 'by the king, for he shall not reign, but by my right inheritance'. Wood then pointed out that, in that case, Latimer, as the eldest brother should inherit first, but William shook his head, saying: 'Nay, my brother shall be slain at one of the said battles, and then shall I have the ward of his son, and have both his lands and the earldom of Warwick.' William continued to prophesy the king's death throughout the weeks when he was in France with Anne Boleyn at the end of 1532 and informed Wood that he should sell his corn and other goods for money and sow no corn that year as it would not be required.

It is clear from Wood's testimony, that William was thoroughly deluded. As well as consulting the necromancer, Jones, he also employed an astrologer called Wade who assured him of his future inheritance. One Nash, a third magician from Cirencester, was also consulted and confirmed the same thing. He further assured William that he would succeed his brother to the title of Lord Latimer. William was also able to enlist the support of another brother, the equally troublesome George, in his consultations with Jones of Oxford and a third brother, Christopher, equally drawn into the delusion, wrote to William as 'my Lord' to signal his future greatness as Earl of Warwick. For all their unwise talk, the three brothers were essentially harmless, but it cannot have pleased Lord Latimer to hear that his brothers had been looking forward to his imminent death. It was also a very dangerous act to predict the death of the king and, while William appears to have meant no harm by it, the dangers of being associated with Latimer's brothers must have been in Catherine's mind as she considered his proposal of marriage.

Catherine's position in her second marriage was very different from her first. When she and Latimer returned to his home at Snape Castle, Catherine immediately found herself as mistress of a household for the first time and responsible both for running of the establishment and for raising her stepchildren, John and Margaret. Margaret, at only around eight years old, quickly became close to Catherine and Catherine always treated her as her own daughter, supervising her education personally and instilling her own reformist religious beliefs in the girl. Margaret's religious beliefs are, in fact, further evidence that Catherine's interest in the religious reform developed early and, at the time of her death in 1545, Margaret's Will displayed her deeply reformist views, clearly a product of her long association with Catherine. Catherine may also have been involved in the negotiations for Margaret's marriage to the son and heir of a neighbour, Sir Francis Bigod, which was agreed in October 1534 and, as Margaret's stepmother, she would at least have been consulted in the arrangements. Catherine's relationship with the older John was more problematic but she made some headway with her stepson.

Catherine's main interests during the early years of her second marriage were domestic and she enjoyed finally having her own household. In her book, *Lamentation of a Sinner,* Catherine later set out her own interpretation of how a good wife should behave and she attempted to follow this model during her second marriage, the most conventional of all her four marriages for a woman of her class. According to Catherine, in order to be one of the Children of God, it was necessary to live by certain rules:

If they are husbands, they love their wives as their own bodies; after the example as Christ loved the congregation, and gave himself for it, to make it to him a spouse without spot or wrinkle. If they are women married, they learn of St Paul to be obedient to their husbands, and to keep silence in the congregation, and to learn of their husbands at home. Also, they wear such apparel as becometh holiness and comely usage with soberness; not being accusers or detractors, not given to much eating of delicate meats, and drinking of wine, but they teach honest things, to make the young women sober-minded, to love their husbands, to love their children, to be discreet, chaste, housewifely, good, and obedient unto their husbands, that the word of God be not evil spoken of.

Catherine was not in love with Lord Latimer, but she was fond of him and attempted to be a good wife for him and measure up to the ideal of a Christian wife. Latimer had no cause for complaint in Catherine and the marriage was a contented one. Catherine, however, must have found herself having to bite her tongue in matters of religion in relation to her husband on a number of occasions. In spite of Catherine's strongly held reformist beliefs and the clear evidence that she was quietly instructing her stepdaughter in her faith, Latimer remained staunchly conservative. In October 1536 her quiet life at Snape Castle was shattered forever with Latimer forced, under duress, to choose between his loyalty to his faith and to his king during the greatest rebellion of Henry VIII's reign, the Pilgrimage of Grace.

4

A PILGRIMAGE OF GRACE:
1 OCTOBER 1536 – JUNE 1537

In order to achieve a divorce from his first wife, Catherine of
Aragon, and marry Anne Boleyn, Henry VIII had made radical
changes to the English Church, breaking with Rome and declaring
himself Supreme Head of the Church in the Pope's place. Henry
himself was by no means a member of the religious reform but,
equally, he was determined to make changes to his Church. In
January 1535 Henry had empowered his chief minister, Thomas
Cromwell, to conduct a visitation of the monasteries in England
in order to report on their conduct. These reports were almost
universally damning, as both the king and his minister had hoped.
Shortly before Easter 1536 Parliament passed the first Act for the
Dissolution of the Monasteries, granting the king all monasteries
in England with a value of less than £200 per year. The king's
agents immediately got to work dissolving the smaller monasteries,
to the horror of the conservative majority in England. The king
was unconcerned with the murmurings against his attacks on
the monasteries but, as the months passed, popular feeling grew
more and more fierce. On 28 September 1536, when Cromwell's
commissioners reached the monastery of Hexham in order to
dissolve it and carry off its treasures, they found the monks armed

and ready to defend themselves. With the local populace in support of the monks there was little that the commissioners could do but retreat, and, within days, worse trouble was to come in England.

Throughout the summer and autumn of 1536 rumours swept up and down the country and Catherine, in conservative Yorkshire, would have heard many of them. These rumours included claims that all the jewels and ornaments of the parish churches would be taken away and that all gold would be taken to the mint for testing and the taking of tribute. Other claims included the closure of many parish churches, rumours that horned cattle would be taxed and that it would be necessary to pay a fine to the king before eating white bread, goose or other luxury food items. There is no evidence that Henry VIII intended carrying out any of this but the claims were widely believed. By the last week of September 1536 there were also three sets of royal commissioners at work in Lincolnshire, a county renowned for its lawlessness. On 2 October one commission, to carry out an investigation into the clergy, was due to arrive at the town of Louth.

On 1 October 1536 the vicar of Louth preached in church of the forthcoming visitation as his congregation listened, grim-faced. After the service, the townsmen assembled to walk in procession behind the three silver crosses belonging to the church. As they did so one Thomas Foster, a yeoman, commented: 'Go we to follow the crosses for and if they be taken from us we be like to follow them no more.' This stirred the crowd and they gathered at the choir door that evening, taking the keys to the church from the church warden 'for the saving [of the chu]rche jewels'. The following day 100 townsmen met outside the church and agreed to ring the common bell in alarm. At that moment, John Hennege, one of the commissioners, had the misfortune to arrive. According to the deposition of a cobbler of Louth, Nicholas Melton, who quickly assumed the leadership of the rebellion under the name of 'Captain Cobbler':

> The people carried him [Hennege] to the church and swore him to be true to God, the king, and the [commo]nalty. They went then to the market place and took divers books from the chancellor's servant and burnt all but one which deponent has. Meanwhile the country resolved to them, and some 40 went to Legbourne [a nearby nunnery] and brought John Bellowe and Mr Mynycente [two servants of Thomas Cromwell] and put them in prison, all the country crying to kill Bellowe.

By the following day thousands of the commons had assembled at Louth before moving on to Caistor where they captured a group of the king's commissioners, with only Catherine's former father-in-law, Thomas Burgh, escaping due to the speed of his horse.

By 6 October around 40,000 men in Lincolnshire were in arms against the king's religious changes and they spent the night in Lincoln, having taken a local landowner, Lord Hussey, to be their captain. The Lincolnshire rebels swore to be loyal to God and the king, but they were determined not to accept the changes ordered to their religion. When Henry received word of the rebellion he immediately sent the Dukes of Norfolk and Suffolk north to raise troops but, with no standing army and lacklustre support, the king's forces were no match for the rebels. It is probable that, had they wished to do so, the rebels could have moved southwards and threatened the king's throne. However, in spite of their rebellion, they were, in the main, loyal to Henry himself and chose instead to wait at Lincoln for the king's response to their petition.

Henry VIII's answer to the Lincolnshire rebels' demands arrived at Lincoln on 11 October and was read to the commons. It is clear, from Henry's response, that he was furious that his subjects should have dared to so defy him and he ranted against the commons' assertion that he should choose counsellors only of noble blood, in a direct attack on his unpopular minister, the low-born Thomas Cromwell. Henry complained:

How presumptuous then are ye, the rude commons of one shire, and that one of the most brute and beastly of the whole realm, and of least experience, to find fault with your Prince for the electing of his counsellors and prelates; and to take upon you, contrary to God's law and man's law, to rule your Prince, whom ye are bound by all laws to obey and serve, with both your lives, lands and goods, and for no worldly cause to withstand: the contrary whereof you, like traitors and rebels, have attempted, and not like true subjects, as ye name yourselves.

Henry also refused to discuss the suppression of the monasteries, declaring that all he had done had been permitted by Parliament before declaring: 'where ye allege that the service of God is much thereby diminished, the truth thereof is contrary; for there be no houses suppressed where God was well served, but where most vice, mischief, and abomination of living was used'. Henry's response cannot have pleased the Lincolnshire rebels, but the delay occasioned by the wait for his answer gave the king time to build his forces. In any event, the Lincolnshire rebellion suffered from a lack of strong leadership and, by 13 October, the rebels had begun to disperse and the rebellion collapsed. With the collapse of the Lincolnshire rebellion, the king's throne still remained far from secure and, by 14 October, Henry had learned that Yorkshire had risen in support of traditional religion.

On the night of 5 October 1536 the Lincolnshire rebels burned beacons which could be seen from the other side of the River Humber in Yorkshire. Yorkshire, as Catherine knew well, was as traditional and conservative as Lincolnshire and news of the rebellion soon spread. Robert Aske, a gentleman from Yorkshire, had been travelling through Lincolnshire on his way to London when the rebellion broke out and he found himself caught up in all that was happening. On his way to the house of his brother-in-law at Sawcliffe, Aske was stopped by a party of rebels and forced to take an oath 'to be true to God, the king, and the commonwealth' before being allowed to continue on his way. Upon his arrival at Sawcliffe he discovered that his brother-in-law had been taken by the commons and the next day he too was roused from his bed by a party of rebels. In spite of the enforced nature of his taking, Aske supported the rebels' demands and, with a promise of loyalty towards them, was allowed to return to Yorkshire to spread the rebellion to the more northern county.

On 7 October Beverley, in Yorkshire, rose in support of the Lincolnshire rebels and Aske hurried to the town to lead them. The townsmen then lit beacons to alert the rest of the country and, by 10 October, Aske had published his first proclamation, ordering the town bells to be rung and declaring that everyone should declare their loyalty to the king, and to preserving the Church. Within days, the rebels had taken York. Aske denied that he and his followers were rebels, instead declaring that they were on a religious crusade for the protection of the true religion and they 'would have it call'd yet only a Pilgrimage of Grace, while, for giving it reputation, certain priests with crosses led the way, the army following with banners, wherein were painted the crucifix, the five wounds, and the chalice'.

Catherine, with her reformist religious beliefs, had no sympathy for the rebels and she watched the progress of the rebellion with anxiety from her home at Snape Castle. Catherine's feelings with regard to the rebels are probably best summed up by the comments of Hugh Latimer, one of Henry's new reformist bishops and one of the men directly complained about by the rebels. According to Latimer:

> In like manner these men in the North Country, they made pretence as though they were armed in God's armour, gird in truth, and clothed in righteousness. I hear say they wear the cross and the wounds before and behind, and they pretend much truth to the king's grace and to the commonwealth, when they intend nothing less; and deceive the poor ignorant people, and bring them to fight against both the king, the church, and the commonwealth.

Within days of the uprising in Yorkshire, the rebels turned their attentions towards Snape Castle and Lord Latimer.

From the earliest days of the Lincolnshire rebellion, the rebels had sought to make the local nobility and gentry their captains, achieving this either through common sympathy or duress. On 4 October 1536, for example, Henry VIII's commissioners who had been captured at Caistor and forced to become leaders of the rebels, wrote to Lord Hussey, a Lincolnshire nobleman, to inform him that the rebels required him to come and lead them. In the event that Lord Hussey would not come of his own free will, he was threatened that 'the commonalty will in all haste come and seek you as their utter enemy'. Shortly afterwards, the rebels came to Lord Hussey's house and threatened his wife, saying that they would burn the house unless she produced her husband. Lord Hussey, in any event, shared the views of the rebels and, although he first became their leader under duress, he gave every appearance of being enthusiastic about the movement. No details survive of a similar visit that was paid to Snape Castle in the early days of October, but it is likely to have followed a similar pattern, with the rebels surrounding the house and threatening to burn it down if Lord Latimer did not become their leader. To Catherine's horror, her husband was forced to swear the rebels' oath, before riding away with them as both their prisoner and their leader.

With Lord Latimer in their custody, the crowd of rebels around Snape Castle melted away. Catherine was already aware that her husband was likely to be a focus for the rebels and, within days of the Lincolnshire rebellion breaking out, Latimer had received a message from the Archbishop of York, warning him to stay his own tenants if necessary. Catherine was terrified by her husband's capture and there is no doubt that she feared for his life. She was also aware that Latimer, while he went with the rebels under duress, fully supported their cause and she knew that, by allowing himself to be carried off, he placed himself in grave danger of being considered a traitor by the king. Once he was with the rebels, Lord Latimer does appear, as did many other noblemen, to have quickly agreed to espouse their point of view and it is difficult to distinguish between duress and freewill in the actions of the lords and gentlemen who were captured and forced to lead the rebels. Certainly, while the rebellion endured, Latimer did not waiver in his leadership of it and, while he was certainly forced to become its leader, he must also have had high hopes that it would succeed and restore the traditional religious practices.

By 20 October, Aske was in control of much of Yorkshire. After leaving York, Aske moved his army on to Pomfret Castle where the leading Yorkshire nobleman, Lord Darcy, and the Archbishop of York had taken refuge. Lord Darcy, who, like Lord Latimer, was a supporter of the rebels' demands, surrendered the castle and both he and the Archbishop were forced to take the oath:

That they should enter into this pilgrimage of grace for the love of God, preservation of the king's person and issue, the purifying of the nobility, and expulsing all villain-blood, and evil counsellors; and for no particular profit for themselves, nor to do displeasure to any, nor to stay nor murder any for envy; but to put away all fears, and take afore them the cross of Christ, His faith, and the restitution of the Church, the suppression of hereticks and their opinions.

As with Lord Latimer, the line between duress and freewill was blurred and Pomfret Castle, which was one of the strongest castles in Yorkshire, was believed to have been surrendered deliberately by Darcy and the Archbishop in their eagerness to join the rebels.

In the days following his capture, Lord Latimer spent his time in organizing his men into an army and, according to Aske's own disposition, while he was at Pomfret Castle 'the lords Nevyll, Latymer, and Lumley then came in, and 10,000 men with them – with the banners and arms of St Cuthbert'. The rebels, with Lord Latimer prominent amongst them, then moved on to Pontefract where around 34,000 or 35,000 men were assembled on horseback by 21 October. The king had a much smaller army of around 8,000 men, under the command of the Duke of Norfolk, waiting at Doncaster. Henry VIII was furious and determined not to give any quarter to the rebels, writing on 28 October to the Earl of Derby that if he found any monks at the monastery of Sawley which had been dissolved by the king but reinstated by the Pilgrims then he should 'without further delay, cause the said Abbot and certain of the chief monks to be hanged upon long pieces of timber, or otherwise, out of the steeple; and the rest to be put to execution in such sundry places as you shall think meet for the example of others'. Norfolk, finding himself confronted by an immense and well-ordered force, was less bullish and agreed to meet with Aske at Doncaster Bridge where he received a list of the rebels' demands and agreed that a truce should be held until the king had had an opportunity to respond.

On 2 November 1536 Henry drew up a response to the rebels' demands in his own hand, complaining, as he had done to the Lincolnshire rebels before them that he marvelled 'not a little that ignorant people will go about or take upon them to instruct us, (which something have been noted to be learned) what the right Faith should be'. In early December, the rebels met again in order to define their articles further. They declared that they wanted the heresies and heretical works of Luther and other reformers to be destroyed, the authority of the Pope to be restored and for Henry VIII's eldest daughter Mary, the daughter of Catherine of Aragon, to be declared legitimate. They also demanded that the suppressed abbeys be restored and that a parliament would be held at Nottingham or York to further address their concerns. Lord Latimer's exact role in the composition of these articles is not recorded, but he was present at the assembly and approved them. Of more concern for Catherine, it was also widely reported that, during the conference Latimer had suggested that the Archbishop of York and other members of the clergy be asked to 'show their learning whether subjects might lawfully move war in any case against their prince'. This was clearly treason and Latimer compounded his offence by then going in person to the Archbishop to ask him to speak upon the subject in his sermon the next day and to declare whether it was ever lawful for subjects to make war against their king. For Catherine, who listened avidly for any news of her husband and the rebellion, this was terrifying.

On the same day that the rebels' articles were drawn up, Robert Aske, accompanied by Lords Latimer, Scrope and Darcy and 300 rebels rode to Doncaster to confer with Norfolk. According to Aske's own account of the meeting, on 7 December:

At the Grey Friars in Doncaster, the said Aske and lords chose 20 knights and esquires and as many commoners to go to the said Duke and Earls. At their coming, the said Aske, by consent of the lords and knights and in the name of them all, made three low obeisances, and all kneeling on their knees requested of the lords to have the king's free pardon for their offences. They then began to discuss the particulars of their petitions, and after order therein taken, by command of the Duke and earls, Aske went to the rest of the commons at the Grey Friars to declare it.

In spite of his anger, and his determination not to treat with the rebels, Henry recognized that it would be necessary to make some concessions and he had reluctantly agreed in advance that Norfolk could offer the rebels a pardon and the promise of further discussions. Norfolk did as he was instructed and Aske, accompanied by Latimer and the other lords, personally proclaimed the result of the negotiations to the rebels on 7 December, reading out their pardon the following day. With the promise that their articles would be further considered, the rebels dispersed and, to Catherine's relief, Latimer was able to return home, unharmed from his time at the head of the rebel army.

Catherine was relieved at the outcome of the rebellion and, while she did not in any way sympathize with their aims, she had been forced into a position of common cause with them by the capture of her husband. As far as the rebels were concerned, Henry VIII intended to act in good faith towards them and, on 15 December the king wrote personally to Aske, inviting him to court for Christmas in order to speak further. Henry showed Aske nothing but charm during the visit and the rebels' captain was entirely won over, writing to Lord Darcy on 8 January from court to assure him that 'the king is a gracious sovereign lord to me and has affirmed his liberal pardon to all the North, by mouth'. Aske also reported that the king had promised to hold a parliament, and have his third wife, Jane Seymour, crowned at York, ending that 'His Grace in heart tendereth the common wealth of his subjects, and extends his mercy from the heart.' Aske was entirely deceived if he believed that the king meant to keep his promises. Lord Latimer, who had had considerably more personal experience of his sovereign than Aske was less convinced by Henry's display of docility and just after Christmas he left Catherine at Snape in order to hurry south to court to try to explain his actions during the rebellion.

Catherine's feelings on being, once again, left alone with her stepchildren and servants can only be imagined but both she and Lord Latimer knew that the commons of the surrounding area were far from pacified and that rebellion was still very much in the air. She certainly had reason to fear both for her husband and her own personal safety, and a letter from Lord Latimer to his friend, William Fitzwilliam, the Lord Admiral of England, shows the dilemma and dangerous situation that both he and his family quickly found themselves in. According to Latimer:

> Thank you for your good report of me in being among the commons against my will. At Buntingford on my way towards London, there met me a letter from my lord Chancellor, my lord Privy Seal, and other of the king's Council, signifying that I should tarry in the North notwithstanding the king's letters to me to come up, because my lord of Norfolk was dispatched. Forthwith I returned homewards, and now, at Stamford, I learn the Commons of Richmondshire, grieved at my coming up, have entered my house at Snape and will destroy it if I come not home shortly. If I do not please them I know not what they will do with my body and goods, wife and children. I beg to know the king's pleasure and shall follow the same whatsoever come of it, likewise as I advertised my coming up now. If it were the king's pleasure that I might live on such small lands as I have in the South, I would little care of my lands in the North.

Lord Latimer's dilemma was very real. In journeying south, he had hoped to persuade Henry that he had acted only under duress. However, the news that he was to be sent back to the north again was a worry. To make matters worse, Latimer's sudden departure worked the commons around Snape into a fury and, convinced that he had betrayed their cause, they vented all their anger on Catherine.

Around 20 January 1537, a mob arrived at the doors of Snape Castle and forced their way inside, abusing Catherine and her stepchildren and servants and quickly taking over control of the castle, ominously making 'inventories of all their goods'. They

asserted that their actions were caused solely by Latimer, with one
rebel later reporting in his examination that

> if Lord Lati[mer] had not removed from Snape in Richmondshire
> a[fter Chris]tmas, and Sir Christopher [Danby] in like case, there
> would have been no insurrection. Item, also the inhabitants were
> so discontent with the departure of the said Lord Latimer and Sir
> Christopher Danby that they would have spoiled their houses.

The commons were angry and the attack on Snape Castle was
the most terrifying experience of Catherine's life. She remained
physically unharmed but it was clear that she and her stepchildren
were to be used as hostages for Latimer's good behaviour and the
air of menace must have been tangible. It was with relief that Lord
Latimer finally made up his mind to act to protect his family, with
or without the king's consent and, hurrying away from Stamford,
he rushed up to Snape to reason with the rebels, assuring them of
his loyalty. Catherine was relieved to see Latimer and glad that his
appearance put an end to her ordeal. She must have been alarmed
when Latimer stayed only briefly before hurrying away to join
Norfolk at Doncaster, as he had been ordered.

Catherine was badly frightened by all that had happened during
the Pilgrimage of Grace and the idea of once again being alone
at Snape Castle filled her with dread. The north was far from
pacified and, while Lord Latimer's direct role ended when he
joined Norfolk at Doncaster, he was still in grave danger. Early
in 1537 a new rebellion broke out when Sir Francis Bigod, the
father of Margaret Neville's fiancé attempted to take Hull and
Scarborough. In spite of the association between the two families,
Latimer played no direct role in the new rebellion and his brother

William was even appointed by the king as one of his agents to pursue Bigod after the failure of his rebellion. Latimer was not the only former rebel leader to shun Bigod's action and Robert Aske wrote to the commons urging them to trust in the king and make no further trouble. Another rebel leader, Sir Robert Constable, wrote personally to Bigod urging him not to rebel.

Bigod's rebellion, which was quickly put down, allowed Henry to repudiate his pardon to the rebels and take his bloody vengeance. On 27 March twelve of the leaders of the Lincolnshire rebellion were tried in London and sentenced to death. In May Henry turned his attentions towards the leaders of the Yorkshire rebellion and Lord Darcy, Robert Aske and Sir Francis Bigod, among others were sentenced to die, suffering execution soon afterwards. Lord Latimer was not amongst the rebel leaders arrested but, by spring 1537, both he and Catherine knew that his life, and the future of his family, hung in the balance.

5

NOT MUCH FAVOUR:
JUNE 1537 – MARCH 1543

For Catherine, the terror of the Pilgrimage of Grace did not end with the dispersal of the rebellion and both she and Lord Latimer were acutely aware of the danger that they and their family faced. Henry VIII was determined to exact vengeance against all those whom he considered to have been at fault in the rebellion.

Catherine remained at Snape Castle with Latimer's children throughout the immediate aftermath of the Pilgrimage of Grace while Latimer stayed with the Duke of Norfolk, hoping to demonstrate his loyalty to the king. Norfolk was content to associate himself with Latimer, viewing him as an enforced spokesman of the rebels rather than as an active participant in the rebellion. Certainly, during June, Norfolk suggested Latimer as one of the peers to sit on a newly formed Council of the North. Norfolk had no intention of endangering his own position through a show of support for Catherine's disgraced husband however and when he received word from the king's chief minister, Thomas Cromwell, that 'the king does not much favour Lord Latimer', he asked what Henry wished him to do with him. Norfolk was not entirely honest with Latimer and merely suggested that he return to London 'as a suitor on his own affairs'. In an attempt to soften

Latimer's reception somewhat, Norfolk did write to Cromwell on 16 June to let him know that the disgraced peer was on his way but to point out that he 'cannot discover any evidence but that he was enforced, and no man was in more danger of his life'. With these words, Latimer was on his own as he made his way slowly towards London, aware that he could expect a frosty reception from the king.

There is no mention that Catherine accompanied Latimer to London and, given the dangerous nature of his journey, it is unlikely that he would have invited his family to go with him. Latimer did not hurry on his journey, only arriving shortly before the end of June, and there is some evidence that he stopped on the way to visit his brother, Thomas Neville, in Aldham in Essex before being arrested. Thomas was aware of his brother's fears about the outcome of the journey and, as ever with Latimer's brothers, he was actively unhelpful. Soon after Latimer's arrival in London Thomas was also arrested. According to the examinations carried out, Margaret Towler, a widow who lived in Aldham as a servant of the parson of the town, asked Thomas Neville whether the parson, who had been arrested, 'should be put to death upon a false wretch's saying'. Thomas shook his head, saying: 'No, Marget, he shall not be put to death, for he hath no lands or goods to lose, then he should lose his life.' Thomas felt his brother's trouble was due solely to the king's desire to obtain Latimer's lands and goods, a treasonous belief. Thomas compounded his offence by telling his wife, in public, on hearing that his brother had been arrested: 'Alas, Mary, my brother is cast away.' He then added, dangerously: 'By God's blood, if I had the king here I would not make him that he should never take men into the Tower.' This comment was enough for Thomas to swiftly join his brother in custody.

Following his arrest, Latimer was immediately taken to the Tower, accused of rebellion against the king. Quite apart from the difficulties that Thomas Neville's comments put him in, he was also damned by association with another of his brothers, Marmaduke, who had preceded his eldest brother to the Tower by some months. On 4 January 1537 the Earl of Oxford reported to Cromwell that he had carried out investigations into comments made by Marmaduke Neville and that he was holding Marmaduke as a prisoner in his house to await the king's pleasure. Marmaduke's troubles had begun in early December when he travelled south to London with the Duke of Norfolk, ecstatic at the outcome of the meeting between the rebels and the king's lieutenant. On 16 December, during a visit to the Abbot of St John's at Colchester, Marmaduke declared that he and the other rebels were not traitors, stating that 'if ye call us traitors, we will call you heretics'. He also claimed that the south had wanted to rise with the north. When reports of this reached Cromwell, he ordered that Marmaduke be immediately sent to the Tower. He was presumably still there when his eldest brother arrived although, like his brother, he survived the danger, receiving an appointment in Catherine's household when she later became queen. It is obvious from this appointment that Catherine retained some fondness for Marmaduke Neville and her old life as Lady Latimer, but, in 1537, she must have lamented the trouble that her husband's brothers were causing, at a time when Latimer could ill afford any more suspicion to fall on him.

Both Catherine and her husband knew that, if Latimer were to save himself, he needed to win the support of Cromwell. As early as 18 January 1537 Latimer had written to his brother-in-law, Sir William Musgrave, on the subject. In his letter, Latimer asked Musgrave to:

Recommend me to my Lord Privy Seal [Cromwell], showing him I was sorry the people spoke otherwise than became them of him. For though he be in the favour of the king it letteth not his Grace to grant what he pleases to the people, and I think his lordship would not be a hinderer of such of their desires as be reasonable. Though I durst not much contrary them, I did my best to reduce them to conformity to the king's pleasure. My being among them was a very painful and dangerous time to me; I pray God I may never see such again.

In the Tower, Latimer continued to maintain that he had acted under duress. There was an element of truth to this as Catherine, who had been present on both occasions when the rebels had come to her house, could attest. However, Latimer's conduct went beyond mere compulsion and, once united with the rebels, he had been an effective and autonomous leader. Both Cromwell and the king were aware of this and the danger to Latimer in the early summer of 1537 was immense.

In spite of the danger that he faced, Latimer was able to secure his own release and no charges were ever brought against him, much to both his and Catherine's relief. The reasons behind Latimer's escape are not entirely clear and it is likely that it was to a large extent due to the difficulties of proving beyond doubt that Latimer had not acted under compulsion. Catherine's contacts at court, through her uncle, her brother and her sister, may also have helped and she petitioned them to support her husband. Finally, Latimer's own conduct contributed to his escape and he was prepared to humble himself completely before the king's chief minister. At some point in 1536 Latimer agreed to pay Cromwell a fee of 20 nobles a year. The timing and reason for this fee is not clear, but it is likely to have been an attempt to secure the influential minister's support towards the end of the year when Latimer was already aware that matters did not look promising for him. In September 1537 Latimer paid Cromwell a further fee of 100 marks which was almost certainly part of a bribe to secure his release. He also ensured that, until the end of Cromwell's life, his annual fee of 20 marks was paid on time and in full. Monetary bribes were not sufficient for Cromwell and the seriousness of Latimer's plight required an even greater sacrifice. On 30 September 1537, at around the time that he paid the cash bribe to Cromwell, Latimer also wrote:

After my most hearty recommendations had to your good lordship. Whereas your lordship doth desire... of your friends my house within Chartreux Churchyard [Charterhouse] beside. So... I assure your lordship the getting of a lease of it cost me 100 marcs, besides other pleasures (improvements) that I did to the house, for it was much my desire to have it, because it stands in good air, out of press of the city. And I do always lie there when I come to London, and I have no other house to lie at. And also, I have granted it to farm to Mr Nudygate (Newdigate), son and heir of serjeant Nudygate, to lie in the said house in my absence. And he to void whensoever I come up to London. Nevertherless, I am contented if it can do your lordship any pleasure for your friend, that he lie there forthwith. I seek my lodgings at this Michaelmas term myself. And as touching my lease, I assure your lordship it is not here, but I shall bring it right to your lordship at my coming up at this said term, and then and always I shall be at your lordship's commandment, as knows our lord, who preserve your lordship in much honour to his pleasure.

Latimer's letter was written when he had already started the long journey home and it seems very likely that it was the promise of the bribe, as well as the signing over of the lease of his house in the Charterhouse to Cromwell's friend, Sir John Russell, which secured his release. In spite of his protestations about the value of the house, both Catherine and Latimer knew that, in reality, he had come away from the Pilgrimage of Grace relatively unscathed and that matters could have been very much worse for him. Angered by the behaviour of their tenants during the rebellion, both Catherine and Latimer were determined to spend as little time as possible on their lands in the north and, during the years between 1537 and 1543, they spent a considerable amount time in London, presumably finding suitable alternative accommodation.

Catherine was pleased to return to London and the city in which she grew up. Upon arrival she immediately sought out her brother. William Parr had become a man of some substance while Catherine had been away. In October 1537, in celebration of the birth of the king's son, Edward, it had been suggested that William be made a peer and finally, on 9 March 1539, he was granted a peerage in his own right, considering the old family name of Lord Fitzhugh before settling on the name of Lord Parr. This was the fulfilment of one of Catherine's mother's dearest hopes and, later that year, both William and his wife, Anne Bourchier, were appointed as prominent members of the reception committee to welcome Henry VIII's fourth wife, Anne of Cleves, to England.

While Maud Parr had wanted to secure a peerage for her son, the title of Lord Parr was not the one that she had had her eye upon. William's marriage to Anne Bourchier was an unmitigated disaster and the couple loathed each other. William always attempted to spend as much time at court as possible, taking mistresses. Anne

Bourchier, with her royal blood and impeccable pedigree, was not prepared to accept this from the husband that had been forced upon her and, at some point during the 1530s, she took a lover herself. According to the report of Parliament in 1542:

> whereas Lady Anne, wife of Sir Wm. Parre Lord Parre, continued in adultery notwithstanding admonition, and, finally, two years past, left his company and has since had a child begotten in adultery, that the said child and all future children she may have shall be held bastards.

The Parrs' marital arrangements were scandalous and Anne had been involved in an affair for some time before she finally decided to break with her husband. It is likely that it was the death of her father, in March 1540, which finally provided her with the opportunity to leave William.

William Parr was, undoubtedly, not sorry to find that he no longer had to live with his wife, but her abandonment brought him very public shame. Catherine must have been equally furious at her sister-in-law's conduct and, as one who had already made two marriages for duty rather than love, she found Anne Bourchier's behaviour difficult to understand. Anne's abandonment of William also had further consequences for the family. On Anne's father's death it had been expected by everyone that William would be made Earl of Essex in his place, the very reason that Maud had expended so much effort and money in securing the marriage. The king, however, perhaps noting the public humiliation heaped upon William following the estrangement from his wife, had other ideas and, on 18 April, just over a month after the death of the old Earl, Thomas Cromwell was created the new Earl of Essex in a glittering ceremony at court.

The loss of what he considered to be his title infuriated William and also angered his entire extended family, including Catherine. The fact that Cromwell was the recipient of the title must also have evoked unpleasant memories of the events of 1537 for Catherine when her husband was forced to debase himself so fully before the king's low-born chief minister. By 1540, Cromwell had been the supreme power in Henry's government for several years and as early as 1532 William Parr had found himself forced to petition humbly to the son of a Putney blacksmith. In one surviving letter by William to Cromwell, it is clear just how far the minister's power extended over the older and more established noblemen and gentry of England. According to William:

> Robert Tarne, a very insolent person, did not only openly and secretly enter my park at Kendal on various occasions, but killed and stole my game and spoke many malicious words to William Redman, my keeper there, who advised him to desist from his unlawful pastime and keep a sober tongue. On which Tarne and he made a fray and the former claimed to be hurt. He purposes not only to trouble Redman, but to sue my cousin, Sir James Labourne, for abetting him, who had nothing to do with it. He is maintained in this by my lord of Cumberland and Sir Thomas Clifford, for the malice they bear my cousin Labourne, for my lord of Richmond's and my poor causes. Whereas it had been ancient custom in the barony of Kendal to administer justice in all strife, as my grandfather, father and uncle, Sir William Parre, always did: now it is that sundry wealthy and malicious persons, for the ill will they bear my lord of Richmond and me, infringe the said custom and send up poor persons to London who cannot afford it. I... write to you for remedy, hoping, whenever such malicious persons

repair to London, they may be remitted to my cousin Laborne who
is deputy steward there [in Kendal].

It rankled with William to have to petition for permission to deal
with the case according to local tradition and his own justice.
The Parr family already had no love for Thomas Cromwell and
Cromwell's creation as Earl of Essex increased this.

Another member of Catherine's family, Sir George Throckmorton,
who had married the half-sister of Catherine's father, Catherine
Vaux, had the misfortune to anger the king's chief minister with
regard to a dispute concerning the boundaries of their neighbouring
manors of Coughton Court and Owsley. It was unwise to earn
Cromwell's enmity and he immediately reported Throckmorton to
the king, accusing him of denying Henry's title of Supreme Head
of the Church. This was a very dangerous accusation, particularly
because Throckmorton's brother, Michael, was in the service of
Cardinal Pole, Henry VIII's greatest enemy. Throckmorton was
arrested and his wife, Catherine's aunt, sent her son to her brother,
William Parr of Horton for safety. She then turned to Catherine
herself for further aid.

The story of Catherine's intervention in the imprisonment of Sir
George Throckmorton is told in the near-contemporary *Legend of
Sir Nicholas Throckmorton*. According to this source, Catherine
was, even by 1540, renowned as 'a woman rare, her like but seldom
seene'. Her aunt came to her in London and 'pray'd her Neice with
watery eyes, to ridd both her, and hers, from endless cryes'. While
the *Legend of Sir Nicholas Throckmorton* was written only a few
years after Catherine's death, it must be pointed out that it was
also written after she had become queen and its author was able to
employ the benefit of hindsight in relation to Catherine's conduct.

At first glance, Catherine Parr, in early 1540, would appear to be a strange choice for her aunt to appeal to for aid and it is therefore possible that the story can only be considered to be family legend. However, while, in 1540, Catherine was only Lady Latimer, she was the wife of a peer and, as such, outranked her aunt. She also, as the daughter of Maud Parr, had had some childhood connection with the court and, following the Pilgrimage of Grace, took steps to reacquaint herself with her former friends at there. It is therefore not impossible that Catherine could have secured an audience with the king, who may well have remembered her from childhood. Equally, by 1540, Cromwell was beginning to lose influence with the king and Henry, angry with the man who he blamed for arranging his marriage to his disappointing fourth wife, Anne of Cleves, may have been prepared to listen to any complaint against the minister. It is therefore not implausible that Catherine could have intervened in the way described. According to the *Legend*, Catherine:

> She, willing of herself to doe us goode,
> Sought out the meanes her Uncle's life to save;
> And, when the king was in the pleasing moode,
> She humbly then her suit began to crave.
> With wooing times denyalls disagree,
> She spake, and sped: my Father was sett free.

This is the first recorded meeting between Catherine and Henry. It is unlikely that Henry harboured any romantic feelings for Catherine on seeing her as Lady Latimer: in early 1540 he was already deeply involved in his affair with the woman who would become his fifth wife, Catherine Howard. Besides, Catherine was a married woman and, while the king may have noted her attractiveness, he would not have considered her as a potential bride. It is also unlikely that the fall of Thomas Cromwell in June 1540 can be attributed to Catherine as has sometimes been suggested. The minister's fall was due more to his inability to supply the king with a divorce from Anne of Cleves. Catherine's intervention occurred at exactly the right moment and she was able to use both Henry's familiarity with her family and his anger at Cromwell to secure her uncle's release.

Latimer gradually returned to favour with the king in the years following his release from prison, being sent to the Scottish borders in the summer of 1542 to assist in the defence of England. Latimer was still present at York in October 1542 when he was chosen as one of the peers to meet with James V of Scotland on his proposed visit to the city. This is clear evidence that Latimer had returned to the king's favour and it is not impossible that this was due, at least in part, to the king's favourable impression of Catherine during their meetings at court. Latimer also received a grant of the stewardship 'of the forest of Galtres and the lawn within the forest and master of the hunt of deer there; with herbage, pannage, windfallen trees and browsings and all accustomed profits' in June 1542, another mark of royal favour. Catherine's whereabouts during Latimer's time at York is not recorded but, given the city's proximity to Snape Castle, it is likely that she returned there with her stepchildren and household. The return was not intended to be permanent and that winter the couple were in London.

Although Latimer was in favour during the summer of 1542, he had little opportunity to enjoy his good fortune because by the autumn he was in poor health. On 12 September 1542, while he was still at York, Latimer made his Will, although he was well enough to return to London some months later. Catherine accompanied her husband and it was with sadness that she watched her second husband's decline. The date of Lord Latimer's death is nowhere recorded but mention was made of it in the official state papers of March 1543. Catherine was close by when her husband died and she grieved for him, arranging his burial in St Paul's Cathedral. Catherine had been an excellent spouse and Latimer rewarded her in his Will, leaving her the custody of his daughter, Margaret, as well as the income from two of his manors. This was a comfortable, if not generous, bequest, and left Catherine independent for the first time in her life. At the time of Lord Latimer's death, she was already aware that her independent widowhood was unlikely to last for long as, by February 1543, she had two suitors waiting for her husband's death to release her for a third marriage.

6

BETTER YOUR MISTRESS THAN YOUR WIFE: MARCH 1543 – 12 JULY 1543

Catherine's second widowhood was to prove very different to her first and, while the death of Lord Latimer did not leave her wealthy, she was comfortably off and had no need to throw herself on the charity of her relations. With Latimer's death, Catherine showed no desire to return to the north, instead remaining in her house in London with her stepdaughter and household. Catherine had already made two marriages out of necessity, but, even before Lord Latimer's death, she had begun to hope that she might finally be able to make her own choice and marry for love.

The origins of the love affair that would dominate Catherine's life are obscure, but, given how deeply she came to feel about her lover in the short period of her second widowhood, it seems certain that they began during the last few months of Lord Latimer's life. Catherine always maintained a virtuous reputation, and it is unlikely that she would have contemplated an affair with another man during her husband's lifetime. However, by January 1543, it was clear to everyone that Lord Latimer did not have long to live and that his wife would soon be available to make a third marriage. Catherine hoped for a swift third marriage and, in 1547, when she was finally truly at liberty to marry the man she loved, she wrote passionately to him that 'I would not have you think that this mine honest goodwill towards you to proceed of any sudden motion of passion; for, as truly as God is God, my mind was fully bent, the other time I was at liberty, to marry you before any man I know'. For the first time in her life, Catherine was in love.

The object of Catherine's affection was a very substantial man in his own right. Thomas Seymour, who was about four years older than Catherine, was the fourth son of Sir John Seymour and his wife Margery Wentworth of Wolf Hall in Wiltshire. The Seymour family was an obscure one, far beneath Catherine's own in status but Thomas, along with his eldest surviving brother, Edward, and his sister, Jane were deeply ambitious and determined to rise at the court of Henry VIII. Thomas's career had begun promisingly enough and, in the early 1530s, he spent time in France in the household of his kinsman, Sir Francis Bryan. His career and status rose remarkably when, in 1536, his sister, Jane Seymour, surprised everyone by becoming Henry VIII's third wife. For Jane's family this meant immediate gains and Edward Seymour was created Viscount Beauchamp. Thomas received a knighthood and an appointment as one of the king's gentlemen of the Privy Chamber. Henry VIII was personally fond of his dashing young brother-in-law and even after Jane's death in childbirth in October 1537, Thomas continued to rise, receiving a number of important offices, as well as grants of land and pensions. As a significant honour, in December 1539 he was appointed as one of the gentlemen to travel to Calais to meet Anne of Cleves on the last stage of her journey to England. In June 1540 he was sent as Henry's ambassador to the King of the Romans, remaining there until his recall to England on 14 January 1543. Thomas arrived back at court soon afterwards and immediately became acquainted with Catherine Parr.

By 1543 Thomas Seymour was one of the most eligible bachelors in England. While, as a younger son, he could expect no great inheritance, as the king's brother-in-law and the uncle of the Prince of Wales, he was a very attractive proposition. In 1538 he attracted the attention of the Duke of Norfolk, the premier peer in England, as a potential husband for his daughter, Mary, Duchess of Richmond, the widow of Henry VIII's illegitimate son. According to a letter written at the time, Norfolk approached the king personally to request his support for the match, making:

A further overture for the maryage of his saide doughter; saying that, lyke as he wolde woyrke, and do nothing therein, contrary to the kinges Highnes pleasure ne without His Graces advyse, so he knew but 2 persons uppon whom he thought mete, or could resolve in his herte to bestowe his saide doughter; the one he names, of whom he saied your lordship had made a mocyon unto him, whose name the Kinges Majestee now remembreth not; thither he sayed, to whom his herte is most inclyned, was Sir Thomas Seymour, on whom, aswell for that he is honestly advaunced by the kinges Majestee, as also for his towardenes, and other his commendable merytes, he could well find in his herte, and wold be glad, stonding so with the kinges pleasure to bestowe his doughter, saying ferther, that, percyvyng there ensueth comenly no grete good by conjunction of grete bloodes togyther, he sought not therefore, nor desired to mary his doughter, in any high-bloode or degree. Whereunto the Kinges Highnes, answered meryly, that if he were so mynded to bestowe his doughter upon the saide Sir Thomas Seymour, he shoulde be sure to couple her with one of suche lust and youth, as should be able to please her well at all poyntes, shewed himself to be right willing and agreeable that the same should take effecte accordingly.

Henry was so pleased with the idea of the match that he raised the subject with Thomas himself, securing Thomas's enthusiastic support. Nothing came of the marriage in 1538, probably due to the Duchess's own opposition. Norfolk, however, remained determined to achieve an alliance with Seymour and in the mid 1540s raised the matter again, suggesting a marriage between Thomas and his daughter, as well as marriages between his grandchildren and Edward Seymour's children. Once again, the Duchess was not interested in the marriage, informing her brother, the Earl of Surrey, that her 'fantasy would not serve her to marry with him'. By 1543 Thomas had not secured an advantageous marriage for himself.

With the exception of Catherine's later letter to Thomas, making it clear that she would have married him after Latimer's death if she could, no other details of the couple's early relationship survive. Thomas Seymour was one of the most handsome men at court and it is not difficult to see what Catherine saw in him. It has been suggested that Thomas's interest in Catherine was due to his desire to attract a wealthy widow, but this seems unlikely. Catherine was, in 1543, not conspicuously wealthy and, as the widow of a mere baron, she was no great catch. Thomas, as the king's brother-in-law, could have aspired to a marriage at the highest level. More likely, Thomas had genuine feelings for Catherine as she was an intelligent and attractive woman. The couple quickly formed a personal relationship.

Henry had originally sent his daughter, Mary, and the other ladies of court away when he discovered his fifth wife, Catherine Howard's, adultery in November 1541. While noblewomen and gentlewomen were still able to visit the court, there was no permanent establishment for them to reside in and take up posts until January 1543 when the king suddenly recalled his eldest daughter, Mary, to act as his hostess. Mary arrived accompanied by a large train of ladies and, while the majority of her household had already been appointed, there were opportunities for other women to join the household. Catherine was four years older than Mary but, given the closeness between the two women's mothers, it is probable that they had known each other in childhood. Catherine's sister, Anne, had also been a lady-in-waiting to Jane Seymour, who had enjoyed a close relationship with Mary and it is likely that, if Catherine were unable to use her own contacts with Mary to open up communication, then Anne was able to recommend her sister for some role in the household. Anne had also married William Herbert, a prominent member of the court, some time before and Catherine's brother-in-law may also have been able to make an appeal on her behalf.

Catherine was attached to Mary's household by 16 February 1543. On that date the king received, and paid, a tailor's bill for a number of fine fabrics for Italian, French, Dutch and Venetian style gowns, as well as pleats and sleeves, hoods and other items of clothing. The bill was originally addressed to Lady Latimer but, about half way down the page, it was inscribed 'for your daughter'. It is arguable that the daughter described may have been Catherine's stepdaughter, Margaret Neville, but that would not explain where Catherine obtained funds to purchase such fine materials for herself and Margaret or why the king decided to pay the bill. More likely, the daughter is Princess Mary and the bill shows that, by the middle of February Catherine was in a position to purchase fine clothes both for herself and for the king's daughter, confident in the knowledge that it was Henry who would pay for them.

Catherine's exact role in Mary's household is not known, but it was almost certainly at court that she first came to meet, and fall in love with, Thomas Seymour, and the couple spent as much time together as possible. Both also had an interest in the religious reform and it is not impossible that they met at religious meetings during the period. For Catherine, in spite of the turmoil surrounding Latimer's illness and death, it was the first time that she had been in love and she gladly returned Thomas's affection, fully intending to marry him once a decent period of mourning had passed for her second husband. To her horror, however, even before Latimer's death, Catherine became aware that she had another, far more powerful suitor to contend with.

By January 1543, Henry VIII had been a widower for nearly a year following the execution of his fifth wife, Catherine Howard, on charges of adultery. Henry's immediate reaction to the revelations concerning Catherine Howard was to shut himself away and grieve. With his previous wives, excepting Jane Seymour, he had been actively seeking ways to rid himself of them at the time of their falls. However, Catherine Howard's conduct had come as a complete shock to him and he was stunned to discover that not only had she not been a virgin at the time of their marriage, but that she had also been carrying out a highly suspect relationship with a gentleman of his privy chamber, Thomas Culpeper. In order to save face, following Catherine's condemnation by Act of Attainder in Parliament, Henry attempted to appear cheerful and the Imperial Ambassador, Eustace Chapuys commented on 8 February 1542 that:

> until then the king has shown no alacrity or joy, not even when he
> first heard of his queen's misdemeanour, but since he was informed

of the trial and subsequent condemnation on the 29th he has considerably changed, for on the night of that day he gave a grand supper, and invited to it several ladies and gentlemen of his court.

At the dinner, Henry made a conspicuous show of his interest in a number of ladies, but he had no candidate for a sixth wife in mind at the time.

Catherine Howard's betrayal plunged Henry VIII into old age and, by early 1543, he was grossly overweight and a virtual invalid, incapacitated by an ulcer in his leg. The king, who had been so handsome in his youth, was, at fifty-one, both melancholy and irascible. In 1540, three years before he turned his attentions to Catherine, he was also described as a tyrant by the French ambassador, Marillac, and few in England would have disagreed with this. Marillac considered Henry to be tainted by a number of vices, including greed and covetousness, considering that 'to make himself rich he has impoverished his people'. Marillac claimed that Henry was blighted by distrust and fear and that, due to the many changes he had wrought in England, he 'does not trust a single man, expecting them all offended, he will not cease to dip his hand in blood as long as he doubts his people'. Finally, and worryingly for anyone who might aspire to become Henry's wife, Marillac concluded that Henry was marred by 'lightness and inconstancy', claiming that he 'has perverted the rights of religion, marriage, faith and promise, as softened wax can be altered to any form'. Henry VIII, by 1543, was a fearsome specimen and, even before Latimer's death, when Catherine was enjoying the early stages of her romance with Thomas Seymour, he turned his attention to her.

Henry's long widowhood following the execution of his fifth wife may not have been entirely his own choice because, after the fall of Catherine Howard, he had passed an act making it treason for a non-virgin to marry the king. As Chapuys sardonically pointed out in early 1542, this narrowed the field somewhat and he claimed that:

> Besides there are few, if any, ladies at court now-a-days likely to aspire to the honour of becoming one of the king's wives, or to desire that the choice should fall on them; for a law has just passed in Parliament enjoining that should the king or his successors wish to marry a subject of theirs, the lady chosen would be bound to declare, under pain of death, if any charge of misconduct can be brought against her.

Henry VIII recognized that, if he wanted a sixth wife, he would have to be content with a widow who could not plausibly be expected to be a virgin at the time of her marriage to him. According to the *Chronicle of Henry VIII*, Henry himself informed his council that: 'Gentlemen, I desire company, but I have had more than enough of taking young wives, and I am now resolved to marry a widow.' The lady that Henry had chosen was Catherine herself, who he noticed from her frequent visits to Mary's household at court.

Within days of Mary's return to court it was noted by observers that the king was showing his daughter a great deal of attention and that he came out himself to meet her when she first arrived. This immediately caused rumours that the king was looking for a bride and, on 22 February 1543, Chapuys was able to report that Henry was continuing to make conspicuous and regular visits to his daughter, stating that 'the king has shown the greatest possible affection and liberality to the Princess, and not a day passes but he goes to visit her in her chamber two or three times with the utmost cordiality'. While Henry was undoubtedly fond of Mary, he had never shown her so much affection before and it is clear that he found something else to interest him in his daughter's household. With the gift of the fine dresses ordered in February 1543 for both Catherine and Princess Mary, it must have suddenly become all too clear to Catherine that Henry's focus was her.

Henry had, of course, come into contact with Catherine back in 1540 but in early 1543 she became a daily presence for the first time. While Catherine was never described as a beauty, she was comely enough. At around thirty, Catherine was about the same age as Anne Boleyn had been when she became queen and both Catherine of Aragon and Jane Seymour had also been past the first flush of youth at their marriages. Henry was always attracted to clever women and Catherine must have seemed a fascinating and highly suitable companion. The only real downside, from Henry's point of view, in choosing Catherine as his sixth wife, was her apparent infertility. At fifty-one, Henry still expected a sexual relationship with his wife, although he was apparently intermittently impotent, and he was hopeful of fathering more sons. As his contemporary, George Constantine pointed out in the late 1530s, 'his Grace might yet have many fayre children to God's pleasure and the comforte of the realme; my father might be grandefather to an elder man than the kynges majestie, and yet ys luste, I thanke God'. Catherine was widely considered to be infertile, with Anne of Cleves, who hoped herself to remarry the king, pointing out that her rival 'gives no hope whatever of posterity to the king, for she had no children by her first two husbands'. Henry VIII, while he always remained hopeful of issue with Catherine, accepted the unlikelihood of the event. Given his own age and sexual difficulties he may have reasoned that since

Catherine was so suitable in all other respects, he could ignore the high probability that they would not have children. There is no evidence that Henry was in love with Catherine, but he was fond of her, referring to her both as 'sweetheart' and by the affectionate nickname of 'Kate' during their marriage.

In the early months of 1543 Catherine was so wrapped up in her love for Thomas Seymour that she may well, at first, not have noticed the interest shown to her by the king. By the time that he made the gift of the dresses to her it must have been clear and deeply worrying. Catherine was still married to Lord Latimer and not yet free to marry Thomas and she felt trapped, desperate to secure the love of her life in the face of the interest of the king. Catherine had no desire to marry Henry and she attempted, as politely as she could, to make it clear that his attentions were unwelcome. Henry always responded more affectionately to women who first refused his advances and Catherine played unwittingly into his hands, increasing his desire to win her as a bride. He also knew that he had a rival in Thomas Seymour and, by early spring he had resolved to get him out of the way, appointing him to act as his ambassador to the Netherlands. News of this appointment was devastating for Catherine but Thomas, aware of the dangers in being a rival to the king, had already begun to back away. In early May he left England, arriving in Brussels on 16 May 1543. For Catherine, this was a bitter blow, but she was still determined not to marry Henry if she could find some way to avoid it.

By early 1543, Henry had a fearsome reputation as a husband, with two divorces and two wives beheaded behind him, as well as a wife who was widely rumoured to have died in childbirth due to lack of care taken by her attendants. The date of Henry's proposal to Catherine is nowhere recorded, but it would have been in the spring, at some point after Lord Latimer's death. Catherine was expecting the proposal and she took the brave step to voice her concerns, responding boldly to Henry when he asked her to become his wife that 'it were better to be your mistress than your wife'. Under ordinary circumstances, this would have been a provocation to the king and Catherine could well have found her life in danger. However, for Henry, excited as he was by his choice of a bride, it was merely evidence of Catherine's modesty in suggesting that she were not good enough to be his queen. Henry was convinced that Catherine was perfect for him, and increased the pressure placed upon her, saying, once again 'Lady Latimer, I wish you to be my wife'. With Thomas Seymour's departure and Henry's dismissal of her objections, Catherine knew that she had no choice but to comply, falling to her knees before answering: 'Your Majesty is my master, I have but to obey you.' While on her knees Catherine also prayed to God for guidance and, after her initial reluctance, she came to see the pressure placed upon her as evidence of God's will, later writing that, while she had intended to marry Thomas Seymour, 'God withstood my will therein most vehemently for a time, and through his grace and goodness, made that possible which seemed to me most impossible; that was, made me renounce utterly mine own will, and to follow his will most willingly.' Catherine saw Henry's proposal as the will of God and, from that moment onwards, she prepared for her marriage with a new purpose, seeing it as an opportunity to do God's work and spread her reformist beliefs.

Catherine was in no way in love with Henry as she prepared for her wedding. In spite of this, with her new sense of religious purpose, she found it within herself to become fond of her new husband, perhaps in recognition of the opportunities that he had opened up for her. In a letter written by Catherine to Henry in the summer of 1544, she set out her heart to him, making it clear that her feelings for him were intricately tied up with her religious devotion. According to Catherine:

Although the discourse of time and account of days neither is long nor many of your Majesty's absence, yet the want of your presence, so much beloved and desired of me, maketh me, that I cannot quietly pleasure in any thing, until I hear from your Majesty. The time therefore seemeth to me very long with a great desire to know how your Highness has done, since your departing hence. Whose prosperity and health I prefer and desire more than mine own. And whereas I know your Majesty's absence is never without great respects of things most convenient and necessary, yet love and affection compelled me to desire your presence. And again, the same zeal and love forceth me also to be best content with that which is your will and pleasure, and to embrace most joyfully his will and pleasure whom I love. God, the knower of secrets, can judge these words not to be only written with ink, but most truly impressed in the heart.

In spite of her attempts to convince herself that she was in love with Henry in the days before her wedding, Catherine was filled with apprehension at just what she was about to embark upon in becoming the sixth wife of such a notorious husband.

In the days before her wedding, Catherine made her final preparations for the change to her life that lay ahead. By late June, she and her sister, Anne, were firmly established at court and, doubtless due to Catherine's influence, Henry recalled his younger daughter, Elizabeth, to join the family group. Catherine spent her time preparing for her marriage and, in the days before the ceremony, ordered presents of a pair of gold bracelets set with diamonds, rubies and emeralds for Henry's elder daughter, Mary, to be given after the wedding ceremony. Catherine later gave Mary a present of £40 which may also have been linked to her marriage and she doubtless made similar gifts to the younger Elizabeth. She also prepared a letter to be sent to her brother, who was absent from court, to inform him of her change in circumstances, 'as the person who has most cause to rejoice thereat'. Perhaps trying to persuade herself, as she prepared for the ordeal ahead, Catherine also assured William that it was her 'greatest joy and comfort'. Henry was also busy with his preparations and, on 10 July 1543, he obtained a licence from the Archbishop of Canterbury to marry Catherine without banns.

The marriage of Catherine and Henry took place on 12 July 1543 at Hampton Court. Unlike the majority of the king's previous marriages, which had been undertaken in secret, the ceremony was a family event with a number of Henry's friends attending, as well as Catherine's sister and brother-in-law, Henry's brother-in-law, the Duke of Suffolk, Henry's two daughters and his niece, Margaret Douglas, and Catherine's friends the Duchess of Suffolk and Lady Dudley. The couple were married by Stephen Gardiner, Bishop of Winchester, a man who would later become Catherine's implacable enemy, but the ceremony itself was a cheerful and successful one. When those assembled were asked if they had any objections to the ceremony, no one said anything and, instead, everyone applauded. Henry then took Catherine's right hand and recited after the Bishop: 'I, Henry, take thee, Katharine, to my wedded wife, to have and to hold from this day forward, for better for worse, for richer for poorer, in sickness and in health, till death us depart, and thereto I plight thee my troth.' Catherine and Henry released hands, before clasping them again as Catherine stated: 'I, Katharine, take thee Henry to my wedded husband, to have and to hold from this day forward, for better for worse, for richer for poorer, in sickness and in health, to be bonayr and buxome in bed and at board, till death us depart, and thereto I plight my troth.' Henry placed a wedding ring on Catherine's finger before the couple left the room, doubtless to sounds of applause once again.

With her marriage, Catherine's life changed dramatically: she was the sixth queen of the elderly and dangerous king. Her reign began well, with one courtier commenting only days after the wedding that Catherine was 'a woman in my judgement, for vertewe, wisdomme and gentilnesse, most meite for his Highnesse; and sure I am his Majesty had never a wif more agreable to his harte then she is'. In the days following her marriage Catherine was acutely aware of the difficulties of her position and the need to live up to both her new role as the wife of Henry VIII and queen of England.

7

CATHERINE THE QUEEN: JULY 1543 – SPRING 1544

Although Catherine was initially reluctant to marry Henry VIII and become a queen, once she had reconciled herself to the inevitable, she was determined to make the most of the opportunity presented to her. Henry had had five wives before Catherine and each had had varying influences over him. Catherine of Aragon and Anne Boleyn, his first two wives, had been very influential in their time and, while Henry's later wives were not allowed positions of such power, Catherine was determined to ensure that her position was one of importance.

One of Catherine's first tasks as queen was to appoint her household. Catherine Howard's household had been disbanded in November 1541 and there had been no queen consort for nearly two years. Catherine was determined to surround herself with friends and family. Her sister, Anne, was appointed as one of the most prominent ladies of the bedchamber for which, in any event, after years of service to Henry's earlier wives, she was well-qualified. Catherine was also determined to keep her young stepdaughter, Margaret Neville, close to her and she was appointed as a maid of honour. Catherine was attended by her friend the Duchess of Suffolk and her cousins Lady Lane and Lady Tyrwhitt.

Catherine's household was nominally frequented by other, far greater ladies and, by May 1546, it was noted that the king's two daughters, Mary and Elizabeth, and his three nieces, Margaret Douglas and Francis and Eleanor Brandon were in attendance on the queen, at least for some of the time. It was her sister Anne and stepdaughter Margaret to whom Catherine was closest. Even when Anne was called away from court Catherine kept in contact with her, with her payments for June 1546 listing the costs of 'five yeomen and two grooms riding to Hanworthe at the [christe]ning of the lady Harbertes [Anne Parr's] child'.

Catherine also sought to promote her kinsmen to positions of honour within her household, again in an attempt to surround herself with familiar faces and ensure the loyalty of those around her. Catherine's hot-headed brother-in-law, Marmaduke Neville, had secured a position in the queen's household by mid 1544 and more prominent posts were given to other family members, with Catherine's uncle, Sir William Parr of Horton, receiving the powerful position of Lord Chamberlain to the queen. Catherine also urged Henry to ennoble her family as he had done previously with the families of his other English wives. In a lavish ceremony on 23 December 1543 at Hampton Court, Catherine's brother, William, was finally granted the title for which Maud Parr had schemed and hoped, with the king appointing him as the Earl of Essex before the assembled court. Catherine's uncle was also elevated to a peerage, receiving the title of Lord Parr of Horton. For Catherine, honours such as these were a vindication of her decision to accept Henry as her husband and she sought to use her influence as queen to benefit those close to her. The *Legend of Sir Nicholas Throckmorton*, states that one of Catherine's cousins, Clement Throckmorton, was appointed as her cupbearer. She also favoured her Throckmorton kin by less official means. According to the *Legend*:

And nowe, because the king and queene did use
By friendlie signes their likeing to displaye,
What men our companie would then refuse?
Our betters then with us did seeke to staye.
For loe! It is a path to dignitie
With Caesar's friend to be in amitie.

Catherine's influence, and that of her influential brother and sister, helped bring the Throckmorton family to prominence at court, with the *Legend* claiming that 'nowe when these call'd us Cousin at each word, The other peeres would friendlie speeche afforde'. Catherine remained dependent on her family during her time as queen and it is telling that, as queen, she always signed her name as 'Katherine the Queen, KP', in reference to her former existence as Catherine Parr.

Catherine retained her deep devotion to the religious reform during her time as queen and she sought to promote her religion through the appointments to her household. In December 1543 one Francis Goldsmith, who had received a place in the queen's household, wrote to Catherine to thank her, demonstrating his reformist beliefs and his admiration for the queen. According to Goldsmith:

If the Queen of the South and Esther will be always remembered, much less will her name be lost by time or the ungrateful oblivion of men. God has so formed her mind for pious studies, that she considers everything of small value compared to Christ. Her rare goodness has made every day like Sunday, a thing hitherto unheard of, especially in a royal palace.

Goldsmith continued praising Catherine's attempts to bring piety to the court. Another of Catherine's servants, a secretary named Richard Butler, was also noted to be on a secret mission to the Lutheran princes in Germany in June 1545, something which also attests to the evangelical nature of Catherine's household. According to the Imperial ambassador, it was believed that Butler's mission 'is to solicit secretly the German princes to form a league with this king, which seems to me, Sire, to be a point of the highest importance, as touching the religious question'.

In spite of Francis Goldsmith's claim that Catherine had made every day like a Sunday, in reality Catherine's household and her time as queen was in no way as joyless as he suggested. For all her reputation as the first truly Protestant queen of England, Catherine was determined to present herself to the world as a queen and this was conveyed in her sumptuous dress. Catherine had always loved fine clothes, as the order for dresses paid for by the king in February 1543 showed. As queen, it was positively Catherine's duty to indulge this interest in order to show the glory of England's queen to the world. In early 1546, for example, Catherine purchased a number of rich fabrics in yellow, red, blue, green, white and black to be made into dresses. Earlier in her marriage, in 1544, Catherine also purchased materials for several new outfits, including over eight and a half yards of purple velvet to make a kirtle for her dress, two yards of purple satin for the bodice and a further ten yards of purple satin for a second kirtle, French sleeves and Venetian stockings. She purchased further purple fabrics later in the year and also black velvet and yellow satin for other clothes.

Catherine employed her own goldsmith and silkwoman, again to ensure that she always looked magnificent. She had an interest in portraiture and is the most painted of all Henry VIII's wives, appearing sumptuously dressed and queenly in every painting.

As well as ensuring that she looked like a queen, Catherine was also determined that those around her should wear clothes to reflect their positions in her household. She is recorded as having purchased black material for a cloak for her stepdaughter, Margaret Neville. At the same time she purchased grey fabric for a coat and red for a petticoat as gifts for two of her fools. The typical livery for Catherine's household was red and she ordered coats in this colour for five of her minstrels and also five members of her personal troupe of players. A list of the liveries and uniforms with which Catherine's footmen were supplied survives and, once again, demonstrates her determination to ensure that the officers of her household looked splendid. Each footman was provided with two and a half yards of scarlet fabric and a further two and a half yards of crimson velvet with which to make a cloak. Further crimson velvet was provided for a coat and a similar fabric for a pair of leg hose. They also received materials for other items, such as doublets, more hose, shirts, hats, caps, garters and shoes, as well as an allowance for having the fabrics made up into clothes. There is however some evidence that, while she was happy to place orders for expensive goods to ensure that she looked like a queen, she was less keen to actually pay her bills, with one member of the court complaining to a member of Henry's council that 'the queen owes me much money', referring to a large sum that she owed to his late wife 'for things delivered' in Catherine's early weeks as queen. Catherine was uninterested in the debt, and the dispute dragged on for several years.

Catherine spent most of her time in her household and she was determined to enjoy herself. She loved music and kept a troupe of minstrels to play for her. She had an interest in drama and her own company of players performed before both her and the court. Like the king, Catherine also employed fools to amuse her, with records noting that in 1546 she had a male fool called Thomas Browne and an unnamed female fool. In June 1544 she paid for Lady Audley's fool to be brought to entertain the court. Catherine kept greyhounds to assist her in hunting and she is recorded as having made presents of venison to a number of courtiers during the summer of 1546, for example. She also kept pet parrots, exotic and extravagant pets, on perches in her rooms. It is clear that, for all her reluctance in accepting Henry's proposal of marriage, she was determined to enjoy her new role.

The relationship between Henry and Catherine quickly settled into a comfortable routine and Catherine was widely praised for her suitability as the king's spouse. According to the *Chronicle of Henry VIII*:

> this lady, Queen Katharine, was quieter than any of the young wives the king had had, and as she knew more of the world, she always got on pleasantly with the king, and had no caprices, and paid much honour to Madam Mary and the wives of the nobles, but she kept her ladies very strictly.

With Henry having selected three of his wives from amongst their predecessor's ladies, it is no surprise that Catherine kept her own ladies strictly under control. She was a great success with Henry in the early weeks of her marriage and he was pleased with his new bride.

Catherine has long enjoyed a reputation as Henry's nurse and the woman who soothed his ills during his old age. There is no real evidence to suggest that Catherine did nurse the king, although she would have attempted to take his mind off the pain of his principal ailment, an ulcered leg. It is less likely that she was relied upon by the king as his sole nurse and carer and it is clear that a nurse was not what Henry was looking for in a wife. Henry expected his wives to be attractive and was always hopeful of children and he would certainly have attempted a sexual relationship with Catherine, although, given the fact that she did not conceive throughout her marriage and the persistent rumours of Henry's impotence, it is possible that attempts to consummate the marriage were unsuccessful. Henry had been unable to consummate his fourth marriage to Anne of Cleves, although there is evidence that he had no such difficulties with his fifth wife, Catherine Howard, who, at one point, was believed to have become pregnant. Anne Boleyn complained of the king's impotency during their marriage several years before he took his sixth wife, although after some delay, Henry's third wife, Jane Seymour, had conceived. Whatever the truth of their relationship, Henry expected a physical relationship with his wife rather than for her to simply act as his nurse.

A relegation of Catherine to the role of nurse would also have been a great disservice to her talents. Henry had allowed his first two wives, Catherine of Aragon and Anne Boleyn, to take very political roles, although he actively discouraged his third wife, Jane Seymour, from doing so. Henry recognised that Catherine was an asset to him and she was allowed to play a prominent role in foreign diplomacy. The Emperor Charles V and Francis I, King of France, had gone to war against each other in 1542 and, as the war dragged on, both became increasingly eager to secure an alliance with Henry. Catherine, perhaps reflecting the king's own partiality towards Charles V, or due to her memories of Catherine of Aragon, the emperor's aunt, was permitted to play an important role in the negotiations with the emperor and Charles himself believed that Catherine was influential, writing to his ambassador, Eustace Chapuys, in March 1544 that 'to conclude, you are doing the right thing in keeping on good terms with the queen; do not fail, whenever the opportunity offers, to address her Our most cordial commendations as well as the Princess'.

In November 1543 Charles wrote personally to Henry 'begging you to let Us also know personal news of you, and of the queen, our good sister'. Catherine was also expected to receive, and entertain, a number of important Imperial visitors and it is evident from the prominence that she was given that Henry was confident in her ability to impress. In December 1543, for example, the emperor wrote to the Duke of Juano, Viceroy of Sicily, who was instructed to go to England, that, on arrival:

> You will offer Our most cordial recommendations to the queen, Our good sister, and also to Madame our cousin [Mary of England], and will thank our sister for the very cordial friendship and favourable treatment of our said cousin. You will, if possible, visit personally the Prince, my nephew, and bring Us news of his health.

The Duke duly visited the court at Hampton Court in Christmas week, where he was well received during his mission to discuss Henry's entry into the war, before leaving, loaded with gifts from the king. Early in January 1544 Catherine also received another Imperial ambassador, Don Luis de Avila. At court, de Avila 'was welcomed and kindly received by the king, by the queen, and by the Princess [Mary]'.

Catherine was permitted to speak regularly with the resident Imperial ambassadors in England and Henry trusted her to say the right thing and further his own policy. In April 1544, for example, when Chapuys informed Henry of the marriage of Charles's son, Philip, to a Portuguese princess, Henry told Chapuys to inform the prince of his goodwill. When the ambassador was admitted to the presence of Catherine and Mary, they both made the 'same offers and protestations of friendship'. A few months later, Chapuys was also questioned individually by Henry, Catherine and Mary on the subject of Philip's marriage, again expressing their goodwill towards the prince and his father. In the summer of 1545, while watching the king hunting in his park at Guildford, Catherine chatted companionably with another Imperial ambassador, Van Der Delft. Catherine attempted to impress the Imperial ambassadors and visitors during her time as queen, both as a means of demonstrating her ability to Henry and also, perhaps, as a mark of her own political partiality towards the Imperial cause over that of the French.

Catherine's assistance to Henry in his foreign diplomacy is most clearly seen in the visit of the Duke of Najera to England in February 1544. The Duke, a high ranking Spanish nobleman, arrived in London on 11 February. Henry was determined to impress the nobleman and, on 17 February, he sent William Parr to dine with the duke and then escort him to an audience with the king. The visit was planned to demonstrate Henry's magnificence and, the duke's secretary, Pedro de Gante, was impressed, recording that:

Before the Duke arrived at the kings chamber he passed through three saloons, hung with tapestry; in the second of which were stationed in order on either side the king's body guard, dressed in habits of red, and holding halberds. In the third saloon were nobles, knights, and gentlemen, and here was a canopy made of rich figured brocade, with a chair of the same material. To this canopy and chair the same respect was paid by all as if the king himself was present, every one standing on foot with his cap in his hand. Here the brother of the queen and other noblemen entertained the Duke a quarter of an hour, until it was announced that he should enter the chamber of the king.

Only the duke and a small number of attendants were allowed to enter the room for an audience with the king. The meeting however, at which the Imperial ambassador, Eustace Chapuys was also present, went well and, immediately afterwards, the duke and his retinue were taken to the queen's apartments to meet Catherine.

According to Chapuys' account, Catherine was ill at the time of the duke's visit, but insisted on coming out of her chamber to entertain him. If she was indeed unwell, she concealed it expertly and the duke's own secretary, who was also present, made no mention of it. The Imperial party found Catherine with her stepdaughter, Princess Mary, and attended by a large number of ladies, including the king's niece, Lady Margaret Douglas. According to the duke's secretary, Catherine put on a regal and spectacular show and her visitors were charmed by her:

The Duke kissed the queen's hand, by whom he was received in an animated manner. From thence they conducted the Duke to another apartment, where stood another canopy of brocade, with a chair of the same. The queen entered with the Princesses and ladies, and having seated herself she commanded the Duke to sit down, and musicians and violins were introduced. The queen danced first with her brother, very gracefully; then the Princess Mary and the Princess of Scotland [Margaret Douglas] danced with other gentlemen, and many other ladies did the same.

The dancing lasted for several hours and Catherine then offered presents to the duke before allowing him to again kiss her hand. Both Catherine and Mary made a great effort to impress during the visit and they were dressed in all their finery. According to the duke's secretary:

> The queen has a lively and pleasing appearance, and is praised as a virtuous woman. She was dressed in a robe of cloth of gold, and a petticoat of brocade with sleeves lined with crimson satin, and trimmed with three piled crimson velvet: her train was more than two yards long. Suspended from her neck were two crosses, and a jewel of very rich diamonds, and in her head-dress were many beautiful ones. Her girdle was of gold, with very long pendants. The Princess Mary has a pleasing countenance and person. It is said of her, that she is endowed with very great goodness and discretion.

Mary was as finely dressed as Catherine in a petticoat of cloth of gold and a violet velvet gown with a bejewelled headdress. Shortly after the Duke of Najera's visit, a further Imperial nobleman, the Duke of Alberquerque arrived to pay court to Henry and, once again, Catherine was called upon to receive him. Catherine's influence was so widely known that, in May 1544, the King of France hoping to win support for himself, sent a ring to be presented as a gift to either Catherine or Mary, although it is not recorded who received the present.

Catherine was an enthusiastic participant in Henry's foreign diplomacy and she was an asset to him, helping to promote his own policy. It is also likely that Catherine's own personal preference was towards the emperor rather than towards France and her fondness for her stepdaughter Mary, the emperor's cousin, and her memories of her own mother and her loyalties to Catherine of Aragon pushed her in the direction of Charles V. What is also evident from the first year of Catherine's marriage is that she was often with her stepdaughter, Princess Mary, and the two women were exceptionally close. Mary was not the only one of Henry's children that Catherine sought to build a relationship with and she did her best to be a mother to Henry's two younger children, Elizabeth and Edward.

8

BELOVED MOTHER: SPRING 1544 – SUMMER 1544

Although she had no children of her own, Catherine had treated Margaret Neville as her own daughter since her marriage to Lord Latimer and, on her marriage to Henry in 1543, she was prepared to adopt the same relationship with her new stepchildren. Mary, who, being only four years younger than Catherine, needed a friend rather than a mother, quickly became a close friend of her stepmother and Catherine also sought to befriend Henry's younger children, Elizabeth and Edward, both of whom had lost their own mothers in infancy.

Catherine was already close to Princess Mary at the time of her marriage. In July 1543 Mary was twenty-seven years old. Small and pretty, she had always been an attractive prize on the European marriage market although her illegitimacy, conferred upon her by her father at the time of her parents' divorce in 1533 hindered any attempts to find her a husband. It is, in any event, unlikely that Henry himself ever had any intention of marrying his eldest daughter to anyone, particularly if it meant a risk of her leaving England. Mary, through her mother, was a cousin of the Emperor Charles V and a significant political figure even after the birth of her half-brother, Edward, in 1537.

While Henry was adamant that his daughter, as the child of his first marriage to his brother's widow, was illegitimate, this was not how she was viewed by the Pope or by her relatives on the continent.

Henry's relationship with his eldest daughter had completely collapsed with the divorce of his first wife but, in the summer of 1536, following the execution of Anne Boleyn and Mary's complete capitulation to her father's will, the princess had been reinstated and remained largely in favour until the end of Henry's reign. Henry could be a doting father when it suited him and, in September 1542, for example, he entertained and feasted Mary and gave her gifts of rings and jewels. Later that year he also 'received the Princess [Mary] in the kindest possible manner, and spoke to her in the most gracious and amiable words that a father could address his daughter'. While Catherine had her sister, stepdaughter Margaret and female cousins to be her companions at court, Mary's presence provided much needed friendship and, in spite of their very different religious beliefs, Mary and Catherine were fond of each other. According to the Imperial ambassador, Eustace Chapuys, in August 1543 'the king continues to treat the Princess kindly, and has made her stay with his new queen, who behaves affectionately towards her'.

Mary had not got on with her previous stepmother, Catherine Howard, and had spent little time at court during that queen's brief reign. During Catherine Parr's time as queen, however, while the princess retained her own separate establishment, her household became loosely attached to the queen's and the two women spent their time largely in each other's company. As well as her own feelings of friendship towards Mary, Catherine was also fond of her stepdaughter for her mother's sake and, in January 1545, she gave her own reasons for her support of Mary. According to Chapuys and his colleague, Van Der Delft, he met with the king on his way to mass one morning:

> When the king had entered his oratory we were conducted, without the slightest hint of desire on our part, to the oratory to the queen, who shortly afterwards herself entered. We conveyed to her your Majesty's [Charles V's] greeting, and thanks for the good offices which she had always exercised towards the preservation of friendship between your Majesty and the king, and also thanked her for the favour she showed to the Lady Mary. The queen answered very graciously that she did not deserve so much courtesy from your Majesty; and what she did for Lady Mary was less than she would like to do, and was only her duty in every respect. With regard to the maintenance of friendship, she said she had done, and would do, nothing to prevent its growing still further: and she hoped that God would avert even the slightest dissension, as the friendship was so necessary and both sovereigns were so good. We afterwards saluted Lady Mary, and gave her your Majesty's greetings, for which she was humbly thankful.

Mary's accounts show that the two women exchanged gifts and when Mary fell ill on a journey between Grafton and Woodstock, Catherine sent her own litter to fetch her stepdaughter to Ampthill where she and the king were staying, presumably to ensure that her stepdaughter received the best possible treatment for her illness. Catherine and Mary also co-operated with each other on a number of occasions, in September 1545, for example, making a joint suit for Mary's chaplain, Richard Baldwin, to receive a position in Newark College in Leicester.

It is also clear from the letters of Catherine's stepson, Prince Edward, that Catherine was considered to have the governance of his eldest half-sister. According to Edward, writing in May 1546:

Pardon my rude style in writing to you, most illustrious queen and beloved mother, and receive my hearty thanks for your loving kindness to me and my sister [Mary]. Yet, dearest mother, the only true consolation is from Heaven, and the only real love is the love of God. Preserve, therefore, I pray you, my dear sister Mary from all the wiles and enchantments of the evil one, and beseech her to attend no longer to foreign dances and merriments which do not become a most Christian princess.

As with Mary, Catherine's relationship with Edward was excellent and, only a few months before, he had written to Mary, who was still staying with Catherine, to assure both her and Catherine of his affections, declaring that 'it is so long since I last wrote to you, my very dear sister, that it may chance so that you may think I have entirely forgotten you, but affection ever holds the chief place in my heart both for you and my dearest mother [Catherine]'.

Henry VIII's beloved only son was five years old at the time of Catherine's marriage and had lost his own mother, Jane Seymour, only twelve days after his birth. Edward, like both his elder half-sisters, was a precocious child and, to his contemporaries, he promised great things. Throughout his life, Edward was the subject of extravagant praise, with his tutor, Sir John Cheke, writing in 1553 that 'should a longer life be allowed him, (and I hope that he may very long enjoy it,) I prophesy indeed, that, with the lord's blessing, he will prove such a king, as neither yield to Josiah in the maintenance of true religion, nor to Solomon in the management of the state, nor to David in the encouragement of godliness'. Another contemporary, John Foxe, was just as lyrical in his praise, declaring that 'on the excellent virtues and singular graces of King Edward, wrought in him by the gift of God, although nothing can be said enough in his commendation'. Foxe continued, stating that Edward, 'a prince, although but tender in years, yet for his sage and mature ripeness in wit and all princely ornaments, as I see but few to whom he may not be equal, so again, I see not many, to whom he may not justly be preferred'. For Henry, Edward was a symbol of his ability to father a healthy son and, also, God's approval. For the people of England he was a symbol of stability and the token that any threat of a civil war with a disputed succession had been averted. For Catherine, however, Edward was always a little boy.

Catherine quickly befriended Edward, becoming the only mother that he was ever to know. Edward, in the main, was a cosseted child, precocious, but with little affection for those around him. Within months of meeting Catherine, however, he was writing her devoted letters:

Most honourable and entirely beloved mother, I have me most humbly recommended unto your grace with like thanks, both for that your grace did accept so gently my simple and rude letters, which do give me much comfort and encouragement to go forward in such things wherein your grace beareth me on hand, that I am already entered. I pray God I may be able in part to satisfy the good expectation of the king's majesty, my father, and of your grace, whom God have ever in his most blessed keeping.
Your loving son, E. Prince.

Of all his letters, only those to Catherine and to his half-sisters show any tenderness and another letter shows how Edward ensured that he always remained in contact with Catherine:

> Perhaps you will be surprised that I so often write to you, and that in so short a time, most noble queen and most dear mother, but by the same rule you may be surprised that I do my duty towards you. However, this I am now doing more willingly, because I have got a suitable messenger, my servant; and therefore I could not help sending a letter to you, in order to testify my respect and affection.

Edward, as the heir to the throne, had his own separate household and Catherine was not expected to take custody of him as she had her other stepchildren. In his diary, written after he succeeded to the throne, Edward wrote that he was raised by women until his sixth year when he began his studies in earnest. Catherine apparently took on some role in the management of Edward's household and, certainly, she took an interest in its members, in 1545 writing in favour of George Tresham, one of Edward's gentlemen, who sought the payment of an annuity. Catherine quickly gained Edward's trust and soon after her marriage she also set about winning the friendship of Henry's younger daughter, Princess Elizabeth.

Like Edward, the nine-year-old Princess Elizabeth had lost her mother in infancy, with the execution of Anne Boleyn when Elizabeth was two years old. Elizabeth, like her half-sister, Mary, had been declared illegitimate by her father and she was largely ignored by him, visiting court only rarely. When Elizabeth visited court for her father's wedding, Catherine sought her out in order to befriend her. Elizabeth, like her half-brother and sister, spent some of the summer under Catherine's guardianship, with the Regent of the Netherlands, Mary of Hungary, asking in December 1543 whether Henry, Catherine, Edward, Mary and Elizabeth 'continued still in one household'. The answer, by December was unfortunately no, because, to Catherine's discomfiture, Elizabeth fell out of favour with her father in some way and was banished from his presence for nearly a year. While the reason for Elizabeth's exile is not clear, it was a major blow to both Catherine and her new stepdaughter although the pair continued to correspond regularly. Catherine continued to speak on behalf of Elizabeth to Henry and, in the summer of 1544, when Henry went to France, Catherine secured his consent to recall Elizabeth to court. In a letter written by Elizabeth to Catherine on 31 July 1544, she poured out her feelings for the stepmother whom she had barely seen but who was already more of a mother to her than anyone had been since her own mother's death. According to Elizabeth:

Inimical fortune, envious of all good and ever resolving human affairs, has deprived me for a whole year of your most illustrious presence, and not thus content, has yet again robbed me of the same good, which thing would be intolerable to me, did I not hope to enjoy it very soon. And in my exile, I well know that the clemency of your highness has had as much care and solicitude for my health as the king's majesty himself. By which thing I am not only bound to serve you, but also to revere you with filial love, since I understand that your most illustrious highness has not forgotten me every time you have written to the king's majesty, which, indeed, it was my duty to have requested from you. For heretofore I have not dared to write to him. Wherefore I now humbly pray your most excellent highness, that, when you write to his majesty, you will condescend to recommend me to him, praying ever for his sweet benediction, and similarly entreating our Lord God to send him best success, and the obtaining of victory over his enemies, so that you highness and I may, as soon as possible, rejoice together with him on his happy return. No less pray I God, that he would preserve your most illustrious highness, to whose grace, humbly kissing your hands, I offer and recommend myself.

Elizabeth signed her letter 'your most obedient daughter, and most faithful servant, Elizabeth' and it is clear that she already held her stepmother in affection. With Elizabeth's forgiveness by Henry, Catherine was able to bring her younger stepdaughter to court much more frequently and, although she did not become a member of the queen's household, Elizabeth found herself inducted into family life for the first time.

Elizabeth and Edward were of a similar age and it has often been suggested that Catherine played a role in arranging their education. Catherine was known to have an interest in education throughout her time as queen. In November 1545 Parliament granted Henry all the colleges, chantries and hospitals in England, allowing him to appropriate their goods and dissolve them if he so wished. This was granted on similar terms to the dissolution of the monasteries and the terror that their colleges would be dissolved gripped Oxford and Cambridge Universities. According to Dr Richard Cox, later the following year, Oxford University decided to appeal directly to the queen for support. There is no record of Catherine's intervention on behalf of Oxford but her response to a similar appeal from the University of Cambridge survives. Catherine answered Cambridge's appeal in a diplomatic and queenly letter stating that she hoped that the university would apply itself to the study of the scripture so that it 'may be accounted rather an university of divine philosophy than of natural and moral, as Athens was'. Once Catherine's letter had dealt with the formalities, she continued, saying that she had petitioned the king:

> For the establishment of your livelihood and possessions, in which (notwithstanding his majesty's property and interest, through the consent of the high court of parliament) his highness being such a patron to good learning doth tender you so much, that he would rather advance learning and erect new occasion thereof than confound your ancient and godly institutions; so that such learning may hereafter ascribe her very original whole conversation to our sovereign lord the king, her only defence and worthy ornament, the prosperous estate and princely government of whom long to preserve, I doubt not but every one of you will in the daily invocation call upon Him, who alone and only, can dispose to every creature.

Catherine spoke for the university to the king and received some partial reassurance of the university's survival, although her intervention did not go as far as the scholars had hoped. Catherine was also asked to intervene in relation to the proposed dissolution of the college of Secular Canons at Stoke, of which she was nominally the patron. Again, in spite of her interest in learning, any appeal that she made was unsuccessful and the college was dissolved.

Prince Edward received an education dominated by the new religion, with a leading reformer, Dr Cox, being appointed as his main tutor. There is no direct evidence to show that Catherine played any direct role in the appointment of Edward's tutors and the prince's education was designed to fit him for his future as king. From the age of six, he studied a rigorous curriculum among tutors who 'sought to bring him up in learning the tongues of the scriptures, philosophy and all liberal sciences'. He also learned modern languages, such as French and, by the time of his death aged fifteen, he was renowned as a scholar, with the famous tutor Roger Ascham commenting that 'if Kyng Edward had liued a litle longer, his onely example had breed soch a rase of worthie learned ientlemen as this Realmne neuer yet did affourde'. It is impossible that Edward's proud and doting father, Henry, would not have had the ultimate authority in the education of his son and, while the reformist nature of his tutors is striking, it may well be that this was less due to any deliberate policy on the king's, or Catherine's, part and more due to the fact that, by 1544 the bulk of the leading university scholars were followers of the religious reform.

While there is no direct evidence for Catherine's involvement in Edward's education, there is no doubt that, in the case of Elizabeth, over whom she exercised much greater parental authority, Catherine helped to ensure that she received an equally good education. During Catherine's time as queen her two youngest stepchildren became close and, while they were often apart, affectionate letters passed between them with Edward writing in one, for example that:

change of place, in fact did not vex me so much, dearest sister, as your going from me. Now, however, nothing can happen more agreeable to me than a letter from you; and especially as you were the first to send a letter to me, and have challenged me to write.

Catherine helped foster their affection for each other simply by allowing the two children to be together, when they visited court, within the secure family environment that she had created.

While it was Henry that was in ultimate governance of the fates and education of his children, Catherine, in seeking to ensure a good relationship between Henry and his daughters, and in bringing them back into the family circle, was able to be of great benefit to her two stepdaughters. Henry had always maintained that his two daughters were illegitimate and thus unfit to inherit the crown. At the time of Catherine's marriage, the existing law was the Second Act of Succession which left the crown to Edward and then any younger children born to Henry, with no place for either Mary or Elizabeth. However, on 16 January 1544, less than six months after Catherine's marriage, Parliament opened in London in order to debate the succession at the king's command. On 7 February 1544 the Third Act of Succession was passed, bequeathing the crown, after Henry's death to Edward and then any son or daughter born to the king by a legitimate wife. The Act continued:

> In the case it shall happen to the king's majesty and the said excellent prince his yet only son prince Edward and heir apparent, to decease without heir of either of their bodies lawfully begotten (as God defend), so that there is no such heir male or female of any of their two bodies to have and inherit the said imperial crown... that then the said imperial crown and all other the premises shall be to the Lady Mary the king's highness' daughter and to the heirs of the body of the same Lady Mary lawfully begotten, with such conditions as by his Highness shall be limited by his letters patents under his great seal, or by his majesty's last Will in writing

signed with his gracious hand; and for default of such issue the said imperial crown and other the premises shall be to the Lady Elizabeth the king's second daughter and to the heirs of the body of the said Lady Elizabeth lawfully begotten, with such conditions as by his highness shall be limited.

While Mary and Elizabeth remained illegitimate under the terms of the Act, the fact that they were reinstated to the succession was a major change in policy and a triumph for Catherine's work in bringing her two stepdaughters back into the royal family. The second Act of Succession had allowed Henry to nominate his successor, if necessary, a provision that could have been used to reinstate Mary and Elizabeth if he chose and the fact that, instead of relying on this as he had done in the past, he chose to enact a new statute is telling concerning Catherine's influence. Soon after the Act was passed Henry commissioned a great painting in which he sits with his queen and his son in a central position, flanked on either side by his daughters. This painting was intended to demonstrate the provision that Henry had made for the succession although, for Catherine, it must have seemed a rebuke that the queen in the picture was a posthumous image of Edward's mother, Jane Seymour, rather than of Catherine herself. In spite of this, Catherine knew that she had succeeded in reinstating her stepdaughters to the royal family, something that was always dear to her heart.

During the first half of 1544 Catherine was very aware of her influence over Henry and, in the summer of 1544 she received a great compliment from the king which demonstrated just how influential she was.

9

REGENT GENERAL OF ENGLAND: JULY 1544 – AUTUMN 1545

Catherine's time as queen coincided with a period of increasing militarism in England and, just over a year after she became queen, she was able to show Henry, and England as a whole, just how able she was.

The first signs that England was heading towards war came before Catherine's marriage and involved England's old enemy, Scotland. Henry's nephew, James V, had been king of Scotland since the death of his father in 1513 in battle against the English at Flodden. As James's uncle, Henry felt that the young king should look towards him for guidance and advice and he was increasingly frustrated with his nephew's seeming lack of respect towards him. In the summer of 1541, during his progress to the north of England, Henry had waited at York for James to meet with him and he was furious when the younger sovereign did not arrive. In August 1542 Henry sent troops north under the command of the Duke of Norfolk. In late November the Scots retaliated, sending a force of 60,000 south into England where they were put to flight in a skirmish at Solway Moss, a disaster for James, who died 'in a frenesy' just over three weeks later, apparently of grief, leaving a six day old daughter, Mary, Queen of Scots, as his heir. Henry immediately decided to unite the two kingdoms through the marriage of the infant queen to his own five-year-old son.

Early in 1543 the Earl of Arran, heir apparent to the Scottish crown, was appointed as both governor and protector of the infant queen, to Henry's disconcertion. With the death of their king and the humiliation of Solway Moss, the Scots had little option but to agree to Henry's demands, concluding in a treaty with Henry that the young queen would be betrothed to Edward and brought to England at the age of ten. Henry was jubilant and turned his attentions towards the continental wars, making a secret agreement with the emperor in February 1543 to invade France in support of his ally, Charles V. In the summer of 1543 Henry sent troops to Calais but he was unable to go in person, aware of the instability in Scotland. He was right to be concerned and, by September 1543 Arran had abandoned the English, repudiating the treaty made for the marriage of Edward and Mary, Queen of Scots.

Catherine played no role in the Scottish wars and negotiations, but it is clear from her later command of the situation in the north that she had given them her whole attention. Henry was determined to ensure that there was stability on his northern border before he embarked on a full campaign in France. The opportunity for this came in the summer of 1544 when he made an alliance with Matthew Stuart, Earl of Lennox, another Scottish grandee. The alliance was cemented by the marriage of Henry's niece, Lady Margaret Douglas, the aunt of the young Scottish queen, to Lennox. Catherine, along with Henry and his children, attended the marriage at court. Henry then sent Lennox north to press the English point of view in Scotland, leaving him free to concentrate on the war between the emperor and Francis I of France.

Henry had always had a romantic ideal of himself as a great war leader. He had made his first wife regent during an earlier campaign in France and he had also considered making his third wife, Jane Seymour, his regent during the Pilgrimage of Grace. Catherine was therefore the obvious choice of regent for the king and she was thrilled at the responsibility offered to her. Henry set off for France on 12 July 1544, leaving Catherine behind in London to rule England in his absence.

Catherine relished the challenge of her regency, immediately focussing her attentions on Scottish affairs. She was not expected to rule alone and Henry provided her with a Council who took much of the burden of affairs, including writing to the Earl of Shrewsbury on 30 July with regard to Scottish affairs and receiving reports from the north in return. It is clear however that Catherine retained the final say in matters and took an active interest herself, receiving briefings from her council and also writing directly to her officers in the north. On 2 September 1544, for example, Catherine wrote personally to Lords Evers and Whartons to say:

> Being appointed Regent of this realm in the king's absence, and understanding from Shrewsbury your diligent service done in the office committed to you, both for defence of the Borders and chastising of the king's enemies, we give you hearty thanks and require you to give the like in our name to the captains and gentlemen who have served you. Requiring you to continue your diligence especially now in the time of their harvest, so as their corn may be wasted as much as may be.

As regent, Catherine ensured that the king's troops in the north received the weapons and other provisions they required, as well as ordering that important strategic towns such as Berwick remained in good repair and fortified. She also issued passports for visitors to Scotland and she kept a firm eye on Scottish affairs, aware that, with the king absent in France, it was possible that England's traditional enemy might see the country as an easy target, as they had done in 1513 under Catherine of Aragon's regency. Catherine's official title was 'Regent generall of Englande in the kinges Majesties absence' and she was determined to assert her authority and repay the trust shown in her by Henry. She was also aware that her regency might prove to be a trial run for future authority as, before he left for France, Henry had made his Will. This Will no longer survives and was replaced before his death but, in light of Catherine's appointment in 1544 as both regent and governor of Prince Edward, it almost certainly included a provision for Catherine to fulfil the role of regent, a role commonly given to the mother of a child king, although rarely accorded to a stepmother.

Henry's trust in Catherine showed both his approval of her intellectual and organizational abilities and his trust in her as his wife. As well as her role in political affairs as regent, Catherine was also entrusted with the governance of the king's three children and she gathered all three to be with her at Hampton Court. Catherine's responsibility for the king's children weighed heavily on her mind and, on 18 September 1544, she issued a proclamation declaring:

> whereas the plague reigns in sundry parts of London and Westminster, no person whose house is infected, or who has been where the plague is, shall come to Court or permit attendants at Court to resort to his house; to avoid danger to the queen, the Prince and other the king's children.

Catherine also sent out servants to survey the surrounding area during the summer to ensure that she and her stepchildren were not exposed to any disease.

Catherine was anxious that she was kept informed of events in France and wrote to Henry soon after he left England. He was well known for his dislike of writing, though, and her hopes of a receiving a direct response from him remained unfulfilled. She had to content herself with letters from the king's council which kept her updated as to the progress of the campaign. Catherine was determined to keep Henry up to date on her actions as regent, both to ensure that her actions received his approval and to set his mind at rest over the state of his kingdom. On 31 July, for example, Catherine wrote to her husband:

> Pleaseth it your majesty to be advertised, this afternoon were brought unto me letters from your majesty's lieutenant of the north, declaring the apprehension of a Scottish ship by certain fishermen of Rye, and in the same certain Frenchmen and Scots, being sent with divers letters and credence towards the French king and others in France. And because I thought this taking of them, with the interruption of the said letters, to be of much importance for the advancement of your majesty's affairs, ordained (I doubt not) of God, as well to the intent your highness might thereby certainly understand the crafty dealing and juggling of that nation, as also mete with the same after such sort as to your huge wisdom shall be thought most convenient.

Catherine sent the Scottish letters to Henry for him to review, flattering him by consulting him on all matters. It is impossible to ignore the triumph in Catherine's letter at her own achievement in assisting the king with the defence of the realm by capturing the ship. Catherine also took the time to inform her husband that 'my lord prince and the rest of your majesty's children are all, thanks be to God, in very good health', before signing her letter as a dutiful wife 'your grace's most humble loving wife and servant, Katherine the Queen, KP'.

Catherine almost certainly received verbal messages from her husband and she was kept fully informed of his campaign in France by his council. Henry was determined to be a conquering hero, like his great predecessor, Henry V, and he wanted to be in the thick of any action. On his arrival at Calais, he divided his army in two, sending the Duke of Norfolk with a smaller force to besiege Montreuil, while he began a siege of the town of Boulogne. The excitement of the war rejuvenated Henry and, for a time, he was able to pretend that he was once again the athlete of his youth. He was also determined to make use of Catherine and, while he got down to the business of making war against the French king to remedy his 'just and lawful quarrels', he also urgently required supplies to continue his campaign. In a letter of 11 August, for example, the king wrote to Catherine's council requesting an immediate loan of funds. Catherine threw herself into action, as she did with regard to all Henry's requests from France. She was also involved in the recruitment of 4,000 footmen requested by Henry and, while these were not in the end required in the campaign, she kept them ready to march at an hour's notice while the future of the war remained uncertain.

Henry was grateful for Catherine's efforts during his campaign and, finally, on 8 September, he took the time to write to her himself. Henry's letter is a matter of fact account of the campaign, though he was both determined to impress his wife with his prowess and aware that she was a woman who would appreciate such detail. According to Henry:

> Most dearly and most entirely beloved wife, we recommend us heartily unto you, and thank you as well for your letter written unto us by your servant Robert Warner as for the venison which you sent then by him, and now last by Fowler, servant unto our dearest son the Prince, for the which we give unto you our hearty thanks, and would have written unto you again a letter with our own hand, but that we be so occupied, and have so much to do in foreseeing and caring for everything ourself, as we have almost no manner rest or leisure to do any other thing.
>
> The cause why we have detained here so long your said servant hath been upon hope to have sent you by him good news of the taking of the town, which no doubt we should have done, by the grace of God, before this time, but that our provision of powder is not come out of Flanders as we thought it would. Within two or three days we look for it here, and then shortly after we trust to write unto you some good news. And yet, in the mean season, we have done somewhat of importance, for we have won, (and that without any loss of men) the strongest part of the town, which is the bray [outwork] of the castle – such a piece, and of such strength, as now that we have it in our hands we think four hundred of our men within it shall be able to keep it against four thousand of our enemies, and yet it is much weaker to the castle side than it was outward to us.

Henry then described the French king's attempts to make peace with him, before adding a jubilant postscript in his own hand, stating that:

We trust, not doubting with God's grace but that the castle and town shall shortly follow the same trade, for as this day, which is the eighth day of September, we begin three batteries, and have three mines going, besides one which hath done his execution in shaking and tearing off one of their greatest bulwarks. No more to you at this time, sweetheart, both for lack of time and great occupation of business, saving we pray you to give in our name our hearty blessings to all our children, and recommendations to our cousin Margaret and the rest of the ladies and gentlewomen, and to our Council also.

Written with the hand of your loving husband, Henry R.

On 18 September Henry entered Boulogne as a triumphant conqueror, and Catherine ordered England to celebrate the king's triumph with a 'solempne generall procession kept at Pawles, with Te Deum songe, for the victorye of the Kinges Majestie, and many fyers made in the citie, and so after in every part of the realme'. Catherine celebrated along with everyone else and she was proud of Henry's triumph, composing a prayer herself in celebration of the campaign:

Our cause being now just, and being enforced to enter into war and battle, we most humbly beseech thee, O Lord God of hosts, so to turn the hearts of our enemies to the desire of peace, that no Christian blood be spilt; or else, grant, O Lord, that with small effusion of blood, and to the little hurt and damage of innocents, we may to thy glory obtain victory. And that the wars being soon ended, we may all with one heart and mind, knit together in concord and unity, laud and praise thee.

For Catherine, acting as regent was hard work but she was also able to enjoy some leisure time while she ran the country in Henry's absence.

The council that Henry had set up to assist Catherine in her regency was headed by Edward Seymour, Earl of Hertford, and Thomas Cranmer, Archbishop of Canterbury. Hertford was quickly summoned to France to assist in the campaign, but Catherine worked closely with the reformist archbishop. After being educated at Cambridge, Cranmer had travelled in Germany where he developed a great interest in the religious reform, even going so far as secretly marrying the niece of a leading German reformer. Catherine's religious beliefs were already well developed by the time that she became queen but, in Cranmer's company, she was exposed to new ideas and Henry's absence gave her a welcome opportunity to extend her religious beliefs. She also found time for family, taking Henry's children on a progress south of London once she had received word of the fall of Boulogne.

While the capture of Boulogne was a triumph for Henry, his victory was marred by the news that his ally, the Emperor Charles V, had, on the very day of Henry's triumphant entry to the city, made a treaty of peace with France which did not include Henry. Henry had always been open with Charles about Francis's overtures of peace during the campaign; for example, in August, he sent a copy of a letter received from Francis to Charles as a demonstration of his friendship. Charles did not extend the same courtesy to his ally and, with peace between the empire and France, Boulogne and Calais, Henry's other territory in France, immediately became the focus of the entire French army. This was a blow for Henry and, with the arrival of the Dauphin to relieve Montreuil, Norfolk was forced to retreat from the city. In spite of this, Henry was confident that Boulogne could be held and, by the end of September, having grown weary of the campaign, he returned in triumph to England and to Catherine.

Catherine was relieved at the safe return of her husband and she immediately adapted again to life as a queen consort rather than a queen regent. No details of the reunion between Henry and Catherine exist but, with Henry rejuvenated by his marshal success, it must have been emotional. Catherine was always determined to be a good wife to Henry, but there was another man whose health and wellbeing that Catherine was also interested in: Thomas Seymour.

Thomas had kept a fairly low profile in the months following Catherine's marriage and the pair tried to stay away from each other, aware of the dangerous precedent set by Catherine Howard. In spite of the two men's rivalry, Henry remained fond of his brother-in-law and, when war broke out in France, he was ordered to join the army there by the king. In recognition of Thomas's abilities, Henry also appointed him as Master of the Ordinance for life, an important role during the military campaign. Thomas's duties kept him largely away from court and, soon after his return to England, he was appointed as an admiral of the king's navy and ordered to ensure that provisions reached Boulogne. This appointment was intended to favour Thomas Seymour and there is no evidence of any hostility by the king towards his younger rival during the second half of 1544. However, it cannot have displeased the king to know that the man who Catherine truly loved was kept as far away from her as possible. Thomas, while an enthusiastic mariner, was not wholly a successful one, and, in November 1544, when his fleet was damaged in a storm, he was forced to write to Henry's council to excuse himself, writing that, from their letters, he perceived that 'I am thowght neclegent in the accomplechement of the kinges heynes plesur. Yf it can be so provede, I am both worthy of ponychement and blame, and having don the best that in me was, I am to be exkewsed'. Thomas was forgiven by the king and he remained in firm favour, and in possession of his naval commission, throughout the dangerous summer months of 1545.

Catherine was determined to do all she could to retain the emperor's friendship for England and any vestige of his support against France. By May 1545, Eustace Chapuys had been the Imperial ambassador to England for nearly twenty years and his health was badly in decline. Early that month he was finally recalled home. According to Chapuys' own report, on receiving his recall:

I immediately sent to Court to request audience in order to take leave of the king, in accordance with your Majesty's instructions. The king fixed the audience for the next morning at 10; but I anticipated the appointment by an hour. When I had entered the back door of the king's apartments, having traversed the garden facing the queen's lodgings, and arrived nearly at the other end, close to the (principal) entrance of the king's apartments, my people informed me that the queen and the Princess [Mary] were following us quickly. I hardly had time to rise from the chair in which I was being carried, before she (Queen Catherine Parr) approached quite near, and seemed from the small suite she had with her, and the haste with which she came, as if her purpose in coming was specially to speak to me.

Catherine and Mary's purpose was indeed to speak to Chapuys. It is clear that the pair, aware of the time of his appointment, had been looking out for him and, on seeing him, rushed out to greet him, accompanied by only four or five female attendants. Catherine told Chapuys that 'whilst on the one hand she was very sorry for my departure, as she had been told that I had always acted well in my office, and the king had confidence in me, on the other hand she doubted not that my health would be better on the other side of the water'. Catherine also pointed out that the ambassador could 'do as much on the other side as here, for the preservation of the amity between your Majesty and the king, of which I had been one of the chief promoters'. Catherine had been briefed on the official line for the ambassador's departure, speaking almost exactly the same words as both the king and the council would later do in their final meetings with Chapuys, and asserting that she was sure that the emperor would:

> realise the importance and necessity of maintaining this friendship. Of which the king, on his part, had given so many proofs in the past yet it seemed to her that your majesty [Charles] had not been so thoroughly informed hitherto, either by my letters or otherwise, of the king's sincere affection and goodwill, as I should be able to report by word of mouth.

Catherine spoke affectionately to the ambassador but, at the same time, she worked hard for Henry, attempting, as he later did himself in his own interview with Chapuys, to ensure the continuing friendship between England and the Empire in the face of increasing French hostility. In spite of the political nature of Catherine's speech, she also showed kindness towards the elderly ambassador, purposefully standing away from Chapuys and Mary while they said their farewells in private, aware of the long relationship between the Imperial ambassador and her stepdaughter. Chapuys had been the ambassador for Charles since before Mary's mother's divorce and the reign of Anne Boleyn and he had always been her great ally and advisor. Catherine also showed concern for Chapuys' health, trying to keep the interview as short as possible so that he would not have to stand for long and refusing his polite request to escort her back to her apartments.

In spite of Catherine's efforts to obtain greater support from Charles V, during the summer of 1545 he had no intention of damaging his new friendship with France in order to support Henry. By June Francis had an invasion fleet of over 200 ships ready to sail for England. Henry was determined to personally oversee the defences and, in the middle of June, he and Catherine set out for the south coast with the court to view the royal navy. Henry also attempted to call on the emperor's support as, under the terms of their alliance, he was entitled to do, writing to Charles to inform him that he was facing imminent invasion from Francis 'for the purpose of avenging himself; if possible, for the attack we as your ally made upon him'. Henry then requested that Charles 'prepare the aid stipulated in case of invasion of the dominions of either of us by a third power'. Henry had little expectation that Charles would comply and, as he travelled with Catherine towards the coast, he ensured that defences were in place in case of invasion, with arrangements made for beacons to be lit on the hilltops to muster between 25,000 and 30,000 men if necessary within two hours.

Henry and Catherine were at Portsmouth, reviewing the English fleet, when the French finally sailed and Henry, who was dining aboard his flagship, the *Great Harry*, was forced to make a hasty retreat when the French ships entered the Solent. The following morning the English and French fleets engaged near Portsmouth and, while Catherine is not recorded as an observer, it is likely that she was there with the king. For Catherine, it must have been a worrying time and both she and Henry watched in horror as Henry's great ship, the *Mary Rose* 'by misfortune by leaving the porte holdes open, as she turned sanke, and all the men that were in her, savinge a 40, were drowned, which were above 500 persons'. The ship sank right in Portsmouth harbour and was a major blow to the king. In spite of immediate attempts to raise the ship, it remained at the bottom of the harbour for over 400 years and, for Catherine, the cries of the drowning must have been terrible to hear. In spite of this disaster, the French were driven back, landing instead on the Isle of Wight on 21 July before, finding themselves unable to conquer the island, moving along the south coast of England.

Hotly pursued by the English navy, the French fleet was unable to land an invasion force and, in spite of everyone's fears, it proved not to be the great danger to the kingdom that had been expected. This was a great relief to both Catherine and Henry and after the summer they were able to return to London safe in the knowledge that Henry was still secure on his throne. For Catherine, the years of 1544 and 1545 were filled with high drama as she played a prominent role in both the war and the security of the realm. In spite of the abatement of the danger, the war itself dragged on into the last months of 1545 and beyond but, for Catherine, with Henry's return and the failure of the French invasion, she was able to hand over much of her responsibility and, once again, focus on her own interests as queen consort, chief of which was always the development and promulgation of her religious faith.

10

THE LAMENTATION OF A SINNER: AUTUMN 1545 – SPRING 1546

Catherine had long held reformist religious beliefs from her early exposure to the ideas during her first marriage and, as queen, she was quick to find ways to promote them.

While Henry VIII had declared himself the Supreme Head of the Church of England and had broken with Rome in order to marry Anne Boleyn in 1533, he was very far from being either a Protestant or a supporter of the religious reform. This was made clear to Catherine in 1543 with the passing of the Act for the Advancement of True Religion. For Catherine, and her fellow supporters of the religious reform, it was crucial that the scriptures be made available in the vernacular language so that their content could be shared by everyone, not just a conservative elite. The 1543 Act, however, can be considered the king's reaction to this movement and it set out 'what persons shall read the Byble in Englische, and how they shall use yt'. Women were specifically excluded from having access to the Bible in English, as were men below the rank of gentleman and it was banned from being read in private. The Act also declared a number of reformist books to be heretical and informed the populace that they must put 'away all other erroneous and hereticall bookes'. Such an Act could never be acceptable to Catherine or the other religious reformers at court, but it is a testament to Henry's continuing conservative views in spite of all that he had done to change the Church.

Although Henry remained conservative in religious outlook, Catherine was encouraged by some aspects of his beliefs. He was, after all, the king that had made the break with Rome and brought about the dissolution of the monasteries, policies of which Catherine heartily approved. Henry had also, on a number of occasions, declared himself determined to root out superstition, in 1541, for example, banning the traditional custom of lighting bonfires on Midsummer Eve in his great hall. At the same time that the Act for the Advancement of True Religion was passed, Henry also unveiled his new model of what doctrine should be: the King's Book. This book rejected Lutheran, and thus, to a great extent, reformist beliefs, for example, refuting the doctrine of justification by faith, something that Catherine herself passionately believed in; but there was also much to support the hopes of those seeking further change to the Church and, once again, superstition was condemned. Catherine and her supporters continued to hope that, with enough persuasion, Henry could be brought to introduce further change but it is clear that he believed in following a policy that has been described as a 'middle way'. This can be seen in Henry's speech to Parliament on Christmas Eve 1545 when he complained:

> Charity and concord is not amongst you, but discord and dissension beareth rule in every place. St Paul sayeth to the Corinthians, in the xiii Chapter, charity is gentle, charity is not envious, charity is not proud and so forth in the said Chapter: behold then, what love and charity is amongst you, when the one calleth the other, heretic and

Anabaptist and he calleth him again Papist, hypocrite, and Pharisee. Be these tokens of charity amongst you? Are these the signs of fraternal love between you? No, no, I assure you that this lack of charity amongst yourselves will be the hindrance and assuaging of the fervent love between us, as I said before, except this would be salved and clearly made whole.

Henry VIII, as the Supreme Head of the Church, viewed himself as the arbitrator of religious doctrine in England and, by 1543, he was neither Catholic nor Protestant.

It is unlikely that Henry was fully aware of Catherine's beliefs at the time of their marriage, although there is no doubt that Catherine saw her elevation as the ideal platform from which to publicize and support the reform. In this, Catherine was following one of her predecessors as Henry's wife, and the close associate of her first father-in-law, Sir Thomas Burgh, Queen Anne Boleyn. Like Catherine, Anne had been an adherent of the reform before she became queen and it was she who first suggested to Henry the possibility of a break with Rome. Once she became queen, Anne sought to advance the reform, for example leaving open an English Bible in her apartments. She also regularly read the Bible in French, a language in which she was fluent, and possessed a number of religious books widely considered heretical. While Anne was interested in religious reform, the movement was still in its infancy in the 1530s and, at the time of her death, she continued to display some traditional religious beliefs, for example, swearing her innocence on the sacrament during her imprisonment in the Tower. She can therefore not be considered to have held fully Protestant beliefs and the honour of being the first Protestant queen of England certainly falls to Catherine Parr herself.

Catherine's religious beliefs were based on humanist traditions which had been active since Henry VII's reign. Humanism essentially involved a reconsideration of religion through a return to the original written sources. To begin with, it was not anticipated that this would lead to a great movement away from traditional doctrine, and Erasmus, the great early humanist, remained largely traditional in his religious works. Catherine was interested in the works of Erasmus and possessed some of them. It has been suggested that she was no true Protestant and that her actions as queen were merely a general patronage of reform in the Church. Catherine used Erasmus as her starting point in religion, as many people of her acquaintance did. She was also passionate about the publication of religious works in the vernacular and in allowing a wider readership of the scriptures. However, it is clear that Catherine's views were wider than this and, while her beliefs were constantly developing and changing, the evidence of those associated with her, her actions and her own written works demonstrate that her beliefs were altogether more radical than all but Anne Boleyn's of her predecessors as queen of England.

Catherine Parr is remarkable as the first queen of England to be a published author in her own right. Catherine's first work, *Prayers or Meditations,* was published in 1545. In order to take the remarkable step of publishing in her own name, Catherine must have secured Henry's consent first and it is therefore reasonable to assume that he read the work himself or, at least, was satisfied as to its contents. *Prayers or Mediations* was a collection of works by the queen, intended to be used by the reader for personal devotions. Catherine's words, at first glance, are conventionally pious, showing the usual humility of the religious writer. In one section, for example, Catherine wrote:

O Lord Jesus, most loving spouse, who shall give me wings of perfect love, that I may fly up from these worldly miseries, and rest in thee? O when shall I ascend to thee, and see and feel how sweet thou art? When shall I wholly gather myself in thee, so perfectly that I shall not, or thy love, feel myself, and above all worldly things; that thou mayest vouchsafe to visit me in such wise as thou dost visit thy most faithful lovers. Now, I often mourn and complain of the miseries of this life, and with sorrow and great heaviness suffer them. For many things happen daily to me which oftentimes trouble me, making me heavy, and darken mine understanding. They hinder me greatly, and put my mind from thee, and so encumber me many ways, that I cannot freely and clearly desire thee, nor have thy sweet consolation, which with thy blessed saints are always present.

Catherine's words contain some autobiographical elements and discuss the personal relationship that she always felt that she had with God. She also wanted to share these feelings with her readers in the hope that it could lead others to as personal a relationship with God as she had. What is most striking about *Prayers or Mediations* though is just how non-controversial the writings were. Catherine intended her work to have a wide readership and hoped that it could be used as a supplement to Bible study by everyone, not just by those interested in reform. She therefore kept any reformist sentiments to a minimum and, while the absence of traditional appeals to saints, for example, is an indication of Catherine's personal beliefs, it is unlikely to have been seen as a striking omission to her contemporaries. Catherine was proud of her work and she commissioned presentation copies from the king's publisher which were bound in gilt and leather soon after the book's publication. Initially Catherine purchased fourteen copies which she distributed to her family and friends and, in the first year of Edward VI's reign, when Catherine's presentation copies had all been given away, she purchased another set, this time bound in white leather and gilt. While Catherine ordered high value copies to be used as gifts, she also ensured that her work was made available in an inexpensive edition and it was a great success, running to several editions and even being available during the reign of Catherine's conservative step-daughter, Mary.

Catherine was keen to involve Mary in her projects and she managed to gain her stepdaughter's involvement in a major religious project. Catherine always had a special interest in the works of Erasmus and, between 1545 and 1548 she was intimately involved in the English translation of the scholar's *Paraphrases upon the New Testament*. This work involved the translation of Erasmus's work on each of the four gospels and Catherine, who appointed the scholar Nicholas Udall as the editor of the work, secured Mary's agreement to translate the gospel of St John herself. The choice of Mary, who was known for her conservative religious views, is surprising and Catherine may have hoped to use it as an opportunity to draw her stepdaughter into her circle of reform-minded aristocratic women. In spite of her misgivings, Mary agreed to carry out much of the work, although it is clear in a letter from Catherine to Mary that the queen had a great deal of difficulty in maintaining Mary's support and interest in the project. According to the letter:

Although, most noble and dearest lady, there are many reasons that earnestly induce my writing to you at this time, yet nothing so greatly moves me thereto as my concern for your health; which, as I hope it is very good, so am I greatly desirous to be assured thereof.

Wherefore, I despatch to you this messenger, who will be (I judge) most acceptable to you, not only from his skill in music, in which you, I am well aware, take as much delight as myself, but also because, having long sojourned with me, he can give the most certain information of my whole estate and health. And, in truth, I have had it in mind before this to have made a journey to you and salute you in person; but all things do not correspond with my will. Now, however, I hope this winter, and that ere long, that, being nearer, we shall meet; than which, I assure you, nothing can be to me more agreeable, and more to my heart's desire.

Now since, as I have heard, the finishing touch (as far as translation is concerned) is given by Mallet to Erasmus's work upon John, and nought now remains but that proper care and vigilance should be taken in revising, I entreat you to send over to me this very excellent and useful work, now amended by Mallet, or some of your people, that it may be committed to the press in due time; and farther, to signify whether you wish it to go forth to the world (most auspiciously) under your name, or as the production of an unknown writer. To which work you will, in my opinion, do a real injury, if you refuse to let it go down to posterity under the auspices of your own name, since you have undertaken so much labour in accurately translating it for the great good of the public, and would have undertaken still greater (as is well known) if the health of your body had permitted.

And since all the world knows that you have toiled and laboured much in this business, I do not see why you should repudiate that praise which all men justly confer on you. However, I leave this whole matter to your discretion, and, whatever resolutions you may adopt, that will meet my fullest approbation.

Mary was evidently less enthusiastic about the project than Catherine as she came to read just what she was expected to translate and she used her poor health as a means to extricate herself with her work only half finished. Mary later banned the work as heretical during her own reign and her involvement in the translation project was probably the first indication for her of the radical religious views held by her stepmother. The two women remained close and Mary sent Catherine the gift of a purse she had embroidered, perhaps to demonstrate her ongoing fondness for her stepmother. However, she did not again involve herself in Catherine's religious projects.

The loss of Mary as a translator for the project was a personal blow to Catherine but the project itself continued. The translator of St Matthew's gospel is not recorded and it has been suggested recently that this was Catherine herself. While this is possible, it is unlikely as Catherine, who had already stated her views on the need for Mary to assert herself as the author of the work, would never have agreed to publish her own work anonymously. Catherine hoped that her involvement in the project would lead to its wider circulation and she took the role of patron rather than translator, as Udall made clear in his dedication on the publication of the translation of St Luke. According to Udall, speaking of Catherine:

> such was her modesty, that she sought nothing less than the fame of her good deeds to be blown abroad. She was of virtuous living from her tender years. She was endued with a pregnant wittiness, joined with right wonderful grace and eloquence: studiously diligent in acquiring knowledge, as well of other human disciplines, as also of the holy scriptures.

According to Udall, Catherine was also:

> Mighty studious to promote the glory of God, and of the holy
> Gospel. These qualities moved King Henry to judge her a meet
> spouse for his majesty, and to pick her out to be his lawful wife
> of so many women of nobility and honour, and high worth. When
> she was queen, she employed herself days and nights in psalms and
> contemplative meditations, in lieu of vain and courtly pastimes and
> gaming. And these she herself set forth in print, for the example of
> all noble women, and to the ghostly consolation and edifying of all
> that read them.

For Udall, Catherine was the model of a Christian queen, devoting
herself to her religion. It is certainly true that Catherine was
devoted to the religious reform but the sudden upsurge in her
activity, marked by, first, the preparation of *Psalms or Meditations,*
may have been due to personal reasons as well.

Thomas Seymour had been largely absent from court since
Henry made his suit towards Catherine plain and the queen
continued to follow her erstwhile lover's career with interest and,
no doubt, some regret. Throughout the summer of 1545 Seymour
had been occupied with the royal fleet, involved in the defence
of England. During this time, Thomas was rarely on shore and
Catherine would have had little, if any opportunity, to see him.
This may have been a blessing for Catherine and, while she had
resigned herself to the role of Henry's wife and queen, the contrast
between her husband and the man she loved only increased with
Henry's growing infirmity in comparison with Thomas's military
reputation. By late 1545, Thomas was back on dry land but kept
fully engaged with equipping Henry's castles and army with

supplies in his role as Master of the Ordinance. He had more of an opportunity to visit the court and, for Catherine, such meetings must always have been hard. Aware of the danger of her position as queen, with the example of her predecessor, Catherine Howard as a constant reminder, Catherine did her best to stay away from him and devoted herself to her studies and her religious works. Both she and Seymour were successful in this dissimulation and Henry, pleased with Thomas's military service, made him the grant at the end of 1545 of a magnificent house in London which Thomas named Seymour Place as a testament to his ambition.

Catherine also suffered a personal loss in March 1545 with the death of her beloved stepdaughter, Margaret Neville. Catherine had raised Margaret since her early childhood and she looked upon her as her own daughter. The cause of Margaret's early death is not recorded but Catherine, as queen, was forced to rise above her grief and show a brave face to the world. Privately, however, she was undoubtedly devastated. Margaret's Will, in which she referred lovingly to her stepmother, fully set out the influence that Catherine had had over her religious beliefs and the girl set out her adherence to the reformed faith. This was some consolation to Catherine and she sought to fill the gap that Margaret had left in her life with her other young stepdaughter, Princess Elizabeth.

Following Catherine's regency, Elizabeth was able to spend a considerable amount of time with her stepmother and, as she had done with both Margaret Neville and Princess Mary, Catherine made attempts to influence her stepdaughter's religious beliefs. As with Margaret, Elizabeth was young and eager to please and Catherine's efforts were wildly successful, as can be seen in Elizabeth's New Year's gift to Catherine in 1545 of a translation, in her own hand, of the reform-minded Margaret of Navarre's *Mirror of the Christian Soul.* In her preface to her work, Elizabeth poured out her fondness for the woman who had become her mother, calling herself Catherine's 'humble daughter' and begging her to excuse and correct any errors that she had made in the work. It is clear that Elizabeth had fully assimilated the message of the radical work and she set out in her preface her own views on the subject-matter of her translation:

> The which book is entitled or named, 'The Mirror, or Glass, of the Sinful Soul', wherein is contained, how she (beholding and contemplating what she is), doth perceive how, of herself and her own strength, she can do nothing that good is, or prevaileth for her salvation, unless it be through the grace of God, whose mother, daughter, sister and wife, by the Scriptures, she proveth herself to be. Trusting also that, through his incomprehensible love, grace, and mercy, she (being called from sin to repentance), doth faithfully hope to be saved.

Margaret of Navarre's work set out the key Protestant doctrine that justification, and salvation, was achieved by faith alone, and Elizabeth's translation of the book is evidence that she knew her stepmother both approved the contents and agreed wholeheartedly with them. Catherine was touched by the work and she continued in her efforts to educate the princess in her own beliefs, introducing her to the religious instruction that went on in her own household while the girl was visiting court. Pleased at the success of her gift, Elizabeth went even further the next New Year, translating into English for Catherine a chapter of one of the works of the great reformer John Calvin. She also set out to please both her father and her stepmother in her gift to the king, translating into three languages Catherine's own *Prayers or Mediations*. Catherine was flattered by Elizabeth's choice of a translation project for her father and pleased at the girl's interest in her own religious beliefs. However, by early 1545 she had already begun to compose a work of a much more radical nature than *Prayers or Mediations*.

During her time as queen, Catherine drew a circle of reform-minded ladies around her and the group shared ideas on the subject of religion. The most prominent of these were Anne Stanhope, Countess of Hertford, Mary Howard, Duchess of Richmond and Catherine Willoughby, Duchess of Suffolk. In later life there was little love lost between Catherine and Anne Stanhope, but she was genuinely fond of the Duchess of Suffolk and the Duchess encouraged Catherine in her literary ambitions. Certainly, the support of these ladies, and Henry's indulgence in allowing her to publish *Prayers or Mediations*, emboldened Catherine and, around 1545 and 1546, she composed her most personal, and radical work, *The Lamentation of a Sinner*.

While *Prayers or Mediations* was not overtly reformist in nature, there is no doubt from *Lamentation of a Sinner* that Catherine held deep Protestant beliefs. The work contained a statement of Catherine's conversion to the reform, which has already been discussed, together with a rejection of the Pope and Catholic tradition. In her work Catherine placed her own emphasis on justification by faith alone, as well as focussing on the reading of the scriptures as a route to God. In *Lamentation*, Catherine complained:

I will now speak with great dolour and heaviness in my heart, of a sort of people which are in the world, that are called professors of the gospel, and, by their words, do declare and show they are much affected to the same. But, I am afraid, some of them do build upon the sand, as Simon Magus did, making a weak foundation. I mean, they make not Christ their chief foundation; professing his doctrine, of a sincere, pure, and zealous mind; but either because they would be called gospellers, to procure some credit and good opinion of the true and very favourers of Christ's doctrine; or to find out some carnal liberty, or to be contentious disputers, finders or rebukers of other men's faults; or else, finally, to please and flatter the world. Such gospellers are an offence, and a slander to the word of God.

Catherine also made plain her views on charity as a necessary means of emulating Christ's example but not, as traditional beliefs would have it, a prerequisite for salvation, declaring:

Charity suffereth long, and is gentle, envieth not, upbraideth no man, casteth forwardly no faults in men's teeth, but referreth all things to God; being angry without sin, reforming others without slanders, carrying ever a storehouse of mild words to pierce the strong-hearted men. I would that all Christians, like as they have professed Christ, would so endeavour themselves to follow him in godly living.

Catherine spoke of her zeal to bring others to the reformed faith, stating:

neither life, honour, riches, neither whatsoever I possess here, which appertaineth to mine own private commodity, be it ever so dearly beloved of me, but most willingly and gladly I would leave it to win any man to Christ, of what degree, or sort soever he were.

The Lamentation of a Sinner is a remarkable document of Catherine's personal religious beliefs and shows her desire to become a missionary for the Protestant faith. She almost certainly intended to publish the work, just as she had done *Prayers or Mediations,* and she believed wholeheartedly that Henry, who she referred to in her work as Moses, who had led his people out of the ignorance of Pharoahic Egypt (or, in this case, bondage to the Pope), would support her and allow her to continue to spread her beliefs. At the beginning of 1546 Catherine was convinced that Henry could be persuaded to fully support her beliefs, ignoring the fact that the king had already set out the limits of how far his Church was to be reformed. As Henry finally turned his attention to his wife's beliefs he found much that concerned him, putting Catherine in grave danger and ensuring that she very nearly followed the path of her two executed predecessors, Anne Boleyn and Catherine Howard.

DANGER FOR THE GOSPEL: SPRING 1546 – JULY 1546

Catherine remained in high favour over New Year 1546. For Catherine, Henry had always been a loving and indulgent husband and she under-estimated him, unaware of just how much danger she would find herself in. 1546 was to prove the most difficult year of Catherine's life and, to her terror, she found out for herself just what a dangerous and unpredictable husband her royal spouse could be.

Catherine saw her role as queen as an opportunity to spread her religious beliefs and she saw no reason to hide this, believing that Henry endorsed, even if he did not entirely share, her views. Henry's behaviour towards Catherine did seem to be a show of support for her beliefs. According to John Foxe, Henry knew that Catherine was interested in reading and studying the scriptures and that she would hold religious services in her own household:

As these things were not secretly done, so neither were their preachings unknown to the king; wherof, at first, and for a great time, he seemed very well to like. This made her the more bold (being indeed very zealous toward the gospel, and the professors thereof) frankly to debate with the king touching religion, and therein flatly to discover herself; oftentimes wishing, exhorting, and persuading the king, that as he had, to the glory of God, and his eternal fame, begun a good and a godly work in banishing that monstrous idol of Rome, so he would thoroughly perfect and finish the same, cleansing and purging his church of England clean from the dregs thereof, wherein as yet remained great superstition.

To begin with, Henry appeared happy to discuss religion with Catherine and the queen hoped that her influence would soften Henry's increasingly conservative religious beliefs.

Catherine knew that, while Henry appeared to tolerate her own interest in the religious reform, there were limits to what he would tolerate in his kingdom. Only weeks after her marriage, she was given an effective warning of Henry's continuing desire to continue his religious policy, promoting a middle way that was neither Catholic nor Protestant. In July 1543 four men of Windsor were tried for heresy. The main charges against the four men were that they denied the miracle of the Eucharist, with one of those accused, Henry Filmer, reported to have said that 'the sacrament of the Aultare is nothing but similitude and a ceremony. And also, if God be in the Sacrament of the aultare, I have eaten twentie Goddes in my life'. Another, John Marbeck, collected writings attacking the mass and the sacrament of the altar. These four men shared many of Catherine's beliefs and it was a worry both to her and her fellow religious reformers when she heard that three of the four men were burned for their beliefs.

The persecution of the four Windsor men was to prove only the first attack on Catherine's co-religionists during her time as queen. Henry also ordered a crackdown on Protestant religious books in England and a number of searches were carried out. In late 1545 a bill was introduced against such books in Parliament which only failed after threats were made against Henry's conservative Lord Chancellor, Henry Wriothesley, and one reforming MP was imprisoned in retaliation. Wriothesley was not daunted by the threats to his life and he, along with his ally, Stephen Gardiner, Bishop of Winchester, became determined to stamp out heresy in the royal court.

The first target that Henry's conservative ministers had in mind was Catherine's ally, Thomas Cranmer, Archbishop of Canterbury. Cranmer's reformist beliefs were well known and, as the leading bishop in England, he would have been an impressive scalp for his enemies to collect. The first attempt against Cranmer occurred soon after Catherine's marriage and may have been linked to the arrests on the four Windsor men. According to the account of Cranmer's secretary, Ralph Morice, Cranmer's religious opinions earned him the enmity of the gentlemen of Kent who resented having an archbishop who showed his reformist beliefs so clearly. According to Morice:

> The kinge on an evening rowing on the Thames in his barge, came to Lambeth bridge and there receyvid my L. Cranmer into his barge, saying unto hym merily, 'Ah, my chaplen, I have newis for you: I knowe nowe who is the greatest heretique in Kente'. And so pulled oute of his sleve a paper, wherin was conteyned his accusation articled against hym and his chaplens and other preachers in Kente.

Cranmer must have turned white as he heard the king's words. Meekly, he responded that the king should appoint commissioners to investigate the accusations and it must have been a relief when

Henry declared that 'I have such affiaunce and confidence in your fidelitie, that I will commit th'examination herof wholie unto you, and suche as you will appoint'. Cranmer survived that attack on his position and he survived a subsequent attack soon afterwards when one Sir John Gostwick accused Cranmer openly in Parliament of heretical preaching. Once again, Henry refused to countenance the accusations, believing that they were the product of malice against his archbishop and he openly raged against Cranmer's accuser, calling him a 'varlet' and threatening him with punishment if he did not submit himself to Cranmer. Henry must have been aware that Cranmer was no conservative and he had appointed him as archbishop back in 1533 for this reason. However, he apparently believed that Cranmer shared his own belief in a middle way. The king's support for Cranmer is less clear cut in a third attack during Catherine's marriage.

According to Cranmer's secretary, as Henry's conservative beliefs became more evident, Cranmer's accusers once again took the opportunity to attack him openly. The third attack against Cranmer was led by members of Henry's council which would have included the Duke of Norfolk, Bishop Gardiner and Wriothesley. The councillors went to the king and informed him that 'the archebisshopp being of his privie counsaile, none man durst objecte matter against hym oneles he were firste committed unto indurance, whiche being don, men wolde be bolde to tell the trueth and say thair consciences'. Henry agreed that Cranmer could be arrested the next morning and sent to the Tower in order for his religious beliefs to be considered.

Henry's motives for agreeing to Cranmer's arrest are unclear but it is worth considering them as they are crucial with regard to his later behaviour towards Catherine. Cranmer was always aware that there was a danger that the truth about his beliefs could be made clear to the conservative king. In July 1539, for example, Cranmer found himself in potential difficulty when a book that he had written, criticizing Henry's Six Articles of faith, fell into the hands of his enemies due to the negligence of his secretary. This book was taken to Bishop Gardiner and it was only through the intervention of Cranmer's ally, the king's chief minister, Thomas Cromwell, that it was recovered. It is clear from this incident that Cranmer, in spite of his privileged position, was acutely aware that his beliefs were not entirely in alignment with the king's and that he was in constant danger that Henry would discover this fact. Henry's agreement to Cranmer's arrest could therefore be seen as a mark of his general attack on heresy during the years of Catherine's marriage although an alternative, and persuasive, view is that he intended to give Cranmer a warning in order to ensure that he remained loyal to royal policy.

The evidence that Henry intended to give Cranmer a warning rather than actually to facilitate his fall can be found in his actions after he had agreed that Cranmer could be committed to the Tower. According to Morice:

At nighte, about xj of the clocke, the same night before the daie he should appere before the counsaile, the kinge sent mr Deny to my lorde [Cranmer] at Lambeth, willing hym incontinently to come unto Westminster to speake with hym. My lorde being abed rose straight waie, and wente to the king into his gallery att Whitehall at Westminster: and there the king declared unto hym what he had don in gyvyng libertie unto the counsaile to commit hym to prison, for that they bare hym in hande [i.e. tried to persuade him] that he and his learnyd men had sowne suche doctrine in the realme that all men almost were infected with heresie, and that no many durst bring in matter against hym being at libertie and one of the counsaile oneles he were committed to prison.

Cranmer was terrified and he thanked the king quietly for the warning. Trying to compose himself, he said that 'he was very well contente to be committed to the Tower, for the trial of his doctrine, so that he mighte be indifferentlie harde [heard], as he doubted not but that his majestie wolde see hym to be used'. Henry was astounded by this answer and exclaimed: 'O Lorde God!' before continuing:

> What fond symplicitie have you: so to permit yourself to be ymprisoned, that every enemy of yours may take vantage against you. Doo not you thincke that yf thei have you ones in prison, iij or iiij false knaves wilbe sone procured to witnes against you and to condempne you.

Henry informed the archbishop that he should go to the council the following day and that, when they attempted to arrest him, he should request an audience with Henry. The king passed a ring from his own finger to Cranmer and told him to produce this at the crucial moment so that 'thei shall well understand that I have taken your cause unto my hande from theym'. Cranmer thanked the king profusely before returning home for a no doubt troubled night.

The following day, as Henry had described, the council summoned Cranmer to attend them in the council chamber. As far as the councillors were concerned, they were to arrest the archbishop and Cranmer's enemies were determined to make the most of this, as they had done with the similar arrest of Thomas Cromwell in June 1540. Cromwell had also been arrested in the Council chamber and his arrest was preceded by a number of slights, including the councillors refusing to remove their hats when Cromwell's was blown off, and in the councillors taking their seats at the council table before Cromwell was present. When Cranmer arrived he was kept waiting outside the door with the serving men for nearly an hour as a mark of the council's contempt for him. When he was finally called, his enemies turned on him, declaring that he was accused with having 'infectid the hole realme with heresie' and that he was to be taken to the Tower. Cranmer, as Cromwell had done before him, asked to be allowed to confront his accusers, but this was denied, and he then produced the king's ring, informing them that, in that case, he would appeal directly to the king.

The council were shocked at the sight of Henry's ring and immediately rushed to him to explain themselves. According to Morice, when Henry took the ring from them he declared:

Ah! My lordes, I had thought that I had hadd a discrete and wise counsaile, but nowe I perceive that I am deceyvid. Howe have ye handeled here my L. of Canterbury? What make ye of him a slave, sitting hym oute of the councell-chamber emonges serving men? Wolde ye be so handeled yourselfes? and after suche taunting wourdes saied, I wold you shulde well understand, that I accompte my L. of Canterbury as faithfull a man towardes me as ever was prelate in this realme, and one to whome I am many waies beholding, by the faith I owe unto God (and so laied his hand upon his breste) and therefore who so loveth me (saied he,) will regarde hym therafter.

Henry made plain his support for Cranmer and this is the last evidence of any open plot against the archbishop during Henry's reign. Cranmer was profoundly shocked by what had happened and he became less open about his beliefs after his escape from arrest. Henry wanted to frighten his archbishop into ensuring that he did not forget just who it was that set religious policy in England. That Henry intended to frighten Cranmer rather than bring him down can be seen from a similar plot against Bishop Gardiner in March 1544. That month, Gardiner's nephew was executed for denying the royal supremacy. Henry's brother-in-law, the Duke of Suffolk, along with Cranmer, Edward Seymour and John Dudley went to Henry and persuaded him that Gardiner must also be guilty of this and Henry gave his permission for Suffolk to order his arrest. As with the plot against Cranmer, news of this reached Gardiner and he rushed to the king, receiving Henry's forgiveness. When Suffolk dared remonstrate with Henry the next day the king calmly responded that it was in his nature to pardon those who confessed that they were at fault, effectively challenging Suffolk to dare deny his authority. Henry was determined that he would decide who should fall and who would survive, but such plots were always terrifying for the victim and, by early 1546, the attacks began to focus on Catherine herself.

The first indication that Catherine was under attack can be seen in the arrest and interrogation of Anne Askew. Anne Askew was a Lincolnshire gentlewoman who had staunch reformist beliefs and had come to London after being thrown out of her house by her husband. Her sister was married to the steward of the Duke of Suffolk and her brother was also a member of the king's household so she had easy access to members of the court. Anne was arrested for her beliefs in March 1545 and, during her interrogation spoke openly of her distaste for the mass. She was, however, more circumspect regarding her beliefs concerning the sacrament and, in order to secure her release, she swore that she did indeed believe in the miracle of the Eucharist. On 24 May 1546 however she was arrested again and, for the first time, Henry's Lord Chancellor, Wriothesley, took an active interest in her interrogation.

Following her second arrest, Anne was taken to be examined before Henry's council at Greenwich. Both Wriothesley and Gardiner were present at the interrogation and they questioned Anne on her opinion of the sacrament. According to Anne herself:

> My answer was this, I believe that so oft as I, in a Christian congregation, do receive the bread in remembrance of Christ's death, and with thanksgiving, according to his holy institution, I receive therewith the fruits also of his most glorious passion. The bishop of Winchester bade me make a direct answer. I said I would not sing a new song of the Lord in a strange land. Then the bishop said, I spake in parables. I answered, it was best for him, for if I show the open truth, said I, ye will not accept it. Then he said, I was a parrot. I told him again I was ready to suffer all things at his hands, not only his rebukes, but all that should follow besides, yea and that gladly.

Anne's response infuriated her accusers and she was examined again the next day. Interestingly, Catherine's own brother, William, as well as the known favourer of reform, John Dudley, were brought in to assist with the interrogation. Anne turned to William and Dudley and said 'that it was a great shame for them to counsel contrary to their knowledge'. Anne was then sent to Newgate and confessed that she did not believe in the real presence of Christ in the sacrament. Her interrogators were very far from finished with her, in spite of the fact that she was condemned to be burned.

Following her condemnation for heresy, Anne Askew was taken to the Tower of London. Anne was immediately questioned by members of the council as to whether she could name any other heretics. Anne refused to name anyone and the interrogators then came to the point, asking her 'of my lady of Suffolk, my lady of Sussex, my lady of Hertford, my lady Denny, and my Lady Fitzwilliams'. These ladies were all associated with Catherine and, for the first time, Catherine's enemies were open about their true targets. Catherine was commonly supposed to share the religious beliefs of that particular group of ladies and Eustace Chapuys later voiced the rumour that Catherine's reformist beliefs had come about through her association with the Duchess of Suffolk, the Countess of Hertford and John Dudley's wife. Anne Askew refused to incriminate the ladies, only admitting that she had received gifts of money while she was in prison from Lady Hertford and Lady Denny. This was not good enough for Wriothesley and, when it became clear that Anne would freely voice no more, he put her on the rack, turning the wheel himself when she refused to speak. In spite of her agony, Anne bravely refused to say anything more, but it is clear that, from the moment of Anne's arrest, an attack on Catherine was a certainty. As the martyrologist, John Foxe, commented, Catherine found herself 'in danger for the gospel'.

By 1546, Henry's health was in deep decline. In March 1546, for example, the king is reported to have suffered from some unspecified ailment which, although not serious, kept him confined to his bed for some time. From the earliest days of their marriage, Catherine had formed the habit of entering into religious debates

with Henry and, in his sickness throughout the early months of
1546, she continued this. According to John Foxe:

> In the time of this his sickness, he had left his accustomed manner
> of coming, and visiting the queen: and therefore she, according
> as she understood him, by such assured intelligence as she had
> about him, to be disposed to have her company, sometimes being
> sent for, at other times of herself, would come to visit him, either
> after dinner or after supper, as was most fit for her purpose: at
> which times she would not fail to use all occasions to move him,
> according to her manner, zealously to proceed in the reformation of
> the church.

In her religious zeal, Catherine failed to notice that Henry was
showing signs of impatience with her. Catherine suspected nothing,
receiving as she left Henry's company, his usual goodbye of
'Farewell, sweet heart!'

At one such interview between the king and queen when Henry
showed his impatience with Catherine, Bishop Gardiner happened
to be present. Gardiner, who was already plotting against Catherine
with Wriothesley, saw his chance, thinking 'that if the iron was
beaten whilst it was hot, and that the king's humour was holpen,
some misliking might follow towards the queen, as might both
overthrow her, and all her endeavours'. Henry was annoyed with
Catherine and commented of himself to Gardiner 'a good hearing,
it is, when women become such clerks; and a thing much to my
comfort, to come in mine old days to be taught by my wife'. This
was all the encouragement Gardiner needed and he immediately
launched into a speech praising Henry's wisdom in matters of
religion and criticizing Catherine's attempts to change the king's

opinions and the dangers of her religious beliefs. He continued saying that:

> Howbeit, for his part, he would not, nor durst he, without good warrant from his majesty, speak his knowledge in the queen's case, although very apparent reasons made for him, and such as his dutiful affection towards his majesty, and the zeal and preservation of his estate, would scarce give him leave to conceal, though the uttering thereof, might, through her and her faction, be the utter destruction of him and of such as indeed did chiefly tender the prince's safety, without his majesty would take upon him to be their protector, and as it were their buckler: which, if he would do (as in respect of his own safety he ought not to refuse), he, with others of his faithful councillors, could within short time disclose such treasons cloaked with this cloak of heresy, that his majesty should easily perceive how perilous a matter it is, to cherish a serpent within his own bosom: howbeit, he would not, for his part, willingly deal in the matter, both for reverent respect aforesaid, and, also, for fear lest the faction as grown already too great, there, with the prince's safety, to discover the same.

Gardiner's speech was well rehearsed and it was intended to raise Henry's suspicions. Gardiner easily obtained Henry's consent for Catherine's arrest and, while preparations for this were made, Henry continued to dissemble with Catherine, allowing her to debate religion with him as she did before. Gardiner also made plans to act against Catherine's sister, Anne, her cousin, Lady Lane, and her kinswoman, Lady Tyrwhitt, who were also well-known to be in favour of reform.

Once it had been agreed by the king that Catherine would be arrested, matters began to take a strange turn, as they did in the earlier conspiracies against Cranmer and Gardiner himself. According to Foxe, one night, after Catherine had left the king, Henry informed his physician, Dr Wendy, of the plot against Catherine, saying that he 'intended not any longer to be troubled with such a doctress as she was'. Henry swore Dr Wendy to secrecy. It seems unlikely that he expected the doctor to keep this vow. Dr Wendy had been Catherine's personal physician since she had become queen and was close to her. An equally unlikely stroke of luck occurred when the articles against Catherine, signed with Henry's own hand, were mysteriously dropped where a member of Catherine's household would find them and brought to Catherine herself. This was the first that Catherine knew of the plot and, like Cranmer before her, she was terrified. According to Foxe, 'for the sudden fear thereof fell incontinent into such sort as was lamentable to see, as certain her ladies and gentlewomen, being yet alive, who were then present about her, can testify'.

Catherine's terror on hearing that her husband, who had already executed two of his previous wives, had ordered her arrest can be imagined. The shock sent her almost out of her wits and her screams and cries were so great that Henry, apparently anxious to see what the matter was, sent Dr Wendy to her. Dr Wendy found Catherine in a pitiful state and he was moved to tell her everything he knew:

> beseeching her most instantly to use all secrecy in that behalf, and exhorting her somewhat to frame and conform herself unto the king's mind, saying, he did not doubt but, if she would do so, and show her humble submission unto him, she should find him gracious and favourable unto her.

This was excellent advice and Catherine, in her distress, resolved to take it. Soon afterwards, Henry came to visit and Catherine explained, humbly to him, that her sudden illness was due to fear lest Henry 'had taken displeasure with her, and had utterly forsaken her'. Henry reassured Catherine that this was not the case and spoke lovingly to her before leaving, but Catherine was left in no doubt that this was not the end of the matter.

In spite of her deeply held religious beliefs, Catherine was no martyr and, after Henry had gone, she ordered that her ladies remove all the forbidden books that she had in her possession. Taking only her sister, Anne, and her cousin, Lady Lane, after supper the following day Catherine made her way by candlelight to Henry's bedchamber. Once inside, she found Henry sitting and talking with the gentlemen of his privy chamber. When the king saw her, he received her kindly and 'began of himself, contrary to his manner before accustomed, to enter into talk of religion, seeming as it were desirous to be resolved by the queen, of certain doubts which he propounded'. Catherine immediately recognized this for the test it was and refused to be drawn on her own beliefs, replying:

Your Majesty... doth right-well know, neither I myself am ignorant, what great imperfection and weakness by our first creation is allotted unto us women to be ordained and appointed as inferior and subject unto man as our head; from which head all our direction ought to proceed: and that as God made man to his own shape and likeness, whereby he, being endued with more special gifts of perfection, might rather be stirred to the contemplation of heavenly things, and to the earnest endeavour to obey his commandments, even so, also, made he woman of man, of whom and by whom she is to be governed, commanded, and directed; whose womanly weaknesses and natural imperfection ought to be tolerated, aided, and borne withal, so that, by his wisdom, such things as be lacking in her ought to be supplied.

Since, therefore, God hath appointed such a natural difference between man and woman, and your majesty being so excellent in gifts and ornaments of wisdom, and I a silly poor woman, so much inferior in all respects of nature unto you, how then cometh it now to pass that your majesty, in such diffuse causes of religion, will seem to require my judgment? which when I have uttered and said what I can, yet must I, and will I, refer my judgment in this, and in all other cases, to your majesty's wisdom, as my only anchor, supreme head and governor here in earth, next under God, to lean unto.

Catherine's response was a perfect wifely submission, but Henry had not finished with her and, smiling, he shook his head, replying: 'Not so by St Mary, you are become a doctor, Kate, to instruct us (as we take it), and not to be instructed or directed by us.' Catherine was once again ready with her response, replying:

If your majesty take it so... then hath your majesty very much mistaken me, who have ever been of the opinion, to think it very unseemly, and preposterous, for the woman to take upon her the office of an instructor or teacher to her lord and husband; but rather to learn of her husband, and to be taught by him. And whereas I have, with your majesty's leave, heretofore been bold to hold talk with your majesty, wherein sometimes in opinions there hath seemed some difference, I have not done it so much to maintain opinion, as I did it rather to minister talk, not only to the end your majesty might with less grief pass over this painful time of your infirmity, being attentive to our talk, and hoping that your majesty should reap some ease thereby; but also that I, hearing your majesty's learned discourse, might receive to myself some profit thereby: wherein, I assure your majesty, I have not missed any part in my desire in that behalf, always referring myself, in al such matters, unto your majesty, as by ordinance of nature it is convenient for me to do.

Catherine's response was exactly what her husband required and he smiled at her, replying: 'And is it even so, sweet heart!, and tended your arguments to no worse end? Then, perfect friends we are now again, as ever at any time heretofore.' Henry then, to Catherine's extreme relief, embraced and kissed her and the couple sat pleasantly together for a time.

It is clear from the account of Catherine's danger that she, like Cranmer and Gardiner before her, had performed exactly as Henry desired in the test that he set. There is no doubt that Catherine, with the example of Anne Boleyn and Catherine Howard looming large in her mind, believed herself to be in real and mortal danger. However, Henry's conduct in talking of the plot with Dr Wendy, whom he must have realized would take the news to Catherine, and in allowing the articles against the queen to be mislaid, makes it clear that he intended to give Catherine a chance to redeem herself in his eyes. When Henry decided that Anne Boleyn and Catherine Howard would be arrested, he refused to see them, leaving the palaces in which they were held and, if he had been truly serious about ending his marriage to Catherine, he would have taken a similar course. Catherine, however, was not to know that she was being tested and simply thanked God for her good fortune in learning of the plot. She also used her own cleverness, in concealing her intelligence and independent mind, to ensure that she was able to reconcile herself with the king. Henry intended to give Catherine the chance to redeem herself, but there was danger in the incident nonetheless and, if Catherine had not acted as she did, her life would have been in danger.

As with his actions in relation to the plots against Cranmer and Gardiner, Henry was also determined to show Catherine's accusers just who was the master. The following day Henry invited Catherine to walk with him in the gardens, a mark of favour that the queen readily accepted. While walking together, Wriothesley approached, accompanied with a number of guards, intending to arrest Catherine and take her to the Tower. Henry, who, in reality, can hardly have forgotten that he had intended to arrest his wife, turned in anger on Catherine's accuser, calling him 'knave! arrant knave! beast! And fool!' Wriothesley was stunned at the sudden change in the king and fled Henry's presence in terror. Catherine, who understood that she was expected to continue to play the game to its very end, smiled sweetly at the king and 'endeavoured to qualify the king's displeasure, with request unto his majesty in behalf of the Lord Chancellor, with whom he seemed to be offended'. Catherine continued saying that 'albeit she knew not what just cause his majesty had at that time to be offended with him, yet she thought that ignorance, not will, was the cause of his error'. Henry, pleased with his wife's performance, replied: 'Ah! Poor soul, thou little knowest how evil he deserveth this grace at thy hands. On my word, sweet-heart! He hath been towards thee an arrant knave, and so let him go.'

Catherine had passed the test, and survived but she knew well that she had been in danger and that she could no longer as openly promote her religious beliefs and opinions as before. As a further emphasis on this, on 16 July 1546, Anne Askew, unable to walk following the torture inflicted on her on the rack, was carried to Smithfield to be burned for heresy alongside three other Protestants. The news of Anne's execution must have caused Catherine to shudder from the knowledge that she had come close to sharing her fate. The incident shattered for Catherine the fond image that she had built of a docile husband and she became fully aware, as her predecessors had done before her, of the dangers of marriage to Henry VIII. For the rest of Henry's reign, Catherine presented herself as an entirely placid and decorative queen, keeping well away from politics and other controversial areas, exactly as Henry had been intending when he set her his test.

12

YIELDED HIS SPIRIT TO ALMIGHTY GOD: SUMMER 1546 – 28 JANUARY 1547

Catherine was thoroughly frightened by the plot against her in the summer of 1546. While she had always striven to be an active and influential queen, at the moment of danger, she took the crucial decision to save her life, even if it was at the expense of her own political influence. She had no intention of being another Anne Boleyn and, for the last few months of Henry VIII's life, she fought hard to save herself by portraying herself as a domestic and passive queen in the same mould as Henry's earlier and, to some extent, favourite wife, Jane Seymour.

The first test of Catherine's new resolve came in August 1546 with the conclusion of peace with France. By October 1545 the war with France had dragged on for well over a year and both Francis and Henry had indicated that they would consider listening to the mediation of Charles V. It was agreed that both kings would send their ambassadors to Charles at Antwerp in the hope that peace could be agreed. Henry was adamant that he would only make terms with Francis if Boulogne remained in his possession while Francis was equally adamant that it must be returned. The negotiations quickly reached stalemate and both sets of ambassadors returned home, unable even to agree a truce with both sides insisting that they should not have to be the ones to request it.

In May 1546 peace negotiations once again opened between the two countries, led by the Admiral of France and John Dudley, Admiral of England. Henry knew that he, in spite of French blustering, had the upper hand, and continued to insist only on a peace in which he kept Boulogne. Finally, in June 1546, a compromise was reached. According to one report:

> the substance of the arrangement is that Boulogne with the whole
> county of Boulognais remain in the hands of the English for eight
> years; after which time they are to be surrendered to the king
> of France, on the payment by him of two million in gold in one
> sum, besides the pensions of 120,000 crowns a year. The peace is
> generally considered shameful and injurious to the king of France,
> but he was obliged to consent to it for want of money.

In reality, the sums required for Francis to ransom Boulogne were so high that it was impossible that he would ever be able to raise them and Henry, along with everyone else, knew full well that Boulogne would remain his indefinitely. In spite of this, the agreement allowed Francis to save face and at least suggested to the world that he had not been forced to make peace at the expense of Boulogne.

Catherine took no direct role in the negotiations for peace. She was however expected to play a prominent, if passive, role in the grand spectacle that was planned to mark the peace with France and Henry's diplomatic triumph in retaining control of Boulogne. On 18 July John Dudley, Admiral of England, travelled to France in order to ratify the peace treaty and was treated to a magnificent reception.

Soon after Dudley's return to England, the Admiral of France set out for England to make a return visit and Henry intended that he should be as magnificently entertained as his English counterpart.

Henry required the entire royal family to take part in the reception of the French admiral and the details of the jewels that he gave to Princess Mary survive, demonstrating that he wanted his daughter to look magnificent. Among other jewels, on 20 July 1546 Henry gave his eldest daughter a diamond cross on a pendant of pearls and a diamond brooch showing the history of Abraham. Later that month he provided still further jewels, delighting the princess with a gift of 100 rubies and 25 diamonds in a gold setting among other things. Catherine also received a great quantity of jewels from her husband, every bit as fine as those provided for her stepdaughter. Henry intended a prominent role for his son and Edward was loaded with expensive presents, including 'chains, rings, jewelled buttons, neck chains, and breast-pins, and necklaces, garments, and very many other things'.

Catherine provided instruction as to how her stepchildren and her household should behave and a letter from Edward to Catherine shows that he valued her input. According to Edward:

Most noble queen and most illustrious mother, I give you uncommon thanks, that you behaved to me so kindly, when I was with you at Westminster. This gentle behaviour doth put my love to the test, although I cannot love you better. Therefore, to me it seems an age since I saw you. Therefore I would entreat your highness to pardon me, that I have not, this long time, written a letter to you. I did indeed wish it, but daily I have been expecting to be with your highness. But, when F__ went away, I had scarcely time for writing to the king's majesty.

> Further, I entreat your highness to let me know, whether the Lord
> High Admiral, who is coming from France, understands Latin well;
> for, if he does, I should wish to learn further what I may say to him,
> when I shall meet him.

Edward was right to be nervous about the reception for the admiral
as it was intended that it should be his first major public duty.

The French Admiral arrived at Greenwich on 20 August in a
fleet of fifteen ships all richly decorated. He was met by a gun
salute from Henry's own navy. He was then taken to Greenwich
where he spent the night, before travelling by water to the Tower
the next day, once again receiving a gun salute. The admiral
rode through the richly decorated streets of the city, watched by
assembled crowds and received a welcome from the people of
London. Prince Edward played his role on 23 August, meeting the
admiral three miles outside Hampton Court with a large escort of
gentlemen. Edward then escorted the admiral to the palace where
both Henry and Catherine were waiting.

The admiral was officially welcomed by the king on 24 August
at Hampton Court, where they dined together. The meeting
was evidently a success and the admiral stayed for some time,
entertained lavishly at Henry's expense. There was 'banqueting and
hunting, and rich maskes everie night with the Queene and ladies,
with dancing in two new banqueting howses, which were richlie
hanged, and had rych cubbordes of gold plate all gold, and set with
rych stones and perles, which shone rychlie'. Catherine loved to
dance and wear fine clothes and she put on a show for the admiral,
as her husband demanded.

Catherine's role during the visit was decorative rather than
political but she, along with everyone, shared the joy that peace

had finally been concluded. There was a sense of occasion to the visit which had not been seen since the early days of Henry's reign and, while neither Catherine or anyone else can have realized it, the Admiral's visit was to be the last great state occasion of Henry's reign.

By late 1546, Henry had ruled England for thirty-seven years and few people in England, including Catherine, could remember the time before he had been king. He remained active following the Admiral's visit and, in September 1546 he and Catherine moved their court to Guildford for a hunting trip. The king obviously enjoyed the trip and, by early October, the court had moved to Windsor, no doubt once again for the sporting pursuits. Catherine, who remained with Henry during his progress, may have started to see a change in her husband and, by December 1546 it was clear that his health was failing. On 5 December 1546, Van Der Delft, the Imperial ambassador, was able to obtain an audience with Henry when the court was staying at Oatlands but, when he tried to see the king again on 14 December, he found that access was denied due to Henry being unwell. His December illness was the recurrence of an earlier ailment at Windsor in mid October and it was obvious to everyone that it was the beginning of the end for the king.

In spite of his illness, Catherine knew that Henry remained as dangerous as ever and during the last few months of 1546 rumours flew around the court that the king was considering ridding himself of Catherine, to replace her with either her friend, Catherine Willoughby, Duchess of Suffolk, or improbably, his discarded fourth wife, Anne of Cleves. Such rumours must have been worrying for Catherine who had only recently survived the plot against her. In early December she was also given a firm example of just how dangerous Henry remained when, on 12 December 1546, the Duke of Norfolk and his son, the Earl of Surrey, were suddenly and shockingly sent to the Tower accused of treason.

Measures against Norfolk and his son proceeded rapidly and, unlike the earlier plots against Cranmer, Gardiner and Catherine, the king did not intend to give the pair the chance to save themselves. Immediately after their arrest Henry's agents were dispatched to Norfolk's principal residence at Kenninghall in Norfolk to search the house and obtain evidence. In spite of his illness, Henry took an active interest, insisting that his commissioners informed him personally of everything that they uncovered. At Kenninghall, Henry's three commissioners found the Duke's daughter, the Duchess of Richmond, and his mistress, Elizabeth Holland. The Duchess, hearing what the commissioners had to say, appeared 'sore perplexed, trembling and like to fall down', before recovering herself and offering to do all she could to assist the investigation against her father and brother. It was not wise to disobey the king as everyone, including Catherine, knew well, and Norfolk threw himself on the king's mercy, writing to declare his innocence and protesting his loyalty, although perhaps not wisely referring in his letter to the king's two former wives, Anne Boleyn and Catherine Howard, when he complained of 'the malice borne me by both my nieces whom it pleased the king to marry is not unknown as kept them in this house [the Tower]'. Feeling angry and unwell, Henry needed no reminders about his difficult past.

It was the Earl of Surrey who was the true focus of the king's wrath and it was claimed that he had attempted to assume the arms of King Edward the Confessor, something that was the prerogative of the king and Prince of Wales alone. Surrey was also reported to have said: 'if God should call the king to his mercy, who were so meet to govern the Prince as my lord his father [i.e. Norfolk]?' Surrey, as the grandson of the Duke of Buckingham, who was executed by Henry purely because of his direct male line descent from Edward III, was already under suspicion, and claims that he had advised his sister, the Duchess of Richmond, to become the king's mistress so that she could rule through him, were dangerous indeed. There is no doubt that Norfolk and Surrey had alienated the faction surrounding Edward Seymour at court and that the prince's senior uncle wanted them out of the way in order to smooth his progress towards a major political role in his nephew's reign. However, the impetus for the arrests can only have come from Henry and, aware, perhaps, that his end was near, he sought to ensure that there was no one who could attempt to assert a better claim to the throne than his son and heir. Henry himself made handwritten alterations to the document listing the charges against the pair and the execution of Surrey on 19 January 1547 was the final action carried out by Henry in his long reign.

Catherine, while no friend of either Norfolk or his son, watched the events of December 1546 anxiously in order to determine what her own future would be in the turmoil at the end of Henry's reign. By early December both Elizabeth and Edward had left her household and Catherine perhaps felt that it was better for the two children to be away from court. Certainly she had reason to fear that she might become politically isolated and, on Christmas Eve, she and her household were abruptly sent away from the king to spend Christmas at Greenwich. This was a great shock to Catherine and the separation caused speculation at court, as a despatch of Van Der Delft declared, pointing out that Catherine:

Has never been known before to leave him on solemn occasions like this. I do not know what to think or suspect. Although the king recently told me, as an excuse for not receiving me when I sought audience, that he had suffered from a sharp attack of fever, which had lasted in its burning stage for thirty hours, but that he was now quite restored, his colour does not bear out the latter statement, and he looks to me greatly fallen away.

Henry was deeply unwell over Christmas 1546 and it was this that caused him to send Catherine away. However, Catherine must have been concerned that others, most notably the king's brother-in-law, Edward Seymour, were still able to obtain access to him. Already, by December 1546 the council had begun to meet at Seymour's house and he started to emerge, in the last days of Henry's life, as a major new power in England.

Catherine spent a gloomy and depressing Christmas with her elder stepdaughter, Princess Mary, and her household at Greenwich. In spite of this, she tried to keep up appearances, sending a New Year's gift and letter to Edward as usual. The boy did not suspect that anything was amiss and, isolated from the court at Hertford, he wrote lovingly to Catherine on 14 January thanking her for her:

Signal and lasting love towards me. And this love you have manifested to me by many kindnesses, and specially by this New Year's gift, which you have lately sent to me, wherein the king's majesty's image and your own is contained, expressed to the life. For it delighted me to gaze upon your likenesses, though absent, whom, with the greatest pleasure, I would see present; and to whom I am bounden, as well by nature as by duty. Wherefore, I

Above: 1. Kendal Castle, Cumbria. By the time of Catherine's birth the castle was in ruins and she is unlikely to have ever visited her family's ancestral home.

Right: 2. The Parr Chapel in Kendal Church. Catherine's family paid for the chapel to be built in the fourteenth century and its splendour shows the wealth of the family and their prominence in Kendal.

Left: 3. The tomb of Sir
William Parr, Catherine's
grandfather in the Parr
Chapel in Kendal Church.

Below right: 4. Catherine
Parr, portrayed as a
Protestant heroine. The real
Catherine loved fine clothes
and jewellery and always
ensured that she was dressed
magnificently.

Above left: 5. William Parr, Marquis of Northampton. Catherine's brother became
one of the leading noblemen in England due both to his advantageous marriage and his
relationship to Catherine.

6. Helena, Marchioness of Northampton. William's Parr's final wife whom he married following a complicated and scandalous marital career.

Right: 7. Princess Mary, daughter of Henry VIII and Catherine of Aragon. Catherine would have known Mary in childhood and the pair later became good friends.

Next page: 8. Catherine of Aragon, Henry VIII's first wife. Catherine Parr's mother served the queen throughout her widowhood and it is likely that Catherine was named after her.

Above: 9. Tomb of Thomas, Lord Dacre at Lanercost Priory. Lord Dacre was a kinsman of the Parrs and sought Catherine as a bride for his grandson, Henry Scrope.

Previous page (bottom) and this page: 10, 11 & 12. Gainsborough Old Hall in Lincolnshire. Catherine spent her first marriage in the comfortable home of the Burgh family which was dominated by her forceful father-in-law, Sir Thomas Burgh.

Previous page and left:
13 & 14.
Interior views of Gainsborough Old Hall. The Hall has been reconstructed to be shown as it appeared at the end of the fifteenth century, shortly before it became Catherine's home.

15. A coverlet supposedly embroidered by Catherine during her time at Sizergh Castle.

Right: 16. Gainsborough Church. The burial place of Catherine's first husband, Edward Burgh.

Below: 17. Sizergh Castle, Cumbria. Catherine spent her first widowhood at the castle as a guest of her kinswoman, Catherine Neville.

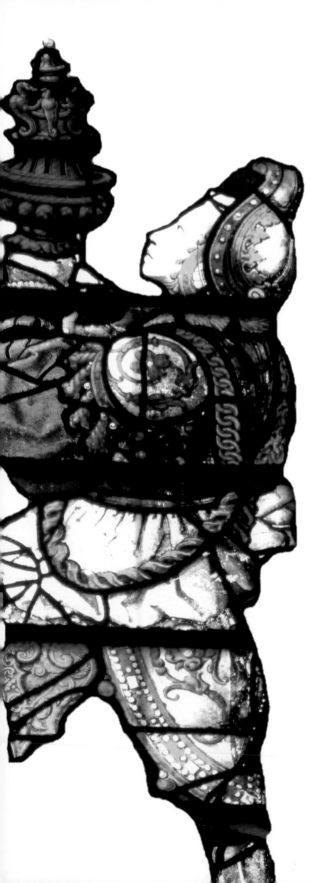

Above: 19. Thomas Seymour. Catherine's true love and the man that she would have married in 1543 if the king had not intervened.

Left: 18. Catherine Howard, Henry VIII's disgraced fifth wife and Catherine's predecessor as queen.

Opposite: 20. Henry VIII in his prime. By the time of his marriage to Catherine the king was elderly and overweight and a shadow of his former self.

HENRICVS.   VIII .

Above and next page top:
21. & 22. Hampton Court.
Catherine and Henry were married
in the grand Tudor Palace.

Left: 23. Anne of Cleves. Henry
VIII's discarded fourth wife.
Catherine's relations with her
predecessor were initially frosty and
Anne disapproved of Catherine's
marriage.

Above: 24. Edward VI. Catherine quickly developed a close relationship with her stepson and he always referred to her as his mother.

Above: 25. Catherine's badge in stained glass at Sudeley Castle. Catherine adopted the image of a crowned maiden emerging from a Tudor rose when she became queen.

Below: 26. Catherine's signature during her time as regent of England.

Previous page: 27. Princess Elizabeth. Catherine became a mother to her youngest stepdaughter and helped to introduce her to the religious reform.

BEATVS vir qui non abiit
in confilio impiorum, & in via
peccatorum non ftetit, & in cathedra pe =
ftilentiæ non fedit

Left: 29. Henry VIII reading. In his old age Henry became increasingly immobile and relied on Catherine to comfort him during his illnesses.

Above: 28. The Family of Henry VIII. Catherine
helped to promote the reconciliation of her two
stepdaughters with their father although she was
replaced by Henry VIII's third wife, Jane Seymour,
in the great dynastic portrait produced to symbolize
the Tudor succession.

Right: 30. Catherine Willoughby, Duchess of
Suffolk. Catherine and the Duchess of Suffolk were
close friends and shared the same religious beliefs
although Catherine was disconcerted by rumours
that Henry meant to replace her with the Duchess.

Above: 31. Greenwich Palace. Catherine was sent to spend Christmas 1546 at the palace away from her dying husband and she never saw him again.

Opposite top: 33. Whitehall Palace. Catherine was present in the palace at the time of Henry's death but she was refused admittance to his presence.

Left: 32. Thomas Cranmer, Archbishop of Canterbury, from his memorial in Oxford. Cranmer helped Catherine to develop her religious beliefs and he found himself in a similarly dangerous position when these beliefs were reported to the king.

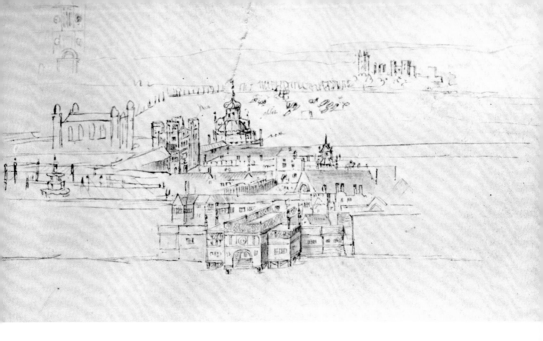

Below: 34. An extract from Henry VIII's Will. While Catherine was pleased that Henry had included both his daughters in the succession, she was shocked to find that she was given no role in Edward VI's minority government.

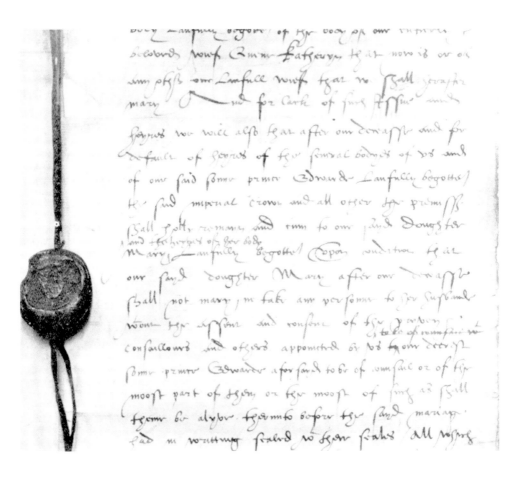

This page spread: 35, 36 & 37. St George's Chapel, Windsor Castle. Henry VIII asked to be buried in the chapel next to his beloved third wife, Jane Seymour.

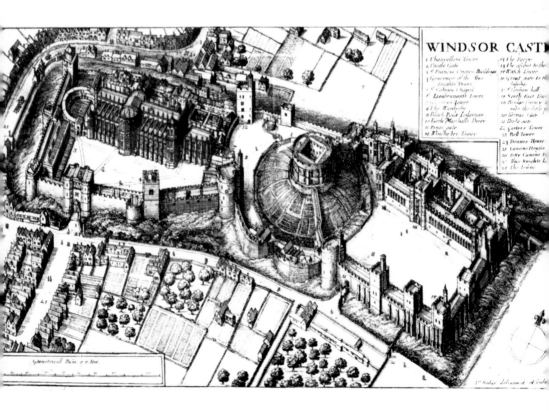

WINDSOR CAST

40. Edward Seymour, Duke of Somerset. Edward VI's Lord Protector disapproved of Catherine's marriage to his younger brother and quarrelled with Catherine on a number of occasions.

Opposite 42. Mary Tudor as queen. Catherine's rapid remarriage following Henry VIII's death alienated her elder stepdaughter.

41. The tomb of Anne Stanhope, Duchess of Somerset, at Westminster Abbey. Catherine and the Duchess were locked in a battle for precedence at the court of Edward VI, ultimately leading to Catherine retreating to the country.

Previous page left: 38. Thomas Seymour depicted in stained glass at Sudeley Castle. The love affair between Catherine and Thomas Seymour was quickly renewed on Henry VIII's death and the pair married secretly.

Previous page right: 39. Catherine Parr depicted in stained glass at Sudeley Castle. In spite of her marriage to Thomas Seymour, Catherine always insisted on being treated as queen throughout the remainder of her life.

MARIA : REGINA .

43. Lady Jane Grey, depicted in stained glass at Sudeley Castle. Catherine provided Henry VIII's great niece with a stable home and influenced the girl's Protestant religious beliefs.

Opposite below: 45. The Tower of London from a drawing by Anthony van Wyngaerde *c.*1543. Catherine's husband, Thomas Seymour, found himself a prisoner in the Tower within months of her death and he was beheaded on Tower Green in March 1549.

Above: 44. Sudeley Castle Chapel. Catherine's burial in the chapel was accompanied by the first Protestant royal funeral service in England.

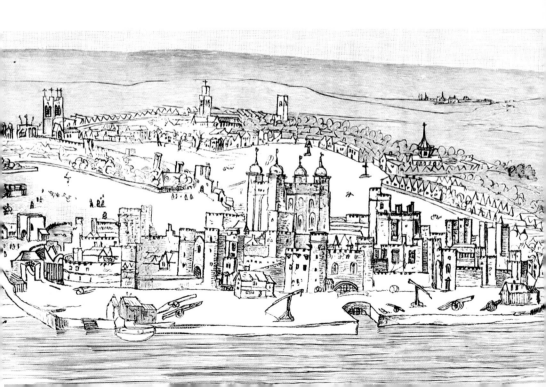

This page spread: 46, 47 & 48. Sudeley Castle. Catherine and Thomas saw the castle as the seat of the dynasty that they hoped to found and Catherine died there after giving birth to her only child.

Previous page and above: 49 & 50. The tomb of Catherine Parr at Sudeley. Catherine's original tomb was destroyed in the seventeenth century and she was eventually provided with a fine replacement.

Next page: 52. Elizabeth I at prayer. Catherine was responsible for Elizabeth's upbringing during her formative years and she is her greatest legacy.

Below: 51. Helena, Marchioness of Northampton, as the chief mourner for Elizabeth I. It was the Marchioness's relationship to Catherine that led to her being selected for the important office of chief mourner at the funeral of Catherine's stepdaughter, Elizabeth I in 1603.

give you greater thanks for this New Year's gift than if you had sent me costly garments or embossed gold or any other magnificent thing.

In sending Edward a picture of the king and herself, Catherine may have hoped to provide her stepson with some token of remembrance of the father that he was soon to lose. She attempted to ensure that her two younger stepchildren were protected from all that was happening in London but, in reality, she was deeply afraid. To increase Catherine's turmoil, Thomas Seymour also returned to court after his long absence near the end of 1546, quickly establishing a prominent presence at court and being appointed to the king's council on 23 January 1547. Catherine's feelings for Thomas had remained as intense as they had always been and the sight of the man she loved can only have served to increase her fear and distress as she, along with everyone else in England, waited to see what would happen next.

Unbeknownst to Catherine, although she may well have suspected it, during her separation from Henry the leading men around him used all their powers of persuasion to shape the future of the realm in a way that suited them. On the night of 26 December 1546 Henry called Edward Seymour, John Dudley and four other members of his council to him and requested that they bring his Will to him. Henry had not updated his Will since leaving for France in 1544, when it is likely that he had paid Catherine the complement of naming her as regent during Edward's minority. When the existing Will was read to Henry, he professed his surprise at the contents and demanded that a new Will be drafted on very different terms. It is almost certain that this surprise was due to the position of power given to Catherine; at the end of 1546, Henry was no longer as fond of her as he had been in the summer of 1544 and had no desire to allow her to rule the kingdom after his death.

The new Will drafted at the end of December 1546 has always been subject to a great deal of controversy. Henry's daughter, Mary, expressed her own concerns about its validity less than six months after his death in a conversation with Van Der Delft. According to the ambassador, Mary told him that:

> She was going to the North by her own desire, as she wished to see personally the estates that had been assigned to her, the value of which she was informed was about twelve thousand ducats (per annum). I said this was a most miserable allowance, and I thought her father had made a far different provision for her by his Will; to which she replied quite frankly that the testament which was said to be that of the late king might or might not be genuine; she did not know. She had heard, however, that the provisions of it, so far as related to her, were not more favourable than those contained in the Will he had made when he was about to cross over to Boulogne.

Mary was uncertain as to whether the Will was genuine and it is clear from her comments that doubt had been thrown on the testament. This is also supported by the fact that the Will is listed as one of the documents recorded as having been signed with a stamp displaying Henry's signature in January 1547. The stamp had been made to spare Henry the burden of having to sign personally all official papers but if it was used on the Will itself it would certainly call the validity of the document into question. The Will has been examined for marks of the stamp but all analysis has proven unclear and it is uncertain whether or not Henry ever actually signed his Will. Henry's younger daughter, Elizabeth, did however appear to have believed in the genuineness of the Will when, in 1559, she wrote to the Dean and Chapter of Windsor to inform them that she wished to carry out one of the bequests in her father's Will and, while it is indeed possible that Henry's new Will was not actually completed in time for him to sign it, it is probable that he already knew and approved its contents.

Henry's Will is, in itself, a remarkable document. As predicted, he left the crown to his only surviving son, Edward, and, in default of Edward's own heirs, to any children that he might have by Catherine, an optimistic and unlikely notion by the end of 1546. In default of such heirs, Henry willed the crown to his daughters, Mary and Elizabeth in turn, before passing over the descendants of his elder sister, Margaret, in favour of his younger sister, Mary. Realizing that he was going to die before his son reached his eighteenth birthday, Henry also put some thought into who would govern England for Edward and eventually decided not, as was conventional, to appoint a Protector for the boy king, and, instead put in place a council of sixteen executors to rule with equal power and to be assisted by a group of assistant executors. This was a radical and, in truth, unworkable arrangement. While Henry handed custody of his Will to Edward Seymour, the Will itself only named Seymour as one of the sixteen executors and gave him no special position as the king's uncle, something that it would undoubtedly have done if Seymour had forged it. It is therefore clear that the decision to excluded Catherine from any role in government came from Henry himself, even if some pressure was brought to bear on him from Catherine's enemies. Henry was prepared to leave Catherine wealthy and to set out in his Will that she should be accorded all honours due to her as a queen, but he left her no power, with the events of the summer of 1546 remaining so fresh in his mind.

Immured at Greenwich away from Henry, Catherine feared that some new plot was planned against her and became increasingly desperate to return to her husband. By 10 January at the latest, both she and Mary were at Whitehall and in the same residence as the king. The contemporary *Chronicle of King Henry VIII* claims that Catherine and Henry had a touching reunion as the king lay on his deathbed with Henry turning to her weakly and telling Catherine:

> it is God's will that we should part, and I order all these gentlemen
> to honour you and treat you as if I were living still; and if it should
> be your pleasure to marry again, I order that you should have seven
> thousand pounds for your service as long as you live, and all your
> jewels and ornaments.

According to the *Chronicle*, Catherine was unable to answer for weeping and Henry ordered her away so that she would not see him dying. While this is a touching scene, and one that would demonstrate that there had truly been a reconciliation between Henry and Catherine, it never occurred. Catherine remained excluded from Henry's presence during his last days even after her journey to Whitehall and, after her departure to Greenwich on Christmas Eve 1546, she never saw him again.

Catherine passed the first few weeks of 1547 in a state of anxiety, powerless to alter anything that was happening around her and fearful that some new plot might be instigated against her. By 8 January 1547 there were already rumours circulating that Henry had died and Catherine feared for the future. While the council circulated counter-rumours, claiming that Henry was showing signs of recovery, Catherine, being more aware of Henry's poor physical state than most, can hardly have believed them. In the early hours of the morning of 28 January 1547 Henry VIII 'yelded up hys spirite to almightie God, and departed thys worlde' with Archbishop Cranmer holding his hand. His death was kept secret and Catherine may at first have been unaware that, for the third and last time, she had become a widow.

13

WEEKS BE SHORTER AT CHELSEA: JANUARY – MAY 1547

For several days after Henry's death, life went on as normal at court with meals continuing to be brought to the king's chamber. For Catherine, Henry's death, while not unexpected, was a shock and she found herself excluded from power in the new reign.

Edward Seymour, Earl of Hertford, had Henry's Will in his possession when the old king died and, at 3 a.m. on 28 January, he and Sir Anthony Browne left London secretly intending to bring the new king, Edward VI, to London. Hertford had only been appointed as one of the sixteen equal executors under Henry's Will and, in order to ensure that he was able to take power it was essential that he obtained possession of his nephew, the young king. On the journey, Hertford succeeded in persuading Browne, a Catholic and not a natural supporter of the reform minded Hertford, to support his bid to become Protector of the realm during the king's minority. Flushed with this success, Hertford obtained custody of his nephew and then rode south to Hatfield where Princess Elizabeth was staying. Once there he informed the two weeping children of their father's death before pressing on for London with the king. Having obtained Browne's support and with Edward VI in his company, Hertford was confident that he would become the new power in England.

On 31 January the chancellor, Wriothesley, announced the death of Henry VIII in Parliament and Paget read out the Will. Later that day Paget met with the Council and secured their consent to Hertford being appointed Protector to the king.

The contents of Henry's Will had been kept closely guarded by Hertford and his ally, Paget, and Catherine was unaware of her husband's last wishes until 31 January when details were finally announced. It must have been a shock to Catherine when she learnt the full extent of her exclusion from power and, far from being named as the sole ruler of the realm as she had hoped, she was not even included as one of the group of executors or their assistants whom Henry intended would govern the kingdom during his son's minority. Catherine's entire exclusion from Henry's executors and Hertford's swift assumption of the reins of power made any political role impossible and she was presented with a *fait accompli*. Mary was with Catherine at the time of Henry's death and the two women retired to mourn the man that had been such a powerful force in both their lives and to share their concerns about the future.

Catherine was not the only person to be excluded from power by the terms of the Will and Hertford's younger brother, Thomas Seymour, found himself equally distant from power. Thomas had been named as one of the assistant executors by Henry VIII but he was not expected by the old king to play a major role. Hertford and his supporters rapidly set about sharing the spoils of the new reign between themselves. On 6 February 1547 the council met at the Tower and, on the assurance of Paget, the minister who had been closest to Henry, that it was the old king's wish, it was agreed that the new members of Edward VI's minority government would be ennobled. According to Paget, Henry had been concerned that 'the nobilitie of this realme were greatly decayed, somme by atteyndours, somme by their owne misgovernaunce and riotous wasting, and some by sickenes and sondrie other meanes'. It was asserted by Paget that Henry intended Hertford to become a Duke, William Parr a Marquis and John Dudley an Earl, as well as other appointments for the other executors. It was agreed that Thomas Seymour would also receive a peerage and the sum of £300 a year but his appointment as Baron Seymour of Sudeley was very far from the dukedom of Somerset that was conferred on his elder brother. Catherine was pleased to find that her brother was promoted to become Marquis of Northampton, only one honour below that of a duke. However, for Thomas Seymour, his new title and even the appointment of High Admiral of England was not enough when he considered the honours bestowed upon his brother.

Thomas Seymour's ambition extended well beyond the honours he received in the weeks following Henry VIII's death and he tried to improve his position by obtaining a royal wife. Within weeks of Henry VIII's death there were rumours that Seymour was attempting to marry Edward VI's elder sister, Princess Mary. By June 1547 these rumours had become urgent enough for the Imperial ambassador, Van Der Delft, to raise the subject with Mary. According to the ambassador's own report, he was pleased to hear that Thomas had in fact made another marriage because:

It meant that she herself (the Princess Mary) had thus escaped an alliance with the personage in question, for which, according to common report, she was at one time designated. She laughed at this, saying that she had never spoken to him in her life, and had only seen him once; and she took in very good part my remark that, but for the perfect confidence I had in her prudence and discretion

I should have come to her and have begged her to bear in mind her great descent and the respect due to her person, which should never tolerate such a degradation.

According to some reports, Mary, as the heir to the throne, was Thomas's first choice of bride. The evidence for this is, however, slight. While it has been claimed that Thomas approached the council or his brother to request their consent to the marriage, there is no record of this and it was not raised later when he found himself in disgrace. As Mary herself admitted, she barely knew Thomas Seymour and, while this may not have been a bar to his ambitions in marrying her, he must have been aware that it was very unlikely that the proud daughter of Henry VIII and cousin of the emperor would condescend to marry him. It appears that the origin of the rumours lies in Edward VI's own remarks when pressed on who he thought his uncle should marry. The boy first replied: 'Anne of Cleves,' before changing his mind to reply: 'Nay, nay, wot you wat? I woold he maried my sister Mary, to turn her opinions.' Thomas, who was deeply ambitious, would undoubtedly have been pleased to have married Mary, but there is no evidence that he actively sought the match and, in any event, his interest lay in a much more promising direction.

Two letters exist which suggest that Thomas showed a great deal more interest in Mary's younger sister, Elizabeth. Both letters are however open to dispute and they survive only as Italian copies in a seventeenth century work. It is indeed possible that they are genuine but, without the originals, they must be considered doubtful. According to the first letter, supposedly written by Thomas Seymour on 25 February 1547 and addressed to the princess:

I have so much respect for you my Princess, that I dare not tell you of the fire which consumes me, and the impatience with which I yearn to show you my devotion. If it is my good fortune to inspire in you feelings of kindness, and you will consent to a marriage you may assure yourself of having made the happiness of a man who will adore you till death.

Elizabeth's response stated:

My lord admiral,

The letter you have written to me is the most obliging, and at the same time the most eloquent in the world. And as I do not feel myself competent to reply to so many courteous expressions, I shall content myself with unfolding to you, in few words, my real sentiments. I confess to you that your letter, all elegant as it is has very much surprised me; for, besides that neither my age nor my inclination allows me to think of marriage, I never would have believed that any one would have spoken to me of nuptials, at a time when I ought to think of nothing but sorrow for the death of my father. And to him I owe so much, that I must have two years at least to mourn his loss. And how can I make up my mind to become a wife before I shall have enjoyed some years my virgin state, and arrived at years of discretion?

Elizabeth finished her letter declaring that 'though I decline the happiness of becoming your wife, I shall never cease to interest myself in all that can crown your merit with glory, and shall ever feel the greatest pleasure in being your servant, and good friend'.

In spite of the doubts over the letters, there is strong evidence that Thomas did at least make enquiries into the possibility of a marriage with Elizabeth. On 17 January 1549 the privy council reported that 'notwithstanding goode advis geven to the contrary aswell by the said Lord Protectour as others his frendes of the Counsail, practised to have in marriage the lady Elisabeth, oone of his Majestes sisters and the second inheritour after his Majeste to the crown'. While this could refer to the period after September 1548, it is more likely that Thomas felt himself in a position to seek advice on the marriage from his brother and the council in the early weeks of Edward VI's reign, before his relationship with the king's government had irrevocably broken down. Thomas was arrested in 1549 and the official charges against him state that he sought to marry Elizabeth before his marriage to Catherine and that he continued this after his wife's death 'by secrete and craftie meanes'. Elizabeth's own governess also later referred to Thomas as the princess's 'old suitor', implying again that he had sought marriage with her in the weeks following Henry's death. It is unlikely that Thomas's tentative enquiries ever reached the stage of a definite proposal and he was rebuffed by his brother for considering a match with the king's sister.

As soon as word reached her of Henry's death, Catherine changed into her widow's clothes again. As a widow, she was expected to remain secluded until after the king was buried and she stayed in London while preparations were made for his elaborate burial on 14 February at Windsor. By convention, Catherine, as Henry's widow, played no direct role in the funeral. On 2 February the body was carried in a procession towards Windsor. Catherine was pleased to see that her own banners, along with those of Jane Seymour, the mother of the new king, were carried in prominent positions alongside the hearse. Again, by convention, Catherine did not travel in the procession but she probably set out from Whitehall at the same time as the funeral procession and she was at Windsor, watching from the privacy of the Queen's Closet in the chapel as her third husband was laid to rest beside the body of his own third wife.

Catherine swiftly returned to London from Windsor, choosing not to remain for too long in the sombre atmosphere of the king's burial place. Mary stayed with her and, soon after the funeral, Elizabeth also joined her from Hatfield. With his accession to the throne, Catherine's relationship with Edward entirely changed and she knew that she would have no further role in his upbringing. In spite of this, she continued to write to him and, on 7 February, even before Henry VIII's funeral, she received a letter of condolence from her stepson showing that his feelings towards his 'mother' remained unchanged. According to Edward's letter:

Many thanks for the letter that you last sent me, dearest mother; which is a token of your singular and daily love for me. And now, as it hath seemed good to God, the greatest and best of beings, that my father and your husband, our most illustrious sovereign, should end this life, it is a common grief to both. This, however, consoles us, that he is now in heaven, and that he hath gone out of this miserable world into happy and everlasting blessedness. For whoever here leads a virtuous life, and governs the state aright, as my noble father has done, who ever promoted piety and banished all ignorance, hath a most certain journey into heaven. Although nature prompts us to grieve and shed tears for the departure of him now gone from our eyes, yet scripture and wisdom prompt us to moderate these feelings, lest we appear to have no hope at all of the resurrection of the dead. Besides, as your highness had conferred on me so many benefits, I ought to afford you whatever comfort I can. I wish your highness abundant health. Farewell, reverend Queen.

Catherine continued her correspondence with her stepson throughout the early months of his reign and was pleased with his continuing affection for her. In a later letter, written at the end of May, Edward assured her:

> since you love my father, I cannot but much esteem you; since you love me, I cannot but love you in return; and since you love the word of God, I do love and admire you with my whole heart. Wherefore, if there be anything wherein I may do you a kindness, either in word or deed, I will do it willingly.

As a dowager queen, it was expected that Catherine would leave court and, by early March, preparations were under way for her to leave London. Mary returned to her own estates and, by April at the latest she had left Catherine. Elizabeth however, at only thirteen was too young to have her own establishment and Catherine was grateful to find herself appointed as her guardian.

While Catherine received no political power under Henry's Will, she was left well provided for with bequests of £3,000 in plate and jewels, £1,000 cash and her dower lands. Catherine was free to choose her own residence and she selected one of her dower houses, the manor at Chelsea, moving there with Elizabeth and the rest of her household, in mid-March. Chelsea manor had been acquired by Henry VIII in 1536 through a property exchange. The Tudor manor was demolished in the early eighteenth century but it appears to have been a fairly modest building which fronted directly on to the street. Henry had spent considerable sums on the gardens and they were particularly fine, planted with fruit trees and roses, as well as borders of sweet-smelling herbs. Catherine was familiar with the manor and Henry had paid it occasional visits during the last decade of his reign. While a smaller residence than she had become used to, Chelsea suited Catherine perfectly, keeping her close to London, as well as allowing her some privacy, something which she had not enjoyed since becoming queen four years before.

For Catherine, privacy was soon to become an essential commodity. In 1543 when she had been forced to abandon her plans to marry Thomas Seymour, both had understood that this must be the end of their relationship and Catherine had no immediate hopes of a resurgence in their relationship. Thomas was still looking for a high profile bride and, within weeks of Henry's death, his thoughts had turned to the queen dowager. For Thomas, there was an obvious advantage in a marriage to the queen and this is likely to have been his primary consideration. However, it is also clear that, back in 1543, the couple had been in love and that Thomas's courtship of Catherine when she had simply been Lady Latimer had had little to do with status and wealth and everything to do with attraction. Shortly after Catherine was widowed he renewed his acquaintance with her, much to Catherine's pleasure.

Catherine and Thomas's relationship is recorded in the letters that they wrote to each other in early 1547 and it is obvious that, on both sides the affection that they had previously known was reawakened. In 1547 Catherine was approaching thirty-five and, after three husbands either chosen for her or forced upon her, she was eager to seize her chance of happiness with the man she loved. A letter of Catherine's written to Seymour during this period shows how serious their relationship quickly became and is worth quoting in full:

My lord. As I gether by your letter delivered to my brother Harbert, ye are in sum fere how to frame my lord your brother to speke in your favour, the denyall of your request schall make hys foly more manifest to the world, wyche will more greve me than the want of his sekyng. I wold not wyssche you importune for hys good wyll, yf yt cum not frankely at the first, yt schalbe suffycyent ones to have require yt, and after to cesse. I wold desire ye might obtayne the kinges letters in youre favour, and also the ayde and furtherans of the most notable of the counsel, such as ye schall thynke convenient, wyche thynge obtained schalbe no small schame to your brother and loving syster, in case they do not lyke. My lord where as ye charge me with a promys wryttin with myne owne hand, to change the two yeres into two monethes, I thynke ye have no such playne sentence written with my hand; I know not whether ye be a paraphryser or not, yf ye be lerned in that syence yt is possyble ye may of one worde make a hole sentence, and yet nott at all tymes after the true meaning of the wryter, as it aperyth by thys your exposycyon upon my writing. When yt schalbe your pleasur to repayre hether ye must take sum payne to come without suspect. I pray you let me have knowledge [o]ver nyght at what howre ye wyll come, that your porteresse may wayte at the gate to the feldes for you. And thus with my humbel and harty comendatyons I take my leve of you for thys tyme gyvyng you lyke thankes for your comyng to the court whan I was thare. From Chelsey.

I wyll kepe in store tyll I speke with you my lordes large offer for Fausterne [one of Catherine's manors] at wyche tyme I schalbe glad to knowe your further pleasur therein.

By her that ys and schalbe your humble, true and loving wyff during her lyf.

Catherine may have signed herself as Thomas's wife but it is clear from her letter that they were not yet married. From the letter it appears that Thomas first renewed their acquaintance when they were both at court and that, when Catherine left court, they agreed that he would come to her at Chelsea when he could. Thomas and Catherine met in the gardens at Chelsea, the easiest place to secure privacy. Thomas would also arrive at night to be let in by the queen herself. Catherine was entirely unaware that she had not, in fact, been Thomas's first choice of bride. It seems likely, particularly from Catherine's description of herself as Thomas's wife, that he would stay the night and that the pair became lovers soon after her arrival at Chelsea. She believed herself to be infertile and can have seen little danger in becoming his lover, and she was anxious to keep up appearances as a dutiful royal widow in her insistence that they wait two years before marrying.

At some point in around early May the couple became betrothed, although Catherine was still determined that no marriage would follow until there had been a decent interval since Henry's death. In spite of her reservations about rushing into marriage, in the spring of 1547 Catherine was the happiest that she had ever been in her life and she was unable to contain herself, telling her sister, Anne, of all that had passed. According to a letter written by Thomas to Catherine, he was surprised to find Anne Herbert a party to the secret:

> After my umbel commedashens vnto your highnes yester nyght
> I sopt at my brother Harbards of whom for your sake besides
> my noun I reseued good cheyre. And after the same I reseued
> from your highness be my sester harbard [Anne Parr] your
> comendashens whiche warre more welcome then they warre sent.

And after the same she waded further with me tochyng my being with your highness at Chelsey which I denyed being with your highness, but that in dede I went by the garden as I went to the beshop of London's house; and at this point, stood with her for a tyme, tyll, at the last, she told me further tokens which made me change colours, who, like a falce wenche, toke me with the maner. Then remembering what she was, and knoyng how well ye trosted her, examined her whether those thyngs came from your highness, and be that knew it to be trew, for the which I render vnto your highness my most umbel and harty thankes; for by her company (in defaught of yours) I shall shorten the wekes in these parttes, which heretofore warre iij days longer in euery of them then they ware vnder the planets at Chelsey.

Thomas was relieved to find a friend in Catherine's sister as both he and Catherine were painfully aware that not everyone would take the news of their relationship well. Catherine found the time that she and Thomas, for appearances sake, had to be apart trying and, in a letter to him, full of impatience, she apologized saying:

I send you my most humble and hearty commendations, being desirous to know how you have done since I saw you. I pray you be not offended with me, in that I send sooner to you than I said I would, for my promise was but once in a fortnight. Howbeit the time is well abbreviated, by what means I know not, except weeks be shorter at Chelsea than in other places.

Thomas was as eager for news of Catherine as she was of him and it is very clear from their correspondence that the affection was mutual. In a further letter written around this period he added:

Yf I knew by what means I might gratify your highness for your goodness to me, showed at our last being together, it shuld not be slakte to declare myne to you agen, and be that intent that I wylbe more bounde vnto your highness I make my request that yf it be nott paynfull to your highness that once in thre days I may rescue iij lynes in a lettr from you, and as many lynes and lettres more as shall seme good vnto your highnes.

Thomas spoke of his hopes of seeing Catherine soon and asking to meet her at the same hour that the letter was written, midnight. Thomas continued to urge Catherine on towards marriage in May 1547 and she found it increasingly difficult to resist.

While still apart from Catherine following their betrothal, Thomas was able to write that 'I perseve that your highness hath ben warmd, wharof I am glad, for that ye shalnot think on the ij yeres ye wrott of in your last lettr before this'. It is unclear when or where the marriage occurred but it may perhaps have been on one of Thomas's midnight visits to Catherine at Chelsea. Certainly the couple were married by the end of May, or the first week of June at the latest, and, for the first time in her life, Catherine threw caution to the wind in an attempt to secure her own personal happiness. Even as the marriage was being celebrated and Catherine experienced her moment of greatest joy, both she and Thomas were aware that the way to acceptance of their marriage was still fraught with danger and, in marrying in secret, they jeopardized, theoretically at least, the succession to the throne itself for, as Thomas was later charged:

he maryed the late Quene so sone after the late Kynges deathe that if she had conceived straight after, it shulde have bene a great doubte whither the childe borne shuld have bene accompted the late kinges or yours [Seymour's], wheruppon a marvaulous daungier and peril might and was like to have ensued to the kinges Majestes succession and quyet of the realme.

By marrying in haste and secrecy Catherine and Thomas were aware that they placed themselves in danger. Both knew that it was imperative that they use Catherine's status and connections to try to secure some measure of approval for their actions.

14

MUCH OFFENDED BY THE MARRIAGE:
JUNE – DECEMBER 1547

In spite of their happiness in their secret marriage, both Catherine and Thomas knew that they still had a long way to go if their union was to be accepted both by Catherine's royal stepchildren and Thomas's elder brother.

Perhaps at Catherine's suggestion, Thomas attempted to persuade Princess Mary to support what he presented as a proposed marriage to the queen. Catherine hoped that Mary, who she knew yearned for a marriage of her own, would support the idea of her stepmother marrying for love. Both Catherine and Thomas were however to be quickly disillusioned and, on 4 June, only a few weeks at most since the date of the marriage, Mary wrote a scathing response to Thomas:

I have received your letter, wherein (as me thinketh) I perceyv strange newes concerning a sewte you have in hande to the quene for maryage; for the soner obtayneng whereof you seme to think that my lettres myghte do you pleasure. My lord in thys case, I trust your wysdome doth consider, that, if it weer for my nereste kynsman and dereste frende on lyve, of all other creatures in the worlde, it standeth lest with my poore honoure to be a meddler in thys matter, consyderyng whose wyef her grace was of late; and besides that, if she be mynded to graunt your sewte, my lettres shall do you but small pleasure. On the other side, if the remembrance of the kyng's magestye my father (whose soule God pardon) wyll not suffre her to grawnt your sewte, I am nothing able to perswade her to forget the loss of hyme, who is yet very rype in myne owne remembrance.

Mary's negative response was not good news and, for Catherine, her stepdaughter's disapproval was deeply wounding. The couple next decided to approach the king himself.

Thomas Seymour approached John Fowler, a member of Edward VI's privy chamber and a man over whom Thomas had some influence. According to Fowler himself, Thomas came to him at St James's Palace and asked: 'Now, Mr Fowler, how does the Kinges majesty?' Fowler replied: 'Well, thankes be to God.' Thomas enquired whether the king ever wondered 'why I married not'. Fowler shook his head at this, saying that the king never asked such a question. Thomas was ready for this and continued, saying: 'Mr Fowler, I pray you, if you have any communication with the Kinges majesty soone, or to-morrow, ask his highness whether he woold be content I shuld mary or not; and if he saye he will be content, I pray you aske his grace whom he woold have to be my wife?'

Fowler duly did as he was asked and it was during his next conversation with the king that Edward suggested that Thomas marry Anne of Cleves or Princess Mary. This was not at all the answer that Catherine or Thomas required and, the next day, when informed by Fowler of the king's reaction, Thomas laughed, asking Fowler to speak to the king again and 'aske his grace if he could be contented

I shuld mary the Quene; and in case I be a sutar to his highness for his letter to the Quene whether his majesty woold write for me or not'. As with his approach with Mary, Thomas pretended that the marriage had not already taken place and that he required the king's consent to the match. Thomas was not entirely prepared to rely on an indirect approach with Edward, which had gone so badly wrong with Mary, and, before Fowler had a chance to speak to the king, Thomas managed to see Edward in private. Thomas persuaded the boy that the idea of a marriage was his own idea and Edward wrote to Catherine pressing his uncle's suit. Catherine was overjoyed and responded to the king's letter, confirming that she would indeed accept his choice of husband for her. This letter drew a favourable response from the king and, on 25 June he wrote to Catherine saying:

> Wee thank you hartely, not onlie for your gentle acceptation of our sute moved unto you, but also for your loving accomplishing of the same, wherin you have declared not onlie a desire to gratifie us, but also moved us to declare the good-will likewise that wee bear to you in all your requests. Wherefore yee shall not need to heare any grefe to come, or to suspect lake of ayde in need; seeing that he, being mine uncle, is of so good a nature that he will not be troublesome on the means unto you; and I of that minde, that of divers just causes I must favour you. But even as without cause you merrily require help against him, whom you have put in trust with the carriage of these letters; so maye I merrily retourne the same request unto you, to provide that he maye live with you also without grefe, which hath given him hoely vnto you.
>
> And I will so provide for you both, that hereafter if any greafe befall, I shall be a sufficient socor in your godlie and praisable enterprises.

Catherine's relief on receiving the letter cannot be overstated and, with the king's assurance of his support, both Catherine and Thomas knew that they were safe from any danger, even if they still feared his brother's reaction to the news.

By early May Catherine's obvious happiness had begun to draw comments and, on 4 May, Van Der Delft, the Imperial ambassador remarked that Catherine no longer wore the deepest mourning for Henry and that she had begun to wear a French hood again and silk dresses. By 16 June the ambassador commented that he had heard a rumour that a marriage was being arranged between Catherine and Thomas. Aware that their secret could be discovered at any time, Catherine urged Thomas onwards and, once he had secured the king's letter of approval, he approached his brother, asking the Protector to speak to the queen to further his suit. Perhaps aware of the king's support for the match, Somerset agreed, although he may have spoken only half-heartedly to the queen. He certainly felt himself duped in late June 1547 when news of the marriage finally became public, later complaining of the 'evill and dissembling nature' demonstrated in his brother by the way he went about pursuing and publicising his marriage.

By early July news of the marriage was finally public and Catherine and Thomas faced the anger of both the Protector and Princess Mary. Mary was furious at what she felt was the lack of respect shown to her father by Catherine's marriage. In early July when the Imperial ambassador visited Mary she asked him 'what I thought of the queen (dowager's) marriage to the Lord Admiral'. Van Der Delft replied that 'it appeared to me to be quite fitting, since the queen and he were of similar rank, she having been content to forget the honour she had enjoyed from the late king'. For Mary, news of the marriage shattered her friendship with her stepmother and the relationship was never the same again. She also doubted Catherine's suitability as a guardian for Princess Elizabeth and a reply written by Elizabeth to her half-sister demonstrates the grave concerns that Mary had expressed over Catherine's marriage. According to Elizabeth:

You are very right in saying, in your most acceptable letters, which you have done me the honour of writing to me, that, our interests being common, the just grief we feel in seeing the ashes, or rather the scarcely cold body of the king, our father, so shamefully dishonoured by the queen, our stepmother, ought to be common to us also. I cannot express to you, my dear princess, how much affliction I suffered when I was first informed of this marriage, and no other comfort can I find than that of necessity of submitting ourselves to the decrees of Heaven; since neither you nor I, dearest sister, are in such a condition as to offer any obstacle thereto, without running heavy risk of making our own lot much worse than it is, at least, so I think. We have to deal with too powerful a party, who have got all authority into their hands, while we, deprived of power, cut a very poor figure at court. I think, then, that the best course we can take is that of dissimulation, that the mortification may fall upon those who commit the fault. For we may rest assured that the memory of the king, our father, being so glorious in itself, cannot be subject to those stains which can only define the persons who have wrought them. Let us console ourselves by making the best of what we cannot remedy. If our silence do us no honour, at least it will not draw down upon us such disasters as our lamentations might induce.

These are my sentiments, which the little reason I have dictates, and which guides my respectful reply to your agreeable letter. With regard to the returning of visits, I do not see that you, who are the elder, are obliged to this; but the position in which I stand obliges me to take other measures; the queen having shown me so great affection, and done me so many kind offices, that I must use much tact in manoeuvring with her, for fear of appearing ungrateful for her benefits.

This letter was apparently written during one of Catherine's visits to court while Elizabeth remained at Chelsea. At first glance, it appears that Elizabeth shared the sentiments of her sister and that both felt that their stepmother had dishonoured the memory of their father. However, Elizabeth, who lived with Catherine, had no desire to leave her and, while she was indeed dissembling, it was to Mary that she dissembled and not Catherine. In spite of this, Catherine would have been very hurt if she had seen Elizabeth's letter and, even if Elizabeth wrote more to appease Mary's concerns and to ensure that she was able to remain with the queen, the sentiments that she set out, attacking Catherine's marriage, were felt by many.

When Van Der Delft told Mary that he thought that Catherine and Thomas were of a similar rank if one ignored her third marriage to the king, he was voicing the view of many. Catherine believed that God had granted her the office of queen and she considered that she was absolutely entitled to the respect due to her in accordance with this rank even after the death of Henry VIII. Certainly, Catherine's position was enshrined in law and the Act that had granted Henry his divorce from Anne of Cleves in 1540 had also confirmed that the highest status woman in England would be his subsequent wife or widow. After her, his daughters were to have priority and then Anne of Cleves, before his nieces and the wives of noblemen vied for status. In the weeks immediately after Henry's death this position was honoured and Catherine, in spite of her lack of political power, was at least still granted all the respect due to a queen when she came to court.

With her marriage, Catherine found that this began to change. Somerset's wife, Anne Stanhope, came from an aristocratic courtly family and she had always resented having to pay court to the former Lady Latimer. With the rise of her husband to the role of Protector, the Duchess's pride in her own position increased and when news of Catherine's marriage reached her she declared that she would no longer hold Catherine's train when she came to court, claiming that 'it was unsuitable for her to submit to perform that service for the wife of her husband's younger brother'. The Duchess considered that she should be the first lady in the land and also declared loudly, for anyone to hear:

> did not Henry VIII marry Katharine Parr in his doting days, when he had brought himself so low by his lust and cruelty that no lady that stood on her honour would venture on him? And shall I now give place to her, who, in her former estate, was but Latimer's widow, and is now fain to cast herself for support on a younger brother? If master admiral teacheth his wife no better manners, I am she that will.

Catherine was a frequent visitor to court during the first few months of Edward VI's reign and she heard of these remarks, to her intense anger. The Duchess was also not content merely to denigrate Catherine's status verbally and, on more than one occasion, she physically pushed Catherine out of the way so that she could pass through a door first in the place of honour.

Catherine was furious at her sister-in-law's conduct and, rightly, insisted that she was still fully entitled to the legal position of queen and that, until the king came to marry, she was the first lady in the land. Catherine's comments on the treatment meted out to her by the Duchess also survive. According to the *Chronicle of Henry VIII*:

> Hardly a year had passed after the marriage of the queen with the Admiral before there was great jealousy between the queen and the Protector's wife, who seeing that the queen was the wife of the younger brother, resolved not to pay the usual honours to her. When the queen saw it she was much annoyed, and said to her husband the Admiral, 'How is this, that through my marriage with you the wife of your brother is treating me with contempt and presumes to go before me? I will never allow it, for I am queen, and shall be called so all my life, and I promise you if she does again what she did yesterday I will pull her back myself.

Catherine was beside herself with anger at the slight. Thomas, who was proud of his wife's status, entirely supported Catherine and approached his brother soon after Catherine complained to him, berating him for allowing his wife to treat the queen as she did. Somerset was angry himself at the way that Catherine and Thomas had gone about their marriage and refused to involve himself in the quarrel, replying: 'Brother, are you not my younger brother, and am I not Protector, and do you not know that your wife, before she married the king, was of lower rank than my wife? I desire therefore, since the queen is your wife that mine should go before her.' The Protector's words signalled open war between the two brothers and their wives and Thomas replied angrily: 'I am sorry there should be any anger between them, but I can tell you that the queen is determined not to allow it, so do not blame me for it.' Catherine and Thomas raged together privately that night as Thomas related his audience with his brother but there was little Catherine could actually do and the next morning in church the duchess once again pushed herself forward to sit in the place of the queen. Catherine was humiliated by this and went away berating herself and saying: 'I deserve this for degrading myself from a queen to marry an Admiral.'

The Protector was also determined to show his displeasure at the marriage. According to the king himself, in his diary: 'Lord Seymour of Sudeley married the queen whose name was Catherine, by which marriage the Lord Protector was much offended.' Somerset was furious that his brother had arranged the marriage and he took this anger out on Catherine, like his wife seeking to denigrate her position as queen. As was usual, during her marriage to Henry VIII, Catherine had stored her substantial collection of jewels in the Tower of London for safekeeping. In the weeks immediately following Henry's death, Catherine had left the jewels where they were but, once the Protector's hostility became clear, she sought their return to her own custody.

When Catherine approached Somerset to secure the release of her jewels she was immediately rebuffed with the answer that they were Crown property of which she, as a widow, no longer had any claim. This was infuriating to Catherine especially as at least some of the jewels were certainly her own possessions. Among the jewels locked in the Tower were a gold cross and some pearl pendants left to Catherine by her mother, as well as her wedding ring, given to her by Henry. The loss of these items of sentimental value was particularly galling to Catherine and both she and Thomas robustly took on the legal case to secure their return. By the summer of 1548 the couple had secured legal opinions setting out her right to the jewels, and Thomas, presumably with the queen's consent, resolved to approach the king to seek the return of the jewels. According to Thomas's usual go-between, John Fowler, Thomas approached him privately at court and asked him to 'tell his grace I wil be a sutar to my lord my brother for certain jewelles which the king that ded is gave the quene, thinking the law woold she shuld have them'. Fowler shook his head at this, being already a party to the bad feeling between the Seymour brothers and replied: 'Alas! My lord, that ever jewelles or muck of this world shuld make you begyn a nue matter between my lords grace and you.' In spite of Fowler's pleas, the matter of Catherine's jewels remained a major bone of contention between the two brothers and their wives.

The pursuit of Catherine's jewels came to dominate both Catherine and Thomas's thoughts and, even after Catherine's death, Thomas pursued the claim, seeking written dispositions from certain gentlemen of Henry VIII's court as to the jewels that Catherine had received from the king and whether these were intended as a gift or loan. Given the terms of Henry VIII's Will, in which he allowed Catherine to keep her jewels and plate, it is a reasonable assumption for her to have made that the jewels belonged to her. Thomas was so obsessed with the return of the jewels that, in the autumn of 1548 he even wrote to Princess Mary 'to learn after what sort the king departed with those jewels that his Highness delivered to the queen at the [French] Admiral's coming in'. Mary did not reply but Thomas persisted until the end of his own life in obtaining lawyer's opinions and other evidence and he was determined to prove Catherine's right to the jewels as just another aspect of his dispute with his brother.

Catherine's jewels were not the only area of dispute that she had with the Protector and he was determined to slight her as a mark of his disapproval in her marriage. Even before her marriage to Thomas, Catherine had found the Protector difficult to work with. According to one of her early letters to Thomas, Catherine complained:

> my lord, your brother, hath deferred answering such requests as I made to him till his coming hither, which he saith shall be immediately after the term. This is not the first promise I have received of his coming, and yet unperformed. I think my lady hath taught him that lesson, for it is her custom to promise many comings to her friends, and to perform none.

To Catherine's anger, it rapidly became clear that Somerset was not prepared to keep his promises on a number of matters and, alarmingly, he also treated her own property as though it remained the property of the Crown.

An extraordinary letter of Catherine's survives showing both the extent of her anger at the Protector's behaviour and the hopelessness of her situation as a powerless queen dowager. According to Catherine, reporting on a visit to court to her husband:

> This shall be to advertise you that my lord your brother hath this afternoon made me a little warm. It was fortunate we were so much distant; for I suppose else I should have bitten him. What cause have they to fear having such a wife? To-morrow, or else upon Saturday, at three o'clock in the afternoon, I will see the king, when I intend to utter all my choler to my lord your brother, if you shall not give me advice to the contrary; for I would be loth to do

anything to hinder your matter. I will declare to you how my lord hath used me concerning Fausterne; and after, I shall most humbly desire you to direct mine answer to him in that behalf. It liked him to-day to send my chancellor to me, willing him to declare to me that he had brought master Long's lease, and that he doubted not but I would let him enjoy the same to his commodity, wherin I should do to his succession no small pleasure, nothing considering his honour, which this matter toucheth not a little, for so much as I at sundry times declared unto him that only cause of my repair into those parts was for the commodity of the park, which else I would not have done. He notwithstanding, hath so used the matter, with giving master Long such courage, that he refuseth to receive such cattle as are brought here for the provision of my house; and so in the meantime I am forced to commit them to farmers.

Somerset was determined to have Catherine's manor of Fausterne for his own purposes and, even before Catherine's marriage, he had made her an offer for it which she had rejected. To Catherine's fury, he overruled her in the matter, securing the lease of Catherine's property for his friend, Master Long, ignoring Catherine's protestations that she used it. Somerset was determined to secure his position as Protector by making grants of land to his allies and Catherine, as her predecessor as queen, Anne of Cleves, also found, was considered fair game by him.

For all her defiance and Thomas's fury, Catherine was unable to effectively respond to the treatment meted out on her by the Protector and his wife and to the general censure that she received at court following her marriage. Catherine, while determined to fight for her rights, became weary of a struggle that she could not possibly win and she increasingly retreated to her dower houses, spending less time at court. At Chelsea, or one of her other properties, Catherine was able to maintain her status as queen. According to the *Legend of Throckmorton*, Catherine's residence remained splendid following her fourth marriage and:

> Her house was term'd a seconde court of right,
>
> because there flocked still nobilitie.
>
> He spared no coste his ladie to delight,
>
> Or to maintaine her Princelie Royaltie.

Thomas was determined to emphasize Catherine's royal status. This is clear from comments made by Thomas after Catherine's death when he commented to his friend, Sir William Sharrington that 'it would be strange to some when his daughter came of age, taking place above [the Duchess of] Somerset, as a queen's daughter, not his'. During Catherine's lifetime Thomas also loudly defended his wife's status at court, declaring when an Act was passed repealing one that forbade people from speaking out against the queen that he would take his fist to anyone who dared to slander her. For Catherine, this was all proof of Thomas's love for her and she entirely approved of his efforts, remaining conscious of her own high status throughout her life. She may, perhaps, not have been aware just how much Thomas's actions were linked to his own ambitions rather than simply being a kindness to her as his wife.

Thomas Seymour was as ambitious as his brother, the Protector. Within weeks of Edward VI's accession he was plotting to ingratiate himself with the king in an attempt to secure a more prominent role in government. Through John Fowler, Thomas supplied the young king with frequent sums of money in order to allow him to make gifts to his servants, something that the Protector did not allow. While Catherine began to retreat from court as the hostility directed at her by the Protector and his wife increased, Thomas became all the more actively involved in plotting his brother's downfall.

15

LADY SEYMOUR OF SUDELEY: WINTER 1547

After the first summer of Edward VI's reign, Catherine spent considerably less time at court, preferring to remain in her own household where she was still treated as queen. In spite of her marginalization as a dowager queen, Catherine was also Lady Seymour of Sudeley and she remained fully interested in politics and in her fourth husband's activities.

Catherine continued to spend much of her time at Chelsea, in the company of her stepdaughter, Elizabeth, and also with Thomas's nine-year-old ward, Lady Jane Grey. Jane was the daughter of Henry VIII's niece, Frances Brandon and her husband, Henry Grey, Marquis of Dorset. Thomas had taken the initiative in securing Lady Jane Grey. According to her father, Dorset's, own report:

Immediately after the king's death [John] Hartington, the lord admiral's [Thomas's] servant, came to my house at Westminster and showed me that the admiral was highly likely to come to good authority and, as the king's uncle, he might do me much pleasure, advising me to report to him and enter more into his friendship. He advised me to allow my daughter Jane to be with the admiral, saying he would have her married to the king. Within a week I went

to the admiral's house at Seymour Place where he persuaded me to
send for my daughter, who remained there until the queen's death.

In January 1547 it seemed likely to everyone that Thomas, as
the new king's uncle, would rapidly come to prominence and
even a great nobleman like Dorset was prepared to bind himself
closely to him. Within weeks of Henry VIII's death Thomas had
already made his displeasure at being excluded from absolute
power known and he saw Jane as a key element in his attempts
to win power for himself, promising Dorset that, if he granted
him his daughter's wardship, he would arrange a marriage for
her with the king. This was a magnificent offer for Jane's parents
and they accepted it willingly, though it is likely that they would
also have extracted some payment from him before agreeing to
part with their eldest daughter. The Dorsets had no son and Jane,
as their senior heiress, was a prize even without her royal blood
and they were determined not to sell her cheaply. The terms of a
later agreement between Dorset and Thomas exist and, following
Catherine's death, Thomas agreed to purchase Jane's wardship
for £2,000, immediately paying Dorset the sum of £500. Money
almost certainly would have changed hands early in 1547.

Based on Dorset's comments, it is most likely that Jane moved
to live with Catherine as soon as her marriage to Thomas was
made known. Catherine is unlikely to have played any direct
role in Thomas's negotiations with Dorset and, at that time, their
marriage was still a secret. However, she must have been aware of
her husband's plans for the girl. The wardships of heiresses were
often bought and sold, usually to an unmarried gentleman or a man
with unmarried sons who intended to either marry the girl himself
or arrange for her to wed one of his sons. Thomas's interest in

Jane was related to her marriageability, something that Catherine recognized. She certainly enquired as to just who Thomas had in mind to marry Jane. Neither Catherine nor Thomas were close enough to the king to know his own thoughts and it is clear that Edward would never have countenanced marrying his cousin. During negotiations for his marriage to Elizabeth of France in 1551, Edward commented in his diary that she 'should be brought at her father's expense three months before she was 12, sufficiently jewelled and stuffed'. Edward was determined to secure a wealthy and prestigious bride and took a strong interest in the negotiations for his future bride's dowry. Lady Jane Grey simply could not compete with the prestige and wealth of the daughter of the King of France but Catherine and Thomas, isolated from Edward's innermost thoughts and persisting in the view that he was wholly controlled by the Protector, were entirely unaware of this.

Catherine welcomed Jane into her household. Catherine was always fond of children and her tiny pale faced great-niece appealed to her. Jane also responded warmly to Catherine's affection. The Dorsets were strict and stern parents, showing little affection to their precocious daughter. According to Jane herself in a conversation with the scholar Roger Ascham in 1550, she spent as little time with her parents as possible, preferring to shut herself away with her studies. Jane told Ascham:

> I will tell you, quoth she, and tell you a truth, which perchance ye will meruell at. One of the greatest benefits, that euer God gave me, is, that he sent me so sharp and seuere Parentes, and so ientle a scholemaster. For when I am in presence of either father or mother, whether I speake, keep silence, sit, stand, or go, eate, drinke, be merie, or sad, be sowing, playing, dauncing, or doing anie thing els, I

must do it, as it were, in such weight, measure, and number, even so perfitelie, as God made the world, or else I am so sharplie taunted, so cruellie threatened, yea presentlie some tymes, with pinches, nippes, and bobbes, and other waies, which I will not name, for the honor I beare them, so without measure misordered, that I thinke my selfe in hell, till tyme cum, that I must go to Mr Elmer [Jane's tutor].

While there might be some element of exaggeration in the then teenaged Jane's outburst to a near-stranger, it is clear that the Dorsets were more concerned with ensuring that their daughter appeared to the world as a credit to them than in her happiness, and a letter written by Dorset to Thomas after Catherine's death shows just how they expected their daughter to be raised:

Nevertheless considering the state of my Doughter and hyr tender yeres, (wherin she shall hardlie rule hyr sylfe as yet without a Guide, lest she shuld for lacke of a Bridle, take to moche the Head, conceave such Opinion of hyr selfe, that all such good behauvior as she heretofore hath learned, by the Quenes and your most holsom instructions, shuld either altogether be quenched in hyr, or at the leaste moche diminished, I shall in most harties wise require your Lordeshippe to commit hir to the Governaunce of hyr Mother; by whom for the Feare and Duetie she owither hyr, she shall most easily be ruled and framd towards Vertue.

That Jane learned 'good behaviour' while she was with Catherine was due more to the kindness and care that she received from the queen than any 'bridle'.

Catherine personally supervised the education of her two royal charges, Elizabeth and Jane. While Elizabeth was four years older than her cousin, it is likely that the two shared some lessons and both were devoted to Catherine, who loved learning and actively encouraged the two girls in their studies. Catherine had played a role in the appointment of William Grindal as Elizabeth's tutor and he moved with the household to Chelsea in early 1547. No account survives of Grindal's methods of teaching his charge but he is known to have been an associate of Roger Ascham, who became Elizabeth's tutor following Grindal's death early in 1548. It is likely that the two followed a broadly similar programme. Ascham followed an enlightened approach to teaching, stating that, where a child does well, the school master should praise them 'for I assure you, there is no such whetstone, to sharpen a good witte and encourage a will to learning, as is praise'. Ascham also commented that, where a child had made a mistake, but showed diligence, he should not be chided, pointing out:

> let your scholer be neuer afraid, to aske you any dout, but vse discretlie the best allurementes ye can, to encourage him to the same: lest, his ouermoch fearing of you, driue him to seeke some misorderlie shifte: as, to seeke to be helped by some other booke, or to be prompted by some other scholer.

Ascham believed that a child required a love of learning to be able to learn, but insisted that scholarship should be carried out in addition to other pastimes and that a child should not always be at their books. This was exactly the ethos that Catherine instilled into her own household, allowing both girls to flourish under her charge. Long after she had left Catherine's household, Ascham was able to comment of Elizabeth that:

It is your shame, (I speak to you all, you young ientlemen of England) that one mayd should go beyond you all, in excellencie of learning, and knowledge of diuers tonges. Pointe forth six of the best giuen Ientlemen of this Court, and all they together, shew not so much good will, spend not so much tyme, bestow not so many howres, dayly, orderly, and constantly, for the increase of learning and knowledge, as doth the Queenes Maiestie [Elizabeth] her selfe. Yea I beleue, that beside her perfite readiness, in latin, Italian, French, and Spanish, she readeth here now at Windsore more Greeke euery day, than some Prebendarie of this Church doth read latin in a whole weeke.

Lady Jane Grey was also renowned as a scholar, in later life carrying out a correspondence in Greek with at least one lady of the court.

Thomas was often at court during the final months of 1547 and the early months of 1548. As the king's uncle, he felt that he should be given a greater share of power than his brother was prepared to allow. One particular area for dispute was over the governorship of the king. Somerset had been appointed both Protector of the Realm and governor of the king in January 1547 and Thomas rapidly became jealous, arguing strongly to anyone who would listen that he should be appointed governor of the king if his brother was to be Protector. Edward VI's first parliament sat between 4 November and 24 December 1547 and Thomas, who had been currying support amongst the nobility and other members of the court for some time, was determined to use the opportunity to put forward his case to be governor of the king. Ominously, he was overheard saying loudly that 'he would make the blackest parliament that ever was seen in England'. He also attempted to make use of his nephew the king, who he had been bribing with sums of money for some time. According to Edward VI's own account Thomas asked him to copy out a piece of paper that he had written. When Edward queried what it was, Thomas assured him that 'it was none yll thing; it ys for the quene's majesty'. The king was unconvinced and refused to copy the letter, saying: 'If it were good, the lordes wold allow it; if it were yll, I wold not wryght in it.' The letter was a direct attack on the Protector and it was framed so as to be a request, direct from the king, that his younger uncle should become his governor in place of the elder. Thomas intended to take the letter down to the Parliament chamber himself but, with Edward's refusal and a warning he received that such an act would be treasonous, he abandoned his plans. He did not, however, abandon his plots against his brother.

According to the Chronicler, John Hayward, the two brothers were their own worst enemies and, while together they could have shared power successfully, divided they brought about each other's ruin. According to Hayward:

> The king had two vncles brothers to Queene Jane his deceased mother, Edward Duke of Somerset, Lord Protector, and Thomas Lord Seymer Baron of Sudley, High Admirall of England, as the Duke was elder in years, so was hee more staied in behauiour. The Lord Sudley was fierce in courage, courtly in fashion, in personage stately, in voice magnificent, but somewhat empty of matter, both were so faithfully affected to the king that the one might well be termed his sword, the other his target. The Duke was greatest in favour with the people, the lord Sudley most respected by the nobility, both highly esteemed by the king both fortunate alike in their advancements, both ruined alike by their own vanity and folly.

Hayward blamed the animosity partly on the rivalry between the two men's wives which was, to a certain extent, true. However, it is clear that Thomas was his own worst enemy and, if anything, Catherine's status protected him from the censure of the Protector.

While Thomas complained publicly that he had not received sufficient honours and powers as the uncle of the king, he neglected his duties as Admiral. As Admiral of England, Thomas was in direct control of the English fleet. In September 1547 the fleet was ordered to sail but, for some reason, Thomas was not at its head, his Vice-Admiral, Lord Clinton instead taking the role. It is possible that, in this case, Thomas did not neglect his duties and that, given the fact that his brother also travelled north to make war on Scotland, his presence was required at home. That his absence might have had a more sinister motive is suggested by Thomas's conduct in July 1548 when the English fleet once again sailed under the command of Lord Clinton. Thomas refused to sail, insisting on remaining in London, in all likelihood to enable him to continue his intrigues against his brother. Thomas and Somerset quarrelled over the admiralty and Thomas's dereliction of duty. According to John Fowler, he was approached at court by Thomas who:

> Asked me whither my lord his brother had byn there or not syns his last being there, and as I remember I said no. Then he told me that my lords grace was fallen out with him concerning th'admiraltie, and how his grace tooke their parte before his, and theis wer my words unto him, 'pray you pacifie yourself, and beare with my lords grace; considering he is the Protector of the realme, and your elder brother, for Goddes love let ther be no unkindnes between you.'

Thomas simply shook his head at this, answering: 'Nay, my lord will have my hed under his girdell.' Fowler again urged the Admiral to make peace with his brother but Thomas refused to answer, merely instructing Fowler : 'I pray you (quoth he) tell the kinges majesty of it, lest my lord shuld tell him, and that his highnes shuld be ignorant of the matter.' Thomas was anxious to ensure that the king saw matters his way and, in a subsequent conversation with Fowler he asked the king's servant to 'put the kinges majesty (as moche as in me lay) in mynde if my lord protector woold tell his highnes any thing against my lord admiral, in that case that his majesty woold take his parte'.

In spite of her personal animosity towards the Protector, Catherine and her brother-in-law had much in common. By the end of Henry VIII's reign Somerset was widely known to be in favour of the religious reform and was described in one letter as 'not very favourable to the priests, and a great enemy to the pope in Rome'. Once in power, Somerset, in close co-operation with Archbishop Cranmer, began the process of undoing Henry VIII's middle way in religion and turned England firmly towards the reformed faith. The first sign of this was in the Injunctions, issued by the government soon after Edward VI's accession to the crown which ordered the removal of images from churches, as well as changes to other traditional practices within the Church. Cranmer and Somerset also sent commissioners across England to attempt to dissuade people from praying to saints or for the dead, and to stop the use of rosaries.

As the months progressed, the religious changes in England became significantly more radical. Later in 1547 the Election of Bishops Act was passed, giving the king the power to appoint new bishops and archbishops. By late 1547 the conservative

Bishop Gardiner had also been imprisoned for his opposition to the religious changes. He was released soon afterwards when he promised to comply with the government before being placed under house arrest and, ultimately, sent to the Tower in July 1548. The changes were not solely government led and in London there was a popular movement towards reform. By December 1547 the people of London had begun to sing psalms in English and, by May 1548, a number of major London churches were conducting their services solely in English. For Catherine, with her reformist beliefs, the last months of 1547 and early months of 1548 were a remarkable time and the speed with which the changes occurred were welcomed by her. During Edward VI's first parliament the first draft of the Protestant Book of Common Prayer was revealed by Cranmer. In July 1548 Cranmer, in a letter to a friend, set out a statement of government policy:

> We are desirous of setting forth in our churches the true doctrine of God, and have no wish to adapt it to all tastes, or to deal in ambiguities; but, laying aside all carnal considerations, to transmit to posterity a true and explicit form of doctrine agreeable to the rule of the sacred writings; so that there may not only be set forth among all nations an illustrious testimony respecting our doctrine, delivered by the grave authority of learned and godly men, but that all posterity may have a pattern to imitate.

Catherine wholly agreed with these sentiments and, after months of having to keep her true beliefs hidden, with the rule of Protector Somerset, regardless of what she thought about him personally, she was finally able to express her views and opinions openly.

Catherine was determined to show herself as an example of a Protestant queen in a way that she had never been able to do before. On 5 December 1547 Van Der Delft, the Imperial ambassador, commented that mass was no longer celebrated in the houses of the Duke of Somerset, John Dudley, Earl of Warwick, or Catherine's. This was a public statement of Catherine's beliefs and she also took steps to ensure that her household remained godly and that everyone there was instructed in the Protestant faith. According to Hugh Latimer, one of the reforming bishops: 'I have heard say, when that good queen that is gone had ordained in her house, daily prayer both before noon, and after noon, the admiral gets him out of the way, like a moth digging in the earth'. Catherine regularly attended the prayer meetings, as she had done before she was queen, and expected her household to follow suit, opening them up to her reformist beliefs. Princes Elizabeth had already been exposed to this during her earlier years in Catherine's household and it was also Catherine who succeeded in evangelizing Lady Jane Grey.

Catherine also patronized leading reformers and, around the time of Henry VIII's death, she took the Protestant John Parkhurst into her service as her chaplain on the recommendation of the Duchess of Suffolk. Parkhurst would later become a leading bishop under Elizabeth I and the pair first became acquainted in Catherine's household. The reformist scholar Miles Coverdale also returned to England in early 1548 and was immediately taken into Catherine's household as her almoner, remaining with her until her death. Catherine's religious beliefs did not remain static during this period and she was prepared to listen to more radical views, to the dismay of many in her household. In a letter written by Parkhurst some time after Catherine's death, he wrote complaining of one such radical influence in the queen's household. According to Parkhurst:

> Robert Cooch is a very accomplished man, and well skilled in music. When I was a preacher in Queen Catherine's household, he was steward of the wine cellar. When King Edward was alive, that most famous physician and very learned divine Master William Turner wrote a book against him in which he refuted his opinion on original sin. At that time he likewise held erroneous opinions on the baptism of infants. He dreamed up strange things about the Lord's supper. He very often troubled Coverdale and myself with these controversies, so much so that we wearied of him. He was extremely verbose. When Jewel and other learned men came to court to visit me, he instantly began to discuss these subjects with them, nor could he make an end of his talking. Now, too, he lives in the queen's [Elizabeth I] court.

Cooch was renowned for his radical opinions and his argument that the Communion was too much like a fast and ought to be a feast was especially controversial. In spite of this, Catherine was fond of him and listened to his ideas, apparently interesting her stepdaughter, Elizabeth, in the scholar.

The driving religious influence in Catherine's household was the queen herself and, while Hugh Latimer's comments about Thomas's ungodliness were certainly slander, he was less committed than his wife. For Catherine, the early months of Edward VI's reign presented her with a golden opportunity to publicize her faith and, towards the end of 1547, she finally felt able to publish her own personal statement of her faith, *The Lamentation of a Sinner*. Catherine took some persuasion to publish the book and, according to the first edition, it was 'set forth and put into print at the instant desire of the right gracious lady, Catherine, Duchess of Suffolk, and the earnest request of the right honourable Lord William Parr, marquis of Northampton'. Catherine was persuaded by the argument that it might help lead others to Protestantism and, according to the preface by Catherine's friend, William Cecil, 'to all ladies of estate, I wish as earnest mind, to follow our Queen in virtue as in honour, that they might once appear to prefer God before the world, and be honourable in religion, who now are honourable in vanities'.

In spite of her joy over the religious changes wrought by Protector Somerset, Catherine was unable to reconcile herself to him during the last months of 1547 and early months of 1548. As Catherine increasingly removed herself from court for the security of her own household, she became more and more reliant for news on her husband and on others that she was close to. Catherine's brother, William, had originally been close to the Protector, being created Marquis of Northampton soon after Henry VIII's death. However, within months he had quarrelled with Somerset over his marital difficulties. Somerset had himself divorced his first wife and William hoped that he would find him sympathetic to his own marital troubles. In April 1547 he petitioned for a divorce from Anne Bourchier, assuming that the process would be nothing but a formality. William was quickly to be disappointed as the Protector ordered an examination which moved so slowly that, in the summer of 1547, William secretly married his mistress, Elizabeth Brooke. Catherine's sympathies lay with William and she was as furious as her brother when he was forced to separate from his second wife by the Council. Catherine agreed to take Elizabeth Brooke into her household while the divorce was debated and she watched events closely as William petitioned the king directly in December 1547 for his divorce. William finally secured his divorce in 1548 and took Elizabeth back again, but the struggle permanently alienated him from the Duke of Somerset.

Somerset continued to extend his power throughout the later months of 1547, being described as 'all but king, but rather esteemed by everyone as the king of the king'. Somerset's increasing power and prominence continued to rankle with Thomas who displayed 'hatred and rivalry against his brother' both in private and in public. Catherine, reliant on her husband for news, soon came round fully to his point of view, coupling this with the poor treatment that she had received from her brother-in-law. Catherine loved Thomas and she trusted him implicitly. It took a devastating shock for this trust to be broken and, by the middle of 1548, only a year after their wedding, Thomas had broken Catherine's heart.

16

THE QUEEN WAS JEALOUS: WINTER 1547 – MAY 1548

Catherine had known Elizabeth since she was nine years old and she continued to look upon the girl as a child. In the autumn of 1547, Elizabeth turned fourteen, an age considered mature enough for marriage in the sixteenth century. If Catherine did not notice that her stepdaughter was growing up, Thomas Seymour certainly did on his visits home from court.

Thomas had already had an interest in Elizabeth before his marriage to the queen, although this was solely due to her status as the king's sister. Once Thomas had married Catherine he became, essentially, Elizabeth's guardian or stepfather and the two regularly came into contact for the first time. Elizabeth was attractive, with pale skin and long red hair and Thomas, in spite of his obvious attraction to Catherine, was in no way averse to flirting with his pretty young stepdaughter.

The first evidence of an attraction between Elizabeth and Thomas appears to have been innocent enough and no one, least of all Catherine, paid any attention to it. In spite of her strict religious observance, Catherine had always loved dancing and she ensured that her favourite pastime was regularly carried out in her own household at her dower houses of Chelsea or Hanworth or at Thomas's London residence of Seymour Place. According to Elizabeth's governess, Katherine Ashley, Elizabeth would often choose Thomas as her partner and then 'laugh and pale at it' with embarrassment. On other occasions, Elizabeth shyly chose Thomas as her partner before she 'chased him away', flushing with embarrassment. This all seemed innocent enough and Catherine, along with Elizabeth's governess, saw no harm in it, laughing with the rest at her stepdaughter's bashfulness. To Thomas, however, it was the first indication that Elizabeth might have feelings towards him.

As Catherine's husband, Thomas was given a great deal more freedom and access to her royal stepdaughter than would ordinarily have been the case and he began a flirtation with Elizabeth almost as soon as his marriage to Catherine had been announced. According once again to Katherine Ashley:

> Incontinent after he was married to the Queene, he wold come many mornings into the said Lady Elizabeth's Chamber, before she was redy, and sometime before she did rise. And if she were up, he would bid hir good morrow, and ax how she did, and strike hir upon the Bak or on the Buttocks famylearly, and so go forth through his lodgings; and sometimes go through to the Maydens, and play with them, and so go forth: And if she were in hyr Bed, he wold put open the Curteyns, and bid hir good morrow, and make as though he wold come at hir: And she wold go further in the Bed, so that he could not come at hir.

For Thomas to even enter Elizabeth's bedchamber was a shocking breach of decency and his behaviour there was scandalous. Worse was yet to come as, not content with merely pretending to join

Elizabeth in bed if he found her there, one morning 'he strave to have kissed hir in hir Bed: And this Examinate [Ashley] was there bade hym go away for shame'. Thomas allowed himself to be chased away on that occasion, as Elizabeth remained giggling in her bed, but it is obvious that his intentions towards his wife's stepdaughter were very far from innocent.

Catherine may not, at first, have been aware of what was happening between her husband and her stepdaughter but his morning visits had been brought to her attention by the time she moved her household to Hanworth, her second dower house, for a change of air. Catherine was still deeply in love with Thomas and she chose to ignore what she heard, seeing it as a malicious interpretation of innocent play between a child and her stepfather. To Catherine, Elizabeth was still the quiet, withdrawn little girl that she had been when she had first met her and she apparently even welcomed the growing relationship between Thomas and Elizabeth, seeing it as harmless fun. According to Katherine Ashley again:

> At Hanworth, he wolde likewise come in the morning unto hir Grace; but, as she remembreth, at all tymes, she was up before. Saving two mornings, the which two mornings, the quene came with hym: And this Examinate lay with hir Grace; and thei tytled [tickled] my lady Elizabeth in the Bed, the quene and my Lord Admyrall.

The image of Catherine and her husband joining Elizabeth in bed in the morning and tickling her is a bizarre one and, deep down, Catherine must have been aware that both she and Thomas were behaving inappropriately. It is impossible now to understand just what her motives could have been in joining her husband in his conduct. Catherine was also involved on another occasion in the gardens at Hanworth when she and Elizabeth came upon Thomas. As the three laughed together, Catherine held her stepdaughter while Thomas drew his dagger and slashed Elizabeth's black dress into a hundred pieces before allowing her to flee. Elizabeth ran back to her governess where she was chided for the destruction of her clothes but, when Elizabeth responded that 'she could not do with all, for the quene held hir, while the Lord Admiral cut it' there was little Mrs Ashley could do but warn her charge to be more careful in future.

Catherine's participation encouraged Thomas to become bolder and, following the incident with Elizabeth's dress, when the household had returned to Chelsea, he renewed his morning visits to the princess's bedroom. As with her behaviour during the dancing, Elizabeth veered between excitement at Thomas's pursuit and embarrassment and, on a number of occasions, Elizabeth, 'on heryng the Pryvie-lock undo, knowing that he wold come in, ran out of hir Bed to hir Maydens, and then went behind the Curteyn of the Bed, the Maydens being there; and my lord tarried to have hyr com out'. When the household moved to Seymour Place in the winter this continued, with Thomas visiting Elizabeth in the morning 'in his Night-Gown, barelegged in his slippers'. Elizabeth would ensure that she was already up and reading, leaving Thomas to go away disappointed.

Elizabeth has often been censured for her conduct in relation to Thomas Seymour. At fourteen, she knew that it was wrong to entertain a flirtation with her stepmother's husband. When the events became common knowledge she received a large proportion of the blame. One contemporary, for example, the hostile Jane Dormer, recalled of Elizabeth:

A great lady, who knew her very well, being a girl of twelve or thirteen, told me that she was proud and disdainful, and related to me some particulars of her scornful behaviour, which much blemished the handsomeness and beauty of her person. In King Edward's time what passed between the Lord Admiral, Sir Thomas Seymour, and her Dr Latimer preached in a sermon, and was a chief cause that the Parliament condemned the Admiral. There was a bruit of a child born and miserably destroyed, but could not be discovered whose it was; only the report of the midwife, who was brought from her house blindfold thither, and so returned, saw nothing in the house while she was there, but candle light; only she said, it was the child of a very fair young lady. There was a muttering of the Admiral and this lady, who was between fifteen and sixteen years of age.

Rumours that Elizabeth bore Thomas a child persisted and, even in the nineteenth century, one writer was able to report with certainty that such a child existed and that Elizabeth was largely to blame for all that happened. It is certain that Elizabeth had feelings for Thomas but there is no evidence to suppose that the pair ever had the opportunity to form a sexual relationship. On the contrary, Elizabeth, despite her personal feelings, did all that she could to resist Thomas, even though pressure was brought to bear on her both by the queen's presence during the romps and by her own governess.

While Katherine Ashley professed herself shocked at Thomas's conduct, she was fond of him and would dearly have loved him to have married Elizabeth before his marriage to the queen. According to Ashley's own report, she came across Thomas in the park at St James's Palace at some point in late May or June

1547. Once there she commented: 'I have ever said that he should have married my lady.' Thomas shook his head saying: 'Nay, I have not to lose my life for a wife. For it has been spoke, but that cannot be. But I will prove to have the queen.' Ashley chided the Admiral pointing out: 'It is past proof, as I hear you are married already.' Mrs Ashley believed that Catherine had stolen Elizabeth's proposed husband from her, commenting to Elizabeth after Catherine's death: 'Madam, now you may have your husband that was appointed you at the death of the king.' Elizabeth simply said: 'Nay' but Mrs Ashley persisted, commenting that 'if all the Council did agree, why not? For he is the noblest man unmarried in this land'. Elizabeth's governess persisted in her attempts to persuade Elizabeth to marry Thomas after Catherine's death.

To her credit, in spite of her fondness for Thomas, Katherine Ashley did realize that something was not right in Thomas's morning visits to Elizabeth. According to her own report:

> And as touching my lord's [Thomas's] boldness in her [Elizabeth's] chamber, the lord I take to record I spake so ugly to him – yea, and said that it was complained on to my lords of the council – but he would swear, 'What do I? I would they all saw it!' that I could not make him leave it. At last I told the queen of it, who made a small matter of it to me, and said she would come with him herself, and so she did ever after.

Catherine continued throughout the early months of 1548 to maintain that she was not concerned by her husband's behaviour with her stepdaughter, but she grew increasingly uneasy, something that may well have been linked to her own changing circumstances.

There is no evidence that in any of her first three marriages Catherine ever conceived a child and she, along with everyone else in England, believed that she was infertile. While Catherine never spoke publicly on the subject, her longing for a child is clear in her actions and in some of her letters. Catherine clearly loved children: she was very close to her sister's children and to her own stepchildren. A letter survives, written by Catherine to Lady Wriothesley on the death of the noblewoman's only son, and it demonstrates Catherine's own feelings on the joys of children and that she sincerely believed that God would reward piety with children. Catherine urged Lady Wriothesley to 'put away all immoderate and unjust heaviness' as her son had now been shown more favour by God than 'that it first pleased him to comfort you with such a gift [of a son]; who can at his pleasure recompense your loss with such a like jewel, if gladly and quietly you submit and refer all to his pleasure'. Throughout her four marriages, Catherine prayed for children. In her heart, however, by early 1548, when she was already approaching thirty-six, Catherine cannot have had any strong hopes that she would conceive a child and she may well therefore have dismissed the early signs that, at last, she was pregnant. Gradually, however, by the end of February 1548 at the latest she was certain that she was pregnant. For Catherine, this was evidence of God's favour both towards her and her marriage to Thomas and she shared the news joyfully with him, all thoughts of his relationship with Elizabeth pushed aside for a moment.

At the age of nearly thirty-six, Catherine was aware that she was unlikely to have an easy pregnancy and the risks to a mother of such a late first-time delivery were great. As with everything, Catherine put her trust in her faith, even when she rapidly became ill during her pregnancy. A letter from Elizabeth to Catherine in

July 1548 makes it clear that Catherine did not enjoy a happy and trouble-free pregnancy:

> Although your highness' letters be most joyful to me in absence, yet considering what pain it is to you to write, your grace being so great with child and so sickly, your commendation were enough in my lord's letter. I much rejoice at your health with the well-liking of the country, with my humble thanks that your grace wished me with you till I were weary of that country. Your highness were like to be cumbered if I should not depart till I was weary of being with you: although it were the worst soil in the world, your presence would make it pleasant. I cannot reprove my lord for not doing your commendations in his letter, for he did it. And although he had not, yet I will not complain on him, for that he shall be diligent to give me knowledge from time to time how his busy child doth, and if I were at his birth no doubt I would see him [Catherine's child] beaten for the trouble he has put you to.

Feeling increasingly uncomfortable and unwell in the early stages of pregnancy, Catherine finally began to look more closely at just what was happening between her stepdaughter and her husband and she became increasingly alarmed at what she saw.

As her pregnancy advanced, Catherine became both worried and angry at what she saw between Thomas and Elizabeth. Finally, in the early months of 1548, she had had enough, summoning Mrs Ashley to her and admonishing her for the care that she took of Elizabeth, complaining that Thomas had told her that he 'loked in at the Galery-Wyndow, and se my Lady Elizabeth cast hir armes about a Man's Neck'. This was a serious accusation to make and Ashley, terrified, rushed back to her charge to confront her.

Elizabeth broke into a fit of weeping and absolutely denied that she had embraced any man as described and begged her governess to ask all the women in attendance on her if it was true. Mrs Ashley, who already had her own suspicions about the story, did as she was bid and everyone denied it. It seems very unlikely that Thomas, who was carrying out a flirtation with his stepdaughter would have risked his position by complaining to Catherine that he had seen Elizabeth embracing a man and, it is clear that Mrs Ashley's own analysis of the situation was correct. According to Ashley:

> She knew it could not be so, for there came no man, but Gryndall, the lady Elizabeth's scholemaster. Howbeit, thereby this Examinate did suspect, that the queen was gelows [jealous] betwixt them, and did but feign this, to thentent that this Examinate shuld take more hede, and be, as it were in watche betwixt hir and my lord Admirall.

Catherine had finally come to see the danger in the growing relationship between Elizabeth and Thomas and she was quickly to find that worse was to come.

For Catherine, the crisis came in May 1548 when she entered a chamber to find Elizabeth and Thomas embracing. Catherine reacted furiously, distraught at the evidence that was finally before her eyes. She was both furious at the betrayal of her husband and her stepdaughter, and broken-hearted. She was also beset by deeper emotions and there is no doubt that she was terrified. Elizabeth, as the king's sister, had been entrusted to her care and she knew full well that both she and Thomas would be in danger if news of the relationship ever broke out.

For Catherine, the solution to the problem was both painful and obvious. Catherine knew that she had to send Elizabeth away and she immediately wrote to her friends, Sir Anthony and Lady Denny to ask them to invite Elizabeth to stay with them at Cheshunt for a time. As soon as she received a favourable response, it was time for the fourteen-year-old princess to leave and Catherine had one final interview with her stepdaughter which is described in a later letter from Elizabeth:

> Although I coulde not be plentiful in giuinge thankes for the manifold kindenis received at your hithnes hande at my departure, yet I am some thinge to be borne withal, for truly I was replete with sorowe to departe frome your highnis, especially leving you undoubtful of helthe, and albeit I answered litel I arrayed more dipper whan you sayd you wolde warne me of all euelles that you shulde hire [hear] of me, for if your grace had not a good opinion of me you wolde not have offered frindeship to me that way, that al men iuge the contrarye, but what may I more say than thanke God for prouiding suche frendes to me, desiring God to enriche me with the long life, and the grace to be in hart no les thankeful to receyue it, than I now am glad in writing to shew it. And although I have plenty of matter, hire I will staye for I know you are not quiet to rede.

Elizabeth signed her letter 'your hithnes humble doughter' and she was desperate to retain the love of the only mother she had really ever known. Although they cannot have been aware of it at the time, this was to be the last meeting between the queen and her stepdaughter. Before Elizabeth departed, Catherine gave Elizabeth a piece of advice that the girl would follow throughout her long life: that she should guard her reputation above all else, and Catherine promised that she would do her best to ensure that all that had happened was not spoken about.

Catherine's advice to Elizabeth was sound and the girl followed it in the months after Catherine's death when, with the queen no longer there to protect her, the whole sorry story came out into the open. In a letter to the Protector of 28 January 1549, Elizabeth showed that she was fully prepared to follow Catherine's advice and fight for her reputation, writing that:

> Master Tyrwhitt and others have told me there goeth rumours abroad which be greatly both against mine honour and honesty, which above all things I esteem, which be there: that I am in the Tower and with child by my lord Admiral. My lord, these be shameful slanders, for the which, besides the great desire I have to see the king's majesty, I shall most heartily desire your lordship that I may come to the court after your first determination, that I may show myself there as I am.

Catherine would have been proud of Elizabeth in her attempts to maintain her reputation as her first priority was always protecting her stepdaughter, her husband, and herself from the fallout of all that had happened. In a subsequent letter to the Protector Elizabeth also demanded that a proclamation be made throughout England in order to declare that the gossip was untrue.

With Elizabeth away from Thomas's dangerous influence, Catherine was determined, for appearances sake, to act as though nothing had happened and she continued to write to Elizabeth and receive letters back from her in return. Surprisingly, Elizabeth also maintained something of a correspondence with Thomas and this may well also have been for appearances' sake. Catherine would certainly not have welcomed direct contact between the two and she may well have insisted on seeing the letters. The correspondence was, in any event, entirely uncontroversial and harmless, with Elizabeth in one letter writing:

> My lord,
>
> You needed not to send an excuse to me, or I could not mistrust the not fulfilling of your promise to proceed for want of goodwill, but only the opportunity serveth not; wherefore I shall desire you to think that a greater matter than this would not make me impute any unkindness in you. For I am a friend not won with trifles, nor lost with the like. Thus I commit you and all your affairs in God's hand, who keep you from all evil. I pray you make my humble commendations to the queen's highness.

Elizabeth always remained true to her promise to Catherine and she refused to have any dealings with Thomas when he attempted to court her after the death of the queen. According to Mrs Ashley, immediately after Catherine's death, Elizabeth refused to write to Thomas to offer her condolences as 'for then she should be thought to woo him'.

Catherine soon realized that she missed Elizabeth and she did not blame her stepdaughter for what had happened, instead bewailing her own negligence and that of Elizabeth's attendants. There is some evidence that Catherine levelled the bulk of the blame at Thomas. While, on the surface, their marriage remained as content as ever, underneath Catherine's heart had been broken and, as she lay delirious and dying later in the year, the full force of her anger and hurt was finally revealed in her deathbed words to her husband.

17

NOT WELL HANDLED: MAY 1548 – MARCH 1549

With Elizabeth's absence from her household and her own advancing pregnancy, Catherine did her best to forget Thomas's faithlessness, but thoughts of the betrayal remained deep in Catherine's mind.

As the months drew on, both Catherine and Thomas grew increasingly excited about the pregnancy. Thomas was often at court, both in his official role as Admiral of England and in order to further his own schemes. He and Catherine kept in regular contact, as their correspondence shows, demonstrating that the relationship remained a fond one, in spite of Thomas's behaviour with Elizabeth. According to one letter written by Thomas Seymour on 9 June 1548 he had been poorly received at court and complained:

That I should nott have justyse of those that I thought woold in all my causes [have] ben parshall, whyche did not a littell trobell me, even so the resayght of your lettr reveyu [revive] my spryttes, partley for that I doo perseve that ye be armed with peyshence how so euer the matter wyll way, as cheiftest that I hear my lettell man doth shake hys belle, trostyng, iff God shall geve hym lyff to leve as

long as his ffather, he wyll revenge such wronges as nether you nor
I can at this present, the wordell [world] ys such. God a mend it!

It is clear from Thomas's letter that Catherine's own letter had
spoken of her joy at her baby kicking and moving and both
parents were convinced that their child would be a boy. Thomas
was also anxious to keep Catherine informed of his doings at
court and of the wrongs that he perceived were done to him, even
suggesting that their son would be the person to avenge them.
Thomas showed a touching concern for Catherine's health, writing
that 'I do deseyr your highness to kepe the litell knave so leane and
gantte [gaunt] with your good dyett and walking that he may be so
small that he may krepe out of a mouse holle'. He finished, stating
'and thus I bid my most dere and welbeloved wyff most hartley
well to fare'.

The couple both displayed a keen interest in Catherine's
pregnancy, using the nickname 'the Little Knave' for their expected
'son'. In spite of being away from court, Catherine was always
anxious for news of what was happening there and her reply to
Thomas's letter contains both domestic concerns and her worries
and anger at the way in which Thomas's affairs at court went:

My lord, this shalbe to desire you to receive my humble and most
harty Recommendatyons and Thanks for your Letter which was
no soner come than welcome. I perceive ye had no lytell Trobell
and Busynes with your mater. I neuer thought the contrary, but
ye shuld have much ado to bringe yt to passe as ye wold have yt;
nevertheless I supposed my lorde Protectour wold have used no
delay with his Frend and naturall Brother in a mater wyche ys
upright and just, as I take yt. What wyll he do to other that be

indifferent to him? I juge not very well. I pray God he may dysceyve me, for hys owne welthe and benefyte more than myne none. Now I have uttered my coler, I schall desire yow, good my lord, with all hart not to unquyett yourself with any of hys unfriendly parts, but bere them for the tyme, as well as ye can; wyche I knowe ys moche better than ether myne advyse or doing can express. I am very sorry for the newse of the Frenche men. I pray God yt be not a lette to our journey. As sone as ye knowe what they wyll do, good my lord; I beseche yow let me here from yow, for I shall not be quiet tyll I knowe. I gaue your lytell knaue your Blessing, who lyke an onest man styred apase after and before; for Mary Odell being a Bed with me had layd her hand upon my Belly to fele it styre. Yt hathe styred thyse thre days every morning and evening, so that I trust when ye come, it wyll make you sum passe tyme. And thus I end, byddyng my swett hart and loving husband better to fare than myself.

Isolated at Hanworth, Catherine was reliant on Thomas for news but by the summer of 1548 he was no longer presenting either a balanced or coherent view of all that was happening at court. Throughout the spring and summer of 1548 Thomas had continued in his attempts to undermine his brother's government. By July 1548 the brothers were in open confrontation and Somerset summoned his younger brother to appear before him and the Council to explain his actions. Thomas, trusting in his nephew's affection for him, refused to attend until he was threatened with imprisonment for his disobedience. Somerset allowed the matter to drop, making it clear that he did so only out of respect for Catherine and in light of her advancing pregnancy. Thomas's behaviour was rapidly beginning to spiral out of both the Protector's and Catherine's control, with it later being described by the Privy Council as the 'great attemptates and disloyall practises of the Lord Seymour of Sudeley, Admirall of England, tending to the daungier of the kinges majeste and the Lord Protectour and Counsaile, and the subversion of the holl state of the realme'. Catherine was unaware of just how serious his behaviour had become.

Throughout the spring and summer of 1548 Thomas continued his effort to ingratiate himself with the king through the medium of John Fowler. In July, while Catherine was still staying at Hanworth, Thomas travelled to court to ask Fowler to speak well of him to the king. Thomas was a regular visitor to court that summer, always taking the time to meet with Fowler privately. According to Fowler: 'He woold come in to the privie buttery and drynke there alone, and aske me whither the king woold say any thing of him? I have answered, "Nay, in good faith"; and then he woold wysshe that the kinges majesty wer v or vi yeres elder'. More sinisterly, Thomas also regularly questioned Fowler about the king's daily routine, including asking him when Edward rose in the morning. Thomas would later be accused of attempting to abduct the king and it is unlikely that his interest in his nephew's routine was entirely innocent. It is unclear how aware Catherine was of all Thomas's endeavours to ingratiate himself with the king and those around him, but Thomas certainly made use of Catherine's status and relationship with Edward. According to Fowler, again speaking of Thomas: 'And at his going in to the country he prayed me to break with the kinges majesty that it woold please him somtyme, when his grace could, to write some little recommendacion with his own hand; for, he said, it will comfort the Quene much and so I dyd'. Edward sent Catherine a brief note, sending his commendations which must have pleased his stepmother. It is telling however that, in a similar note addressed to Thomas, he asked his uncle for money, something that he had become accustomed to his uncle providing. In order to ensure that he did not lose any influence with his nephew while he was away from court, Thomas made arrangements for Catherine's receiver to supply the king with money whenever he required it.

The summer of 1548 was unusually warm and by July the country was engulfed in a drought and plague had begun to rage in London. With Catherine's advancing pregnancy, she was undoubtedly worried about disease and, also, uncomfortable in the heat and she made plans for her confinement away from the capital. The place chosen by Catherine and Thomas for the birth of their child was an obvious one and, around 13 June 1548, the couple, with a household well in excess of 100 people, set out from Hanworth to make the journey to Thomas's baronial seat of Sudeley Castle in Gloucestershire. Sudeley was a symbol of the dynasty that they hoped to found with the birth of their first son.

Sudeley Castle had been granted to Thomas at the beginning of Edward VI's reign when he was created Baron Seymour of Sudeley. Catherine had never visited the castle before July 1548, although Thomas had on at least one occasion, and had already carried out a series of building works intended to ensure that it was a fitting residence for a queen. By July 1548 a set of rooms had been prepared for Catherine at the south-east end of the inner quadrangle. These were connected by a covered corridor to the kitchens and servants' quarters which allowed Catherine's extensive household to be housed comfortably. The castle contained a banqueting hall and a chapel and was intended to be a comfortable country retreat for the couple. Sudeley Castle itself is still inhabited although much of what Catherine knew is gone. In spite of this, it is easy to see that it was a pleasant spot for Catherine to spend the weeks while she awaited the birth of her child.

The summer months of 1548 were a time of relaxation and rest for Catherine. With Elizabeth absent from her household and her excitement about the anticipated birth, she allowed thoughts of her husband's betrayal to slip to the back of her mind and engaged in a friendly correspondence with Elizabeth. Catherine also enjoyed something of a rapprochement with her elder stepdaughter, Mary, after their estrangement over Catherine's marriage. Mary wrote to Catherine, on 9 August 1548, in an attempt to put the angry feeling between the two behind them:

Although I have troubled your highness lately with sundry letters, yet that notwithstanding seeing my lord Marquess [William Parr] who hath taken the pains to come to me at this present intendeth to see your grace shortly, I could not be satisfied without writing to the same, and especially because I purpose to-morrow (with the help of God) to begin my journey towards Norfolk, where I shall be farther from your grace, which journey I have intended since Whitsuntide, but lack of health hath stayed me all the while, which, altho' it be, as yet, unstable, nevertheless I am enforced to remove for a time, hoping, with God's grace, to return again about Michaelmas, at which time or shortly after, I trust to hear good success of your grace's condition, and in the mean time shall desire much to hear of your health, which I pray Almighty God to continue and increase to his pleasure as much as your own heart can desire; and thus, with my most humble commendations to your highness, I take my leave of the same, desiring your grace to take the pain to make my commendations to my lord-admiral.

Mary's letter is signed 'Your highness' humble and assured loving daughter, Marye' and it is obvious from its tone that Mary wanted to be friends with her stepmother again. Catherine was relieved at the sign that the estrangement was over and it may have been at this time that she first asked Mary to stand as godmother for her unborn child. Catherine was now on good terms with all her stepchildren again, although it was with her husband, and Lady Jane Grey, that she spent the bulk of her time at Sudeley.

While Catherine and Thomas both eagerly anticipated the birth of their 'Little Knave', Catherine was nervous about the approaching birth, knowing that being in her late thirties at the time of her first confinement was far from ideal. She saw her pregnancy as a miracle and a sign of God's favour and she doubtless hoped that He would also ensure her safe delivery. Catherine was lucky with her labour and there is no indication that it was difficult. On 30 August 1548 Catherine finally gave birth to her longed for child, apparently without any danger to herself, although, for both her and Thomas, the sex of the child was a surprise as it proved to be a girl. Both parents, relieved at the baby's good health, and that of her mother, did not seem unduly concerned, hoping that their daughter would be followed by brothers in due course. Thomas immediately sent word of the birth to London, receiving a letter of congratulations back from his brother shortly afterwards in what was, as with Mary's earlier letter to Catherine, intended to be a letter of reconciliation. According to Somerset 'we are right glad to vnderstand by your lettres that the quene your bedfellow hath had an happie hower, and, escaping all daunger, hath made you the father of so pretie a daughter'. Somerset did however continue by saying that he would have preferred Catherine's baby to be a boy, although he hoped that she would soon bear his brother a number of sons. It was no doubt gratifying to the Duchess of Somerset, who was still recovering from her own confinement, that she had given birth to a son while her sister-in-law and rival had produced a 'mere' daughter.

No record of Catherine's thoughts about the birth of her daughter survive but the choice of the name, 'Mary', was almost certainly hers and intended as a compliment to the child's stepsister and godmother. As Somerset's letter shows, immediately after the birth it was announced that Catherine was recovering well. Following the birth, Catherine showed no immediate signs of danger but, by 3 September, she was grievously ill. According to Catherine's friend and kinswoman, Lady Tyrwhitt, on the morning of 3 September she came to Catherine who asked her 'where I had been so long?' Before Lady Tyrwhitt could answer, Catherine continued saying 'that she did fear such things in herself that she was sure she could not live'. Lady Tyrwhitt, disconcerted by the change in her friend, merely shook her head, saying 'that I saw no likelihood of death in her'. Lady Tyrwhitt was unaware that, at that stage, Catherine had already dictated her Will.

When Lady Tyrwhitt entered Catherine's bedchamber, she found Catherine lying in her bed, with Thomas and other members of the household present. In her Will, Catherine proclaimed:

> that she, then lying on her death-bed, sick of body, but of good mind, and perfect memory and discretion, being persuaded, and perceiving the extremity of death to approach her, gives all to her married espouse and husband, wishing them to be a thousand times more in value than they were or been.

Catherine's Will was brief and to the point and the queen was unable to even sign it, indicating that she no longer had the strength to do so. Catherine had succumbed to puerperal, or childbed, fever, the same condition that ended the life of her sister-in-law and predecessor as queen, Jane Seymour.

By the time that Lady Tyrwhitt entered Catherine's bedchamber, the queen was already suffering from the delirium characteristic of puerperal fever. Thomas was holding Catherine's hand and attempting to calm her, but her mind was entirely distracted. According to Lady Tyrwhitt, Catherine said: 'My lady Tyrwhitt, I am not well handled, for those that be about me care not for me, but stand laughing at my grief, and the more good I will to them the less good they will to me.' Thomas continued to hold Catherine's hand and, concerned by her comments, shook his head, saying: 'Why, sweetheart, I would you no hurt.' Catherine, in her delirium, would have none of this answer and turned and railed at her husband, saying: 'No, my lord, I think so,' before whispering loudly in Thomas's ear, 'but, my lord, you have given me many shrewd taunts.' Lady Tyrwhitt had previously admitted that she believed that Catherine spoke in her delirium, but this comment she believed Catherine 'spake with good memory, and very earnestly; for her mind was sore disquieted'. Lady Tyrwhitt, as a close confidante of Catherine, was aware of the whole sorry saga involving Thomas and Elizabeth and she recognized that it was this to which Catherine referred in her distress.

Thomas was upset by Catherine's venom towards him and he took Lady Tyrwhitt aside to ask what he could do to comfort her. On his own initiative, he then decided 'that he would lie down on the bed by her, to look if he could pacify her unquietness with gentle communication'. Lady Tyrwhitt agreed that this might help and Thomas lay down beside Catherine, trying to comfort her. In her delirium, all of Catherine's usual quiet prudence was abandoned and she once again turned on her husband, complaining sharply: 'My lord, I would have given a thousand marks to have had my full talk with Hewyke [Dr Huicke, her physician] the first day I was delivered, but I durst not for displeasing you.' Catherine elaborated no further on this, but Lady Tyrwhitt was deeply troubled by what she heard, as was everyone else who had assembled around the dying queen.

While Catherine almost certainly voiced her thoughts only because of her fever, it is likely that these were her genuine beliefs. She had been deeply wounded by Thomas's conduct towards Elizabeth and while she had been able to carry on as before, and even continue to behave lovingly towards him, deep down her heart had been broken and she accused her husband of cruelty towards her as she lay dying. In spite of his conduct with Elizabeth, Thomas undoubtedly loved Catherine to some extent, and her accusations deeply wounded him. Immediately after Catherine's death, Thomas found himself completely at a loss as to what to do with himself, as a letter from him to the Marquis of Dorset on 17 September 1548 shows. According to Thomas: 'whereby my last lettres unto the same, written in a tyme when partelye with the Quene's Highnes Death, I was so amazed, that I had smale regard eyther for my self or to my doings'. Thomas rather spoiled the effect by implying, later in his letter, written less than two weeks after Catherine's death, that he had now recovered from her death but it is clear that he was shocked and saddened by his sudden loss. He also later informed his friend, Sir Richard Cotton, that he 'would wear black for one year, and would then know where to have a wife'. Once again, this does not suggest that Thomas was broken-hearted, but there is no doubt that he had some feelings for her and was grieved by her illness and death.

Catherine remained in a state of delirium throughout 3 and 4 September. In spite of her anger towards her husband at the memory of his conduct with Elizabeth, she still loved him dearly and, during her lucid intervals, she was comforted by his presence. There was nothing that anyone could do for her and, as the hours passed, she grew steadily weaker and was aware of her surroundings less and less. In the early hours of Wednesday 5 September, between two and three o'clock in the morning, Catherine Parr, the last queen of King Henry VIII, passed quietly away, only six days after the birth of her daughter and at the age of just thirty-six.

No one who had been in attendance on Catherine during the previous few days was shocked by her death, but everyone was deeply saddened by it as Catherine had been loved. It was still central to Thomas's ambitions to display Catherine's high rank and he ordered that a royal funeral be prepared for her in the chapel at Sudeley Castle, with all ceremony as befitted a queen. Catherine would have been glad of this and she would have been equally pleased to know that her funeral was conducted wholly in accordance with the reformed rites of the Church.

Shortly after Catherine's death, her body was embalmed and she was placed in a lead coffin. The chapel was 'hanged with blacke clothe garnished with schoocheons of maryages, vizd. King Henrye th'eight and her in pale under the crowne, her own in lozenge under the crowne. Allso th'armes of the lord Admyrall and hers in pale without crowne'. The chapel seats were covered in black cloth and a hearse was prepared, surrounded by tapers, on which Catherine's coffin was to rest during the service. When everything was ready, the coffin was carried in procession into the chapel with the black-clad members of Catherine's household following solemnly. Thomas, by convention, was absent, and the most conspicuous of the mourners was the tiny, ten-year-old Lady Jane Grey who acted as chief mourner.

Once inside the church, the choir sang psalms in English and three lessons were read, again in the vernacular. The mourners then made an offering of alms, in accordance with their ranks, and Catherine's almoner, the famous reformer Miles Coverdale, took to the pulpit to make a sermon. Coverdale's sermon was intended to reinforce the queen's Protestant beliefs and he took great care to:

> declare unto the people howe that thei shulde none there thinke seye nor spredde abrode that the offering which was there done was don anye thinge to perfytt the deade but ffor the poor onlye. And also the lights which were carid and stode abowte the corps were ffor the honour of the parsson & for none other entente nor purpose.

Catherine would have heartily approved of these sentiments as they were at the core of her own beliefs. Following the sermon, Coverdale led the mourners in prayers before a Te Deum was sung for Catherine, again in English. The mourners then departed while Catherine was left, alone in her tomb. Coverdale himself composed a fitting epitaph to the much loved queen:

> In this new tomb the royal Kath'rine lies,
> Flower of her sex, renowned, great, and wise;
> A wife, by every nuptial virtue known,
> And faithful partner once of Henry's throne.
> To Seymour next her plighted hand she yields
> (Seymour who Neptune's trident justly wields);
> From him a beauteous daughter bless'd her arms,
> An infant copy of her parents' charms.

When now seven days this tender flower had bloom'd,
Heaven in its wrath the mother's soul resum'd.
Great Kath'rine's merit in our grief appears,-
While fair Britannia dews her cheeks with tears,
Our loyal breast with rising sighs are torn,
With saints she triumphs, we with mortals mourn.

Catherine's influence was missed by everyone in her household, but it was missed most dearly by her husband, Thomas Seymour.

Catherine's rank had always protected Thomas from punishment and, without her presence, he was dangerously exposed. He was informed of this bluntly by the Earl of Rutland shortly after Catherine's death as the pair rode together to visit the Marquis of Dorset at his seat at Bradgate in Leicestershire. According to Rutland: 'we talked of the queen; I said I thought his power much diminished by her death'. Thomas failed to heed this warning, answering that 'the Council never feared him as much as they do now'. Almost as soon as Catherine was buried, Thomas turned once more to his schemes against his brother and, within days of her death, his thoughts also turned to marriage.

The first marriage that Thomas intended to resurrect was that of his ward, Lady Jane Grey, to the king. In his grief at Catherine's death, Thomas, believing that he would have to break up Catherine's household, had sent Jane back to her parents. However, he quickly realized the error that he had made, first speaking to Catherine's brother, William Parr, of his desire to obtain again the marriage of Lady Jane Grey and then writing urgently to her father. Once he had time to think, Thomas realized just how valuable Jane was to his schemes and requested that she be returned to him, offering to bring his mother up from her home in Wiltshire to act as chaperone to Jane and offering himself to 'contynewe her haulf Father and more'. Dorset, who was as aware as anyone how far Thomas's status had been diminished with Catherine's death, initially refused to return his daughter, but he was finally persuaded on the promise of a payment of £2,000. With Lady Jane Grey safely returned to his custody, Thomas once more attempted to persuade Elizabeth to marry him, aware that he needed another royal bride to carry his plans to fruition. Elizabeth, deeply regretting the hurt that she had caused her stepmother, always refused to see Thomas.

Thomas, though disappointed by his failure to arrange a marriage to Elizabeth, considered that he would have plenty of time to persuade her in the future. His plans to dominate the king moved rapidly in the months following Catherine's death. Throughout the autumn and winter of 1548 Thomas took active steps to build a party around him. According to a later report of the privy council, he:

> reteyned yonge gentlemen and had yeomen to a great multitude, and farre above suche number as ye permitted by the laws and statutes of the realme, or were otherwise necessarie or convenient for your service, place or estate, to the fortifying of yourself towards all your evill ententes and purposes; to the great daungier of the kinges Majestie and peril of the state of the realme.

It is clear that Thomas was planning some action against his brother and the government and, by January 1549, it was believed that he was able to raise 10,000 men to fight for his cause. Thomas was also later charged with fortifying his castle at Holt with provisions to feed his army and, by the end of 1549, he was deeply involved in high treason.

While Catherine had always been supportive of her husband's political ambitions and fully shared his discontent with his brother, she would never have endorsed the course that Thomas decided upon in late 1549 and, with her death, the last restraining hand on Thomas's ambition was removed. The circumstances of Thomas's arrest in January 1549 are far from clear and, it is possible that he actually made an attempt to kidnap the young king. Van Der Delft, the Imperial ambassador, writing on 27 January 1549 claimed that:

I have heard here that the Admiral of England, with the help of some people about the court, attempted to outrage the person of the young king by night, and has been taken to the Tower. The alarm was given by the gentleman who sleeps in the king's chamber, who, was awakened by the barking of the dog that lies before the king's door, cried out 'Help! Murder!'

Everybody rushed in; but the only thing they found was the lifeless corpse of the dog. Suspicion points to the Admiral, because he had scattered the watch that night on several errands, and because it has been noticed that he has some secret plot on hand, hoping to marry the second daughter of the late King, the lady Elizabeth, who is also under grave suspicion.

There is no other direct evidence to corroborate Van Der Delft's claims, but it is not impossible that Thomas's plans had advanced so far. He had already shown detailed interest in the king's routine and was able to come and go freely at court. He had also obtained a bride for the king, an act designed to ensure that Edward remained under his control, and it is certain that he wanted the king in his own custody. One member of Edward's council, Paget, may also have corroborated Van Der Delft's claims when he spoke to the ambassador and told him that Thomas had 'been a great rascal' and that he had intended to kill Edward and Mary in order to claim the throne as Elizabeth's husband. While it is odd that the charge of actually entering the king's chamber with the intent of kidnapping him was not laid against Thomas, this does not mean it did not happen and the Council, embarrassed that Thomas had been able to get so close to the young king, may well have hushed it up.

Regardless of what actually happened in the king's bedchamber one night in January, Thomas's actions had become too dangerous for the Protector and the Council to allow him to remain at liberty. On 17 January the Council met to decide Thomas's fate and, unanimously, they agreed that he be arrested and sent to the Tower. Without Catherine's status and influence to help him, Thomas was doomed. He was also furious and refused to answer the charges against him unless he was brought to open trial. Once it became clear that he would be granted no trial, he grudgingly told the council that the previous Easter he had:

> saide to Fowler, as he supposeth it was, that if he might have the king in his custodie as Mr Page[t] had he wolde be glad, and that he thought a man might bring him through the Galery to his chamber, and so to his howse, but this he said he spoke merely meaning no hurte.

This was all that Thomas would admit to, but he was undoubtedly guilty of high treason. He may never have realized the gravity of his actions, relying on the fact that he had always been forgiven any offence in the past, and was therefore shocked and angered when he was informed that both Edward VI and Somerset consented to his condemnation and death. Somerset at least had the decency to ask to be excused from the session of parliament that condemned his brother, 'for natural pities sake'. Edward VI showed no such compunction in the matter of his 'favourite' uncle, stating coldly that he desired that justice be done.

Thomas Seymour had had a cosseted life, first as brother of the queen, then favoured brother-in-law of the king and, finally, husband of the queen. With Catherine's death, he was finally on his own and on 20 March 1549 he was led out onto the scaffold at Tower Hill to die. Unable to believe that this was finally the end, Thomas died badly, refusing, as was customary, to admit his guilt and instead making a last ditch appeal to the princesses, Mary and Elizabeth, to avenge his death. According to Bishop Hugh Latimer, Thomas 'died very dangerously, irksomely, horribly; and to conclude, that God had him left to himself'. Thomas died with two strokes of the axe. Thomas caused Catherine deep grief, but she also loved him dearly and, while she lived, she protected him even at the cost of her own reputation and her relationship with her beloved stepchildren. Her death left Thomas alone to his fate and that he would follow her shortly to the grave was always something that was all but inevitable.

18

HOW MANY HUSBANDS WILL SHE HAVE?

Catherine's death came as a surprise to everyone and it rapidly led to the fall and death of her fourth husband, Thomas Seymour. In spite of the suddenness of her death, Catherine left a legacy both in her daughter and surviving family and her stepdaughter, Elizabeth I.

With Thomas Seymour's execution, Mary Seymour, at less than six months old, was left an orphan. The Act of Attainder that was passed, condemning Thomas to death, also confiscated all his property and Catherine's little daughter was left penniless. Catherine had always greatly desired a child and, when she knew that she was expecting Mary, she made elaborate preparations. A list of the child's personal belongings survives and the majority would have been chosen for her by her mother before her birth:

The said plate and stuff were, two pots, three goblets, one salt, parcel gilt, a maser and a band of silver and parcel gilt, and eleven spoons, a quilt for the cradle, three pillows, three feather beds, three quilts, a testor of scarlet embroidered with a counterpoint of silksay belonging to the same, and curtains of crimson taffeta, two counterpoints of imagery or the nurses's bed, six pairs of sheets, six fur pieces of hangings within the inner chamber, four carpets for the windows, ten pieces of hangings of the twelve months within the utter chamber, two cushions of cloth of gold, two wrought stools, a bedstead of gilt, with a testor and counterpoint, with curtains belonging to the same.

Mary Seymour, as the daughter of a queen was entitled to the highest rank among non-royal ladies in England. Although she had no lands to support her, on her father's arrest, Mary's rich possessions went with her to the household of her uncle, Protector Somerset, where she spent some time before transferring, at Thomas's express request, to the household of Catherine's friend, the Duchess of Suffolk.

The Duchess of Suffolk made Mary welcome at her house at Grimsthorp in Lincolnshire, but the baby was a burden to her. As befitted her status, Mary arrived with a large household of attendants, including her governess, a nurse, two maids and other servants. The Duchess received no financial assistance from either of Mary's uncles, Protector Somerset or William Parr. By 27 August 1549, the Duchess had had enough of being forced to support Catherine's daughter herself and wrote to appeal for aid from her friend, the influential William Cecil, complaining that Mary's governess and servants continually begged her for their wages, which she could not afford to pay. The Duchess continued:

It is said, that the best remedy to the sick, is first plainly to confess and to disclose the disease. Wherefore both for remedy, and again for that my disease is so strong that it will not be hidden. I will discover me unto you. First, I will, as it were under benedicites, and in high secrecy, declare unto you, that all the world knoweth, though I go never so correctly in my net, what a very beggar I am.

This sickness, as I have said, I promise you, increaseth mightily
upon me; amongst other the causes thereof, if you will understand
not the least, the queen's child hath lain and yet doth lie at my
house with her company, wholly at my charges.

There is no evidence that the Duchess was anything but a kind
guardian to Mary Seymour, but it is evident that the burden irked
her and Mary's circumstances were very far from what Catherine
would have wished for her daughter.

Mary Seymour, as the queen's daughter, and the niece of the
Protector, was never likely to remain penniless for long and,
later in 1549, she was restored to her lands and titles by an
Act of Parliament. The council also granted money to Mary for
household wages, servants' uniforms and food on 13 March 1550.
This is the last evidence for Mary's continued survival. In the
nineteenth century a number of historians claimed that she had
lived to marry a courtier called Sir Edward Bushel, and bore him
children. One recent writer has gone so far as to claim descent
from Mary, again through the supposed marriage to Edward
Bushel. These writers have explained the absence of records for
Mary by suggesting that she slipped quietly into obscurity and
did nothing of note. However, for the daughter of a queen, this
is simply impossible. Mary Seymour, although not royal herself
would have been considered a kinswoman by Catherine's royal
stepchildren and Elizabeth, when she came to the throne in 1558
would certainly have favoured Catherine's daughter. The fact that
there is no further mention of Mary Seymour at all suggests that
she, like so many infants in her time, died of some unspecified
illness in her early childhood. Catherine's much longed for child
survived her parents by, at most, little over two years.

While Catherine would have hoped that her daughter would live to be her legacy, it is in the descendants of her sister Anne that her bloodline survives. Anne's husband was created Earl of Pembroke in 1551 and their eldest son succeeded to the earldom on his father's death and was prominent in the reign of Elizabeth. He enjoyed something of a narrow escape when he married Catherine Grey, the younger sister of Lady Jane Grey just before the latter assumed the crown and it was only a rapid divorce procured by his father that ensured that he escaped any punishment. Catherine's brother, William, also survived until well into Elizabeth's reign. Elizabeth Brooke, his second wife, died in 1565 and, in 1571, he surprised everyone by marrying a young Swedish noblewoman. His second and third marriages proved as childless as his unhappy first. He did not survive his marriage long but his widow became a close friend of Queen Elizabeth and, on Elizabeth's death in 1603, it was William's widow, as the sister-in-law of Elizabeth's beloved stepmother, who was chief mourner, an important role usually reserved for the deceased's closest relatives.

Protector Somerset was widely criticized for allowing his own brother to be put to death. In 1550 he was removed from office as Protector but the following year was readmitted to the Council. Edward VI's new chief minister, John Dudley, Earl of Warwick and, later, Duke of Northumberland, plotted against his rival and, on 16 October 1551, Somerset was arrested and sent to the Tower. Edward VI proved just as unemotional about the fate of his senior uncle as he had been about the younger one, merely noting in his diary on 22 January 1552 that 'the Duke of Somerset had his head cut off upon Tower Hill between eight and nine o'clock in the morning'. A number of commentators saw the origins of Somerset's fall in his treatment of his brother and at least one commentator, John Hayward, remarked that the deaths of both men were a direct consequence of the rivalry of their wives, commenting: 'O wiues! The most sweete poison, the most desired evill in the world.' Someone that Catherine undoubtedly cared about a great deal more than Somerset, Lady Jane Grey, was also caught up in the political turmoil of Edward VI's long minority and, on the king's death in July 1553, she was pushed onto the throne by Northumberland, to reign for nine days before being abandoned by everyone in favour of Princess Mary. She, like so many others that Catherine knew, ended her life on the block.

While Catherine's husband and daughter did not long survive her, she did leave one lasting legacy. Her stepdaughter, Elizabeth, became perhaps the greatest monarch that England ever had. Catherine was the first person to be a mother to Elizabeth since the death of her own mother in her infancy and, in spite of her conduct with Thomas, Elizabeth loved Catherine. It was Catherine who supervised Elizabeth's education and raised her during her formative years and it was to Catherine that Elizabeth looked when she sought a model of just what a queen could be. For Elizabeth, Catherine was also another cautionary tale from her childhood as to the dangers of marriage.

Following the execution of Catherine Howard back in 1542, one of the ladies of Henry's court exclaimed, incredulously: 'How many wives will he have?' In 1547, after the publication of her fourth marriage, a commentator could have equally exclaimed of the queen: 'How many husbands will she have?' Catherine still holds the distinction of being England's most married queen.

There is one more bizarre postscript to Catherine's tumultuous life. The chapel at Sudeley Castle was destroyed during the Civil War in the seventeenth century and all record of Catherine's burial place was lost. In May 1782, some curious visitors to the ruins of the chapel discovered the site of Catherine's tomb and, digging down two feet in depth came across her lead coffin. Once the lid of the coffin had been cleaned, an inscription was found that confirmed that the grave was indeed Catherine's, saying 'K.P. VIth and last wife of King Hen. The VIIIth, 1548'. Catherine's coffin excited curiosity among the party and they opened it to find the body still perfectly preserved under its shroud, with the flesh of Catherine's arm described as 'white and moist'. It does not appear that the observers uncovered Catherine's face and, alarmed to find her so uncorrupted, they hurriedly resealed the coffin and covered it over once again with earth. In the summer of 1783 Mrs Bockett, a friend of the owner of Sudeley, Lord Rivers, returned to Catherine's grave and ordered the coffin to be opened once more. According to her account she 'found Lucas's account of the coffin and corps to be just as he had represented them; with this difference, that the body was then grown quite fetid, and the flesh where the incision had been made was brown and in a state of putrefaction, in consequence of the air having been let upon it'. Once again, Catherine's tomb was hurriedly sealed but in May the following year it was opened once again and nothing was found except Catherine's bones. In 1786 she was disturbed again by curious onlookers. By the late eighteenth century the chapel ruins were used for keeping rabbits which further damaged Catherine's grave. It was only in 1863, when the chapel had been rebuilt and rededicated, that Catherine was finally given the fine tomb in which she now lies and she remains permanently at rest, her posthumous adventures almost as turbulent as those of her life.

Catherine Parr is remembered as one of the greatest of Henry VIII's queens. She was the last wife that he married and is often credited with providing him, at last, with the stable home life that he had long desired. Catherine was a reluctant queen and, while she accepted the fate that Henry decided for her, her final marriage for love is testament that her heart always belonged to Thomas Seymour. Catherine Parr survived a dangerous husband through her clever management of him and her intelligence. Throughout her adult life she sought happiness for herself but rarely found it. Finally, in marrying for love she hoped to choose her own destiny and enjoy, at last, the freedom that she had always longed for. She was destined to be deeply disappointed and, after three husbands chosen for her, Catherine proved to be a very poor judge of her fourth. Catherine Parr, Henry VIII's reluctant queen, was one of the best that he had, but her time as queen was fraught and filled with danger and she was never able to find the peace and contentment that she desired.

NOTES

L&P refers to *Letters and Papers, Foreign and Domestic of the Reign of Henry VIII*. CSP Spanish refers to *Calendar of State Papers, Spanish*. ACP refers to *Acts of the Privy Council of England*.

1. THE PARRS OF KENDAL

Annals of Kendal (1861:84) describes the history of the Parr family. The survey of Kendal Castle is in Farrer 1923:95–6. That the Parr family were second only to the king in Kendal is evidenced by a letter of Catherine's brother, William, to Cromwell, dated 20 April 1532, recording the tradition that his family administer local justice (Farrer 1923:62). Evidence of William de Parr's wealth in 1396 and on his death is in Farrer 1923:32 and 34. Commission to Thomas Tunstall 1413 (Farrer 1923:40) records the purchase of Thomas de Parr's wardship in 1413. Farrer 1923:49 notes the death of Thomas Parr and his son's inheritance. Farrer 1923:32 records that Catherine's grandfather accompanied Edward IV to France. Gordon p1, Nicholson 1861:323, and Kemeys and Raggatt 1993:5 claim Kendal as Catherine's birthplace. Thomas Parr's place at Henry VII's funeral is in *L&P I*:13. *L&P I*:37 notes that Parr was made a Knight of Bath and his place at the coronation is in *L&P I*:421. *L&P I*:924 records Thomas Parr's service on the French campaign. Henry's cancellations of the debts owed by Parr and Vaux are in *L&P I*:112, *L&P I*:281 and *L&P I*:533–4. The quote on Henry's decision to release debts is in *L&P I*:142–3. The grant to the Parrs of a manor in November 1510 is in *L&P I*:358. The grant in March 1516 is in *L&P II*:480–1. *L&P I*:776 records the controversy over Thomas Parr taking the title Lord Fitzhugh. Lord Dacre to Henry VIII, 12 April 1516 (*L&P II*:498) and Thomas Alen to the Earl of Shrewsbury, 6 May 1516 (*L&P II*:533) records Thomas's participation in the escort for Margaret, Queen of Scotland. *L&P II*:790 and *L&P II*:1187 notes Thomas as sheriff of Warwickshire and Leicestershire. Thomas Alen to the Earl of Shrewsbury, 23 November 1517 (*L&P II*:1193) records Thomas Parr's death. Thomas Parr's Will is from Farrer 1923:57–8. Maud's inclusion in the queen's household is noted in *L&P III*:170 and *L&P III*:180. Her attendance at the Field of the Cloth of Gold is in *L&P III*:245. Privy Purse expenses for Henry VIII 1530 (Farrer 1923:62) contains Maud's gift of a coat to the king. Withrow 2009:29 suggests that Catherine was educated with Princess Mary. The quote concerning Maud's reputation as an educator is from Lord Dacre to Lord Scrope, 17 December 1523 (Nicholson 1861:92–3). Prince Edward's comments on Catherine's Latin are in his letter of 10 June 1546 (Halliwell 1848:12-13). Catherine Parr to the University of Cambridge (Strype 1822 vol II pt II:337)contains Catherine's comments on her Latin. Fraser 2002:446 considers that Catherine was educated up to a point but that she was not fluent in Latin. The quote from Elizabeth's letter is in Wood 1846:178–9. The Duke of Richmond's Council to Wolsey,

2 August 1525 (*L&P IV*:692) gives Richmond's stay at Maud's household. Nash 1789:3 notes the length of Catherine's coffin. De Gante 1831:354 described Catherine as lively and pleasing. The story concerning the fortune teller is quoted from Nicholson 1861:323.

2. MISTRESS BURGH OF GAINSBOROUGH OLD HALL

The letters between Maud and Lord Dacre are in Nicholson 1861:90–3. Lord Dacre's letter to Lord Scrope is from the same source (p92–3). William's marriage is described in Starkey 2003:697. Gordon p5, Martienssen p44 and Strickland 1844:10 claim that Catherine married the grandfather. Details of the Burgh family are from *Complete Peerage* vol II 1912:422. *L&P IV*:3077 contains the grant of Kirton Lyndsey to Thomas and Edward Burgh. *L&P V*:703 lists Edward as a commissioner of the peace for Lindsey. In the parliament of 1543 Thomas Burgh's daughter-in-law, Elizabeth, was publicly declared an adulteress and her three children illegitimate (*L&P XVIII pt1*:46). *L&P II*:1187, *L&P II*:1395 and *L&P IV*:367 record Thomas Burgh's appointments as Sheriff of Lincolnshire. Thomas Burgh's role at the funeral of Henry VII is in *L&P I*:15. Thomas Burgh's role in the defence of Berwick is attested by Sir Raufe Ever, Thomas Burgh, Robert Carre, William Langton, Thomas Strangways and Robert Musgrave to the Council, 15 July 1513 (*L&P I*:952). The quote from Burgh's letter during the Pilgrimage of Grace is from *L&P II*:216. Christopher Ascugh to Cromwell, 6 October 1536 (*L&P XI*:225) claims Burgh's escape was due to a good horse. Burgh's role in the Pilgrimage of Grace is also discussed n Dodds and Dodds 1915, vol I. The rebels' attack on Gainsborough Old Hall is from Earl of Shrewsbury to Henry VIII, 4 October 1536 (*L&P XI*:217) and Christopher Ascue to Cromwell, 6 October 1536 (*L&P XI*:225). *L&P VI*:249 and *L&P VI*:465 contain Thomas Burgh's attendance at Anne Boleyn's coronation and Princess Elizabeth's christening. William Gardner to Lord Brough, 10 October 1533 (*L&P VI*:513) reports slander against Anne Boleyn. Burgh's seizure of Catherine of Aragon's barge is in Chapuys to Charles V, 29 May 1533 (*L&P VI*:241). *Lamentation of a Sinner* (1831:32-4) records Catherine's conversion.

3. LADY LATIMER OF SNAPE CASTLE

William's participation in the wedding of Lord William Howard is noted in William London to Lord Lisle, 30 June 1536 (St Clare Byrne 1981:440–1). Anne Parr is mentioned in a number of sources, including John Husee to Lady Lisle, 29 January 1538, John Husee to Lady Lisle, 29 June 1537 and John Husee to Lady Lisle, 3 August 1537 (St Clare Byrne 1981:79, 147 and 157). Scott 1908 recounts the history of the Strickland family and Catherine's time at Sizergh. Strickland 1844:14–5 gives details of Catherine's apartments there. Commission for the Council of the North, 1530 records Tunstall's appointment to the council (Williams 1967). The Commissioners of the North to Wolsey, 27 March 1525 lists Lord Latimer's father as one of its members (*L&P IV*:532). The Complete Peerage vol VII 1929:479 recounts the history of the Latimer family. Latimer's father's presence is recorded in Ceremonial upon Wolsey's receiving the Cardinal's hat, 15 November 1515 (*L&P II*:304). *L&P IV*:2929 contains the petition to the Pope requesting that he grant Henry VIII a divorce. *L&P IV*:3062 describes the legal action taken by Latimer's brothers over their father's estate. Accusations declared by Thomas Wood, gentleman, against William Nevyll, 30 December 1532 (*L&P V*:694) contains William Neville's activities. The quote from *Lamentation* is from p62.

4. A PILGRIMAGE OF GRACE

The Ten Articles are in Bray 1994:162–70. Elton 1977 discusses the dissolution of the monasteries. Williams 1967:770–1 contains the Act for the Dissolution of the Monasteries and Wriothesley's Chronicle vol I p43 records the passing of the Act. The trouble at Hexham is in *L&PXI*:203–4. Information on the Lincolnshire uprising comes from Dodds and Dodds 1915 vol I and St Clare Byrne 1968:140. Some of the rumours are contained in Captain Cobbler's Depositions, November 1536 (*L&P XI*:389). Nicholas Melton's deposition (*L&P XI*:321–3) contains details of the uprising. Christopher Ascugh to Cromwell, 6 October 1536 (*L&P XI*:225) records that by 6 October 40,000 men were in arms in Lincolnshire. Henry's 'Answer to the Petitions of the Traitors and Rebels in Lincolnshire' is in St Clare Byrne 1968:141. Darcy to Henry VIII, 6 October 1536 (*L&P XI*:223) states that the Lincolnshire beacons could be seen in Yorkshire. *L&P XII ptI*:4–8 contains Aske's deposition. Aske's first proclamation is from Dodds and Dodds 1915 vol I:148. Herbert 1870:596 states that Aske called the rebellion a Pilgrimage of Grace. Dent p26 contains the quote by Bishop Latimer. Sir Robert Tyrwhyt and Others to Lord Hussey, 4 October 1536 (*L&P XI*:218) contains the threat to Lord Hussey. The attack on his house is in Lord Hussey to the Council, October 1536 (*L&P XI*:341). Aske, in *L&P 12 pt I*:4 notes that Lords Latimer, Lumley and Westmoreland had been taken by the commons. The declarations of Archbishop Lee (*L&P XII pt*

2:465) contains the warning to Latimer to stay his tenants. Herbert 1870:598 describes the capture of Pomfret Castle and the rebels' oath. Aske's deposition (*L&P XII pt I*:5) contains Latimer's arrival with an army at Pomfret. Henrys response to the rebels' petition is in St Clare Byrne 1968:151-155. Dodds and Dodds 1915 vol I:377 contains Latimer's query about making war against the king. Aske's Deposition (*L&P XII pt I*:7–8) contains the meeting with Norfolk at Doncaster. Henry VIII to Robert Aske, 15 December 1536 (*L&P XI*:529) invites Aske to visit court. Aske to Darcy, 8 January 1537 (*L&P XII pt I*:22) records his discussions with Henry. Latimer's dilemma following the attack on Snape is in his letter to the Lord Admiral, 20 January 1537 (*L&P XII pt*2:74–5). Shrewsbury to Henry VIII, 20 January 1537 (*L&P XII pt 2*:73) reports the attack on Snape. The rumours that Latimer had fled are contained in two contemporary reports of Hallam's Rebellion (*L&PXII pt 2*:92 and 104). Norfolk to the Earl of Sussex, 8 February 1537 (*L&P XII pt*2:150) states that Latimer was at Doncaster. Dodds and Dodds 1915 vol II:60 describes Bigod's rebellion. Sir Ralph Eure to Henry VIII, 25 January 1537 (*L&P XII pt 2*:114) notes William Neville's pursuit of Bigod. Aske to the commons, January 1537 (*L&P XII pt I*:63) and Sir Robert Constable to Francis Bigod, 18 January 1537 (*L&P XII pt I*:66–7) contain the attempts by the Pilgrims' leaders to end Bigod's rebellion.

5. NOT MUCH FAVOUR

Norfolk to Cromwell, 2 June 1537 and 16 June 1537 contain discussions regarding Lord Latimer (*L&P XII pt 2*:7 and 35). John Earl of Oxford to Cromwell, 8 September 1537 (*L&P XII pt 2*:244) contains the examinations into Thomas Neville's conduct. John Earl of Oxford to Cromwell, 4 January 1537 (*L&P XII pt I*:12), Dodds and Dodds 1915 vol II:25, *L&P XI*:25 and *L&P XII pt1*:17 records Marmaduke's arrest. *L&P XIX pt2*:405 records payments made to Marmaduke Neville by Catherine in September 1544. The quote of Latimer's letter to Sir William Musgrave is from *L&P XII pt I*:62. Bribes to Cromwell are contained in Latimer to Cromwell, 12 April 1537 (*L&P XII pt 2*:414), Cromwell's Accounts from 1537 to 1539 (*L&PXIV pt 2*:320) and Latimer to Cromwell, 30 September 1537 (Strickland 1844:20). John Husee to Lord Lisle, 16 October 1537 (St Clare Byrne 1981 vol IV:425) suggests that William Parr receive a peerage. His appointment to a peerage is in John Husee to Lord Lisle, 7 March 1539, John Husee to Lady Lisle, 9 March 1539 and John Husee to Lord Lisle, 12 March 1539 (all St Clare Byrne 1981:412, 415, 417). William's role at the reception of Anne of Cleves is in *L&P XIV pt2*:200–1. *L&P XVIII pt I*:47 contains the quote on Anne Bourchier's adultery. William's letter to Cromwell dated 20 April 1532 is in Farrer 1923:62-63. The *Legend of Sir Nicholas Throckmorton* (Nichols 1874:6–8) contains Catherine's intervention on behalf of her uncle. Strickland 1844:24 claims that Catherine was responsible for Cromwell's fall. A number of records refer to Latimer's presence at the border, including L&P XVII:229 and 387. The Privy Council to the Commissioners at York, 1 October 1542 (*L&P XVII*:512) states that Latimer had been chosen to meet James V. The grant of the forest to Latimer is in *L&P XVII*:256. *L&P XVIII pt I*:199 refers to Latimer's death.

6. BETTER YOUR MISTRESS THAN YOUR WIFE

Catherine's letter to Seymour referring to her desire to marry him in 1543 is from Crawford 2002:222. For a discussion of the

Seymour family, see Seymour 1972 and Norton 2009a. MacLean 1869 describes Thomas's rise to prominence. Sir Ralph Sadleir to the Lord Cromwell, 14 July 1538 (MacLean 1869:4) sets out Norfolk's hopes of arranging a marriage between his daughter and Thomas in 1538. Norfolk to the Council, December 1546 (*L&P XXI pt2*:283) records that the Duke raised the marriage again in the 1540s. Sir Gawen Carew's Deposition, December 1546 (*L&P XXI pt2*:285) states that the duchess did not want to marry Seymour. Chapuys to Charles V, 19 November 1541 (*CSP6 pt2*:396) records that Henry sent the ladies from court when he learned of Catherine Howard's adultery. Chapuys to Charles V, 15 January 1543 (*L&P XVIII pt I*:30) contains the recall of Princess Mary. A tailor's bill addressed to Lady Latimer dated 16 February 1543 is in *L&P XVIII ptI*:266. Strickland 1844:27 suggests that Catherine and Thomas met at religious meetings. For details of the attempts made by Anne of Cleves and her family to obtain a re-marriage, see Norton 2009b. Chapuys to Charles V, 9 February 1542 (*CSP 6 ptI*:468) records Henry's entertainment of ladies following Catherine Howard's condemnation. Chapuys to Charles V, 25 February 1542 (*CSP 6 ptI*:473) states the ambassador's opinion that it was unlikely that Henry was contemplating a swift remarriage. Smith 1971:231 comments on Henry's ill health. Henry's contemporary, George Constantine, mentioned the king's sore leg in the late 1530s (1831:75). Marillac's Impression of Henry VIII is in Williams 1967:393–4. Chapuys to Charles V, 25 February 1542 (*CSP 6 ptI*:473) contains the quote about the lack of virgins at court. *Chronicle of Henry VIII* (p107) states Henry's desire to marry a widow. Chapuys' despatches of 15 January 1543 and 22 February 1543 (*L&P XVIII ptI*:30 and 107) record Henry's attentions to Princess Mary. Chapuys to Charles V, 27 July 1543

(*L&P XVIII ptI:444*) reports Anne of Cleves' claims that Catherine was 'inferior to her in beauty'. George Constantine 1831:59–60 comments on Henry's hopes of fathering more children. Gordon p15 records Catherine's comments about preferring to be Henry's mistress than his wife. *Chronicle of Henry VIII* (pp107–8) contains Henry's proposal to Catherine. Catherine Parr to Thomas Seymour (Crawford 2002:222) records Catherine's belief that she was called by God to marry Henry. Catherine's letter to Henry is from Savage 1949:91. Lisle to Parr, 20 June 1543 (*L&P XVIII pt I:418*) states that Catherine and her sister were prominent at court and that Elizabeth was also there. Privy Purse Expenses of Princess Mary (Madden 1831:185) note Catherine's gifts to Mary. In Catherine to Lord Parr, 20 July 1543 (*L&P XVIII pt I:498*) she informs her brother of her marriage. The marriage licence is in *L&P XVIII pt I:478*. Catherine and Henry's wedding is described in *L&P XVIII pt I:483*). Wriothesley to the Duke of Suffolk, 16 July 1543 (*L&P XVIII pt I:490*) contains the favourable report of Catherine.

7. CATHERINE THE QUEEN

Strickland 1844:35 records the appointment of members of Catherine's family to her household. The *L&PXXI pt I:478* lists the queen's ladies. *L&P XIX pt 2:484* lists Catherine's payments for messengers to her sister. *L&P XVIII pt II:272* records the ennoblement of Catherine's brother and uncle. The quotes from the *Legend of Sir Nicholas Throckmorton* are from pp10–15. Francis Goldsmith's letter to Catherine is in *L&P XVIII pt II:283*. Van Der Delft to Charles V, 18 June 1545 (*CSP 8:130*) records Catherine's secretary in Germany. Records of Catherine's purchases of material for clothes are in Bill of Huettson, draper (*L&P XXI pti:321*) and

Bill of Symond Loo, Mercer (*L&P XIX pt II*:400). Catherine's silkwoman and goldsmith are referred to in *L&P XIX pt 2*:404. Bill of George Brystow, draper (*L&P XXI pt I*:321) records Catherine's purchase of material for Margaret Neville's coat, clothes for her fools and livery for her minstrels and players. *L&P XX pt2*:911 outlines Catherine's footmen's uniforms. Vaughan's letters to Paget of 4 January 1545 (*L&P XX pt I*:10), 5 January 1545 (*L&P XX pt I*:14), 17 June 1545 (*L&P XX pt I*:470) and 7 January 1546 (*L&P XXI ptI*:13) refer to the debt owed by Catherine to Vaughan's wife for items delivered. Catherine's minstrels, players and two of her fools are mentioned in the bill of George Brystow, draper (*L&PXXI pti*:321). *L&P XIX pt2*:404 lists the payment for Lady Audley's fool. It also includes references to Catherine's greyhounds, her gifts of venison and her parrots. The quote on Henry's satisfaction with Catherine is from the *Chronicle of Henry VIII* p108. Charles V to Chapuys, 5 March 1544 (*CSP 7*:70) states that Catherine was influential. Charles's request for personal news of Henry and Catherine is in his letter of 8 November 1543 (*CSP 6 pt2*:519). Charles's instructions to the Duke of Juano are in *CSP 6 pt2*:537–8. The visit is recorded in *Hall's Chronicle* 1904:345. Chapuys to Granvelle, 1 January 1544 (*CSP 7*:13–4) contains the reception of Don Luis de Avila. Chapuys's letters to Philip of Spain, 13-22 April 1544 and 10July 1544 (*CSP 7*:110 and 243–4) records Catherine's pleasure at the news of Philip of Spain's marriage. *CSP 8*:232 records Van Der Delft's discussion with Catherine at Guildford. The visit of the Duke of Najera is recorded in Chapuys to Charles V, 18 February 1544 (*CSP 7*:55) and De Gante 1831. Chapuys to Granvelle, 27 May 1544 (*CSP 7*:182) describes the visit of the Duke of Alberquerque. Anonymous letter of an Englishman, 22 May 1544 (*CSP 7*:174) contains Francis's gift of a ring.

8. BELOVED MOTHER

Henry's favourable treatment of Mary is in Chapuys to Mary of Hungary, 24 September 1542 and 23 December 1542 (*CSP 6 pt2*:138 a d 190). Chapuys to Charles V, 13 August 1543 (*CSP 6 pt2*:459) records that Catherine treated Mary favourably. The quote in which Catherine told Chapuys that she did her duty towards Mary is in *CSP8*:2. Strickland 1844:37 records Catherine's concern when Mary was ill. The suit made for Richard Baldwin is in *L&P XX pt2*:184. Edward's letter to Catherine concerning Mary's interest in foreign dances and his letter to Mary are in Nichols 1862:9 and 2. Sir John Cheke to Henry Bullinger, 1553 (Williams 1967:395) and *A Description of Edward VI* by John Foxe (Williams 1967:394) praise Edward. Edward's letters to Catherine are in Halliwell 1848:4 and 9. *Diary of Edward VI* (North 2005:15) records that Edward began his studies at six. Catherine's letter of 28 February 1545 (*L&P XX ptI*:117) contains her appeal in favour of George Tresham. Mary of Hungary's enquiry about whether the royal family remained together is in Layton to Henry VIII, 16 December 1543 (*L&P XVIII pt2*:269). Elizabeth's letter to Catherine is in Wood 1846:176–7. *Hall's Chronicle* 1904:353 records the grant of the colleges, chantries and hospitals to Henry. Cox to Paget, 29 October 1546 (*L&P XX pt2*:147) notes the appeal planned by Oxford University. Catherine's letter to Cambridge University is dated 26 February 1546 (Crawford 2002:220). Catherine's letter to the Dean and Fellows of Stoke dated 24 March 1544 (Withrow 2009:136) and her letter to the Dean, Dr Matthew Parker dated 14 November 1544 (Withrow 2009:145–6) demonstrate that she maintained an interest in the college. Matthew Parker to the Queen's Council, May 1546 (*L&P XXI ptI*:14) appeals to Catherine. Haugaard

1969:347 suggests that Catherine was involved in the appointment of Edward's tutors. Strickland 1844:37 comments on the similarity between Edward and Catherine's handwriting. Dowling 1987:60 points out that there is no evidence that Catherine appointed Edward's tutors. Ascham's comments are from 1934:119. Edward's letter to Elizabeth is dated 5 December 1546 (Halliwell 1848:21). *The Acts of Succession* are in Williams 1967:452–6.

9. REGENT GENERAL OF ENGLAND

The war with Scotland is described in Scarisbrick 1968:560–3 and *Hall's Chronicle* 1905:323–39. Shrewsbury and others to the Queen and Council, 2 August 1544 (*L&P XIX pt 2*:3) contains Catherine's interest in Scottish affairs. The Queen to Lord Evers and Wharton, 2 September 1544 (*L&P XIX pt2*:89) contains the quote on the defence of the borders. The Council with the Queen to Shrewsbury, 11 August 1544 (*L&P XIX pt2*:29) contains Catherine's orders for the provisioning of troops. Catherine's issue of passports is in the Council with the queen to Shrewsbury, 21 August 1544 (*L&P XIX pt2*:54). The Council with the King to the council with the queen, 5 September 1544 (*L&P XIX pt2*:101) records Catherine's official title as regent. Catherine's proclamation about the plague is in *L&P XIX pt2*:127. *L&P XIX pt2*:405–6 records that Catherine sent servants to enquire about the plague. Catherine's letters to Henry are dated 31 July 1544 and 25 August 1544 (Wood 1846:173–4 and 174–5). Henry VIII to the Privy Council and Others, 11 August 1544 (St Clare Byrne 1936:362–3) refers to just and lawful quarrels and requests supplies. The Council with the King to the Council with the Queen, 14 September 1544 (*L&P XIX pt2*:119) refers to the recruitment of 4,000 troops. Henry's letter to Catherine is in St Clare Byrne 1936:365–6. *Wriothesley's Chronicle vol I* 1875:149 contains Catherine's orders that England celebrate Henry's victory. Catherine's prayer during the French campaign is in Strype 1822 vol II pt I:205–6. Cranmer's life is described by his secretary, Ralph Morice 1859:239 and Foxe (Nichols 1859). Henry VIII to Wotton, 5 August 1544 (St Clare Byrne 1936:368–9) contains Henry's determination to keep Charles informed of all offers of peace received from Francis. MacLean 1869:20 contains details of Thomas Seymour's conduct during the war. Catherine's last meeting with Chapuys is recorded in his despatch of 9 May 1545 (*CSP* 8:103–10). *Wriothesley's Chronicle vol I* 1875:157 records Francis's attempt to capture Boulogne in July 1545. Henry's letter to Charles on 23 June 1545 is in *CSP* 8:140. The preparations for the defence of England are in Van Der Delft to Charles V, 18 June 1545 (*CSP* 8:130). *Wriothesley's Chronicle vol I* 1875:157 recounts the French invasion. Attempts to raise the Mary Rose are described in Suffolk to Paget, 1 August 1545 (*L&P XX pt2:2*) and Lisle and St John to Paget, 9 August 1545 (*L&P XX pt2:39*).

10. THE LAMENTATION OF A SINNER

Bernard 2007:579–89 discusses Henry's beliefs during the 1540s. Henry's last speech to Parliament is in St Clare Byrne 1936:420. A discussion of Anne Boleyn's religious beliefs can be found in Norton 2008. A contemporary account of Anne's religion is in Latymer 1990. Kingston to Cromwell, 18 May 1536, letter VI (Singer 1825:229) records that Anne swore her innocence on the sacrament. There is a discussion of Humanism and Catherine's beliefs in Dowling 1987. McCornica 1965 claims that

Catherine was not a true Protestant. The extract from *Prayers or Meditations* is from Parr 1831:18. King 1985:47 discusses *Prayers or Meditations*. Two bills for the presentation copies for *Prayers or Meditations* are printed in Rose-Troup 1911:40–3. Haugaard 1969 discusses the non-controversial nature of the work and its popularity. Catherine's letter to Mary is dated 20 September 1544 and is in Wood 1846:181–2. James 2008:206 suggests that Catherine translated the Gospel of St Matthew. Nicholas Udall's praise of Catherine is in Strype 1822 vol II pt I:203. A number of records of the privy council in the summer and autumn of 1545 refer to Seymour in relation to the navy, for example of 1 June, 9 June, 18 June, 9 July, 1 October and 3 October (*APC I*). Thomas Seymour was kept busy as Master of the Ordinance, for example, the privy council minutes for 29 December 1545, 7 January 1546, 20 January 1546, 24 January 1546, 22 February 1546 and 4 May 1546 refer to requests made to Seymour for supplies (*APC I*). Seymour 1972:101 notes the gift of Seymour Place. Elizabeth's preface to her translation of Margaret of Navarre's work is in Wood 1846:177–9. Elizabeth's preface of John Calvin is in Marcus, Mueller and Rose 2002:10. Mueller 1988:23 and Haugaard 1969:356–7 discuss *Lamentation of a Sinner*. The extracts from are from pp57, 52 and 64.

11. DANGER FOR THE GOSPEL

The quote from Foxe is from p553–4. *Hall's Chronicle* 1904:342–3 contains details of the arrests of the men in Windsor. Starkey 2004:755–6 notes the threats against Wriothesley. The attack on Cranmer is in the account of his secretary, Ralph Morice (Nichols 1859:251–5). Foxe (Pollard 1903:29–35) gives the story concerning Cranmer's secretary and his book attacking the Six Articles. The arrest of Cromwell is described in the *Chronicle of Henry VIII* pp97–9. Smith 1971:31 describes the plot against Bishop Gardiner. The Examinations of Anne Askew by John Bale 1831:5–7 describes her arrest and interrogation. Details of her life are in Fraser 2002:473. Anne's arrests and interrogations are recorded in her own accounts 1831:10–20, 22 and 27–8. The rumour that Catherine's religious beliefs came from her ladies is from Chapuys to Mary of Hungary, 29 January 1547 (*CSP* 8:555). Dowling 1987 discusses the plot against Catherine. Henry's illness in March 1546 is from Van Der Delft to Charles V, 13 March 1546 (*CSP* 8:320). The plot against Catherine is from Foxe pp555–61. *Wriothesley's Chronicle* 1875:170 records the death of Anne Askew. Levin 1986:125 points out that Catherine survived by hiding her intelligence.

12. YIELDED HIS SPIRIT TO ALMIGHTY GOD

Henry VIII to Charles V, 13 October 1545 (*CSP* 8:267) and Charles V to St Mauris (Imperial Ambassador to France, 25 November 1545 (*CSP* 8:277) discuss the emperor's offers to mediate. *Wriothesley's Chronicle* 1875:174 records Dudley's visit to France. Madden 1831:186–9 details the jewellery given to Mary by Henry. The gifts to Prince Edward are noted in his letter of 4 August 1546 (Halliwell 1848:15). Edward to Catherine Parr, 12 August 1546 (Halliwell 1848:15–16) contains his enquiries on how best to receive the French Admiral. The French Admiral's visit is recorded in *Wriothesley's Chronicle* 1875:172–4 and *Hall's Chronicle* 1904:359–60. *Hall's Chronicle* 1904:354 records the reception of Henry's last speech. His speech is from St Clare Byrne 1936:418–9. Selve's reports of 14 and 25 September 1546 (*L&P XXI Pt* 2:37, 67) note that Henry was hunting in Guildford. His reports of 5 and 12 October 1546 (*L & P XXI Pt* 2:107 and 122) mentions the move to Windsor and his audience with Henry. Van Der Delft to Charles V, 14 December 1546 (*CSP* 8:523) records Henry's illness. *Wriothesley's Chronicle* 1875:176 describes the arrests of Norfolk and Surrey. John Gate, Sir Richard Southwell and Wymond Carew to Henry VIII, 14 December 1546 (*L&P XXI Pt* 2:277) records the visit of the commissioners to Kenninghall. Norrfolk to the Council, December 1546 (*L&P XXI Pt II*:283) contains the duke's submission. The evidence obtained against Surrey is in *L&P XXI Pt* 2:284-5. The charges against Norfolk and Surrey are in St Clare Byrne 1936:422-3. Edward to Elizabeth, 5 December 1546 notes that the two children had been separated (Halliwell 1848:21). Van Der Delft to Charles V, 24 December 1546 (*CSP* 8:533) speculates on Catherine spending Christmas away from Henry. Edward to Catherine Parr, 14 January 1547 (Halliwell 1848:23) thanks her for her New Year's gift. *APC I*, 23 January 1547 p566 details Thomas Seymour's return to court and his appointment to the Privy Council. Van Der Delft to the Queen Dowager, 10 February 1547 (*CSP* 9:19) singled out Hertford, Wriothesley, Dudley and Paget as the new powers in England. Scarisbrick 1968:629 discusses Henry's new Will. Van Der Delft to Charles V, 10 July 1547 (*CSP* 9:123) contains Mary's doubts on the Will. Smith 1971 and Levine 1964 discuss the validity of the Will with differing arguments. The Will is in St Clare Byrne 1936:424. *Chronicle of King Henry VIII* 1889:152 claims that Catherine and Henry had an emotional reunion. Selve and La Garde to Francis I, 10 January 1547 (*L&P XXI Pt II*:360) reports that Catherine and Mary were not allowed to see Henry. The quote on Henry's death is from *Hall's Chronicle* 1904:361.

13. WEEKS BE SHORTER AT CHELSEA

Jordan 1968:51 records the activities of Edward Seymour after Henry's death. *ACP II*:15–17 contains the council meeting on 6 February 1547. The new honours proposed are in *ACP II*:35 for 18 February 1547. Thomas's appointment as High Admiral of England is in the minutes for 10 February 1547 (*ACP II*:28). Van Der Delft to Charles V, 16 June 1547 (*CSP* 9:123–4) claims Thomas planned to marry Mary. John Fowler's Deposition (Nichols 1862: cxv–cxvi) contains Edward VI's opinion on who Thomas should marry. The quote from Thomas's letter to Elizabeth is from Seymour 1972:216. Elizabeth's response is in Wood 1846:191–2. Privy Council report 17 January 1549 (*ACP II*:238) and The Articles of High Treason and other Misdemeanours against the Kynges Majeste and his Crowne objected to Sir Thomas Seymour, knight, Lord Seymour of Sudeley, and High Admiral of England (*ACP II*:251, 23 February 1549) record Thomas's attempts to marry Elizabeth. An account of Henry's funeral is contained in a book in the College of Arms (Strickland 1844:85–6). Edward's letters to Catherine are dated 7 February 1547 and 30 May 1547 and are from Halliwell 1848:25–6 and 33–4. Van Der Delft to the Queen Dowager, 7 March 1547 (*CSP* 9:48-49) records Catherine's plans to leave London. Van Der Delft to Charles V, 27 April 1547 (*CSP* 9:85) notes that Mary had left Catherine. Chelsea manor is described in Colvin 1982. Catherine and Thomas's letters are from MacLean 1869:46, 44–5 and Crawford 2002:221–2). The Articles against Thomas (*APC II*:251) claim that he married Catherine too soon after Henry's death to be sure of any child's paternity.

14. MUCH OFFENDED BY THE MARRIAGE

Mary's letter to Thomas is from MacLean 1869:47. John Fowler (Nichols 1862:cxv) contain Thomas's attempts to gain Edward VI's support for the marriage. Article 23 of the accusations against Thomas speaks of the contents of Edward's letter (*APC II*:252). Edward's letter responding to Catherine's in which she accepted Thomas is dated 25 June 1547 (Strype vol II part I 1822:208–9). Van Der Delft to the Queen Dowager, 4 May 1547 (*CSP* 9:88–9) observes the change in Catherine's mourning clothes. The rumour that Catherine and Thomas planned to marry is in Van Der Delft to Charles V, 16 June 1547 (*CSP* 9:104). Somerset's agreement to speak to Catherine to further Seymour's suit is in article 23 of the accusations against Seymour in 1549 (*APC II*:252). Van Der Delft to Charles V, 10 July 1547 (*CSP* 9:123) contains Mary's comments on the marriage. Elizabeth's diplomatic response to Mary is in Woods 1846:193–4. The rivalry between Catherine and the Duchess of Somerset is detailed in Strickland 1844:100. *Chronicle of Henry VIII* (p160) records Catherine's comments on her treatment by the Duchess. Edward VI's Diary (North 2005:20–1) notes that Somerset was offended by the marriage. John Fowler (Nichols 1862:cxvii) discusses the dispute over Catherine's jewels. Deposition of William Wightman, 23 January 1549 (*Hatfield MSS Pt XIII* 1915:24–5) claims Thomas sought written depositions on Catherine' jewels and approached Mary for support. Catherine's letters to Thomas (Crawford 2002:222, Strickland 1844:98–9 and Haynes 1740:61) contain Catherine's complaints about Somerset's behaviour. Somerset's confiscation of Anne of Cleves' properties are discussed in Norton 2009b. The quote from The *Legend of Sir Nicholas Throckmorton* is in Nichols 1874:17. Thomas's comments on his daughter's status are in The Deposition of Sir

Richard Cotton (Knighton 1992:84). John Fowler (Nichols 1862: cxvii) refers to the money given by Thomas to Edward.

15. LADY SEYMOUR OF SUDELEY

Deposition of Henry Grey (Knighton 1992:83) records Thomas's request for Jane's wardship. Edward VI's Diary (North 2005:91–5) discusses the king's proposed marriage to Elizabeth of France. The Scholemaster (Ascham 1934:97–8) contains Jane's comments on her parents. Dorset to Seymour (Haynes 1740:78) notes Dorset's views on discipline for Jane. Ascham's comments are from p73, 78 and 120–1. Lady Cecil to Jane Grey (Knighton 1992:286) is evidence of a correspondence in Greek. Strype 1822 vol I pt I:194 contains Thomas's comments on the blackest parliament. Edward VI's testimony against Thomas Seymour (Nichols 1862:57) records Thomas's attempts to involve the king in his plots. MacLean 1869:58 details Thomas's plot to become Edward's guardian. John Hayward 1993:97–8 contains the quote on the Seymour brothers. Van Der Delft to Prince Philip, 18 August 1547 (*CSP* 9:136) suggests that Thomas did not sail as he was required at home. Van Der Delft to Charles V, 7 July 1548 (*CSP* 9:277) notes Thomas's refusal to sail in July 1548. John Fowler (Nichols 1862: cxvi) refers to the quarrel between the brothers. The quote on Somerset not being favourable to priests is in Richard Hilles to Henry Bullinger, 25 February 1547 (Robinson 1846:257–8). Locke 1911 and Bush 1975 describe Somerset's religious changes. John Hayward 1993:68 discusses the Edwardian Injunctions. The text of the injunctions is in Bray 1994. Jordan 1968:171 discusses the Book of Common Prayer. The quote from Cranmer's letter to John A Lasco is dated 4 July 1548 (Robinson 1846:17). Van

Der Delft to Charles V, 5 December 1547 (*CSP* 9:221) comments that Catherine no longer heard mass. The Seventh Sermon Before King Edward, 19 April 1549 by Latimer 1824:145 contains Hugh Latimer's comments on Catherine's household. Houlbrooke 1974:21–2, 83 details Catherine's employment of John Parkhurst. The quote from Parkhurst's letter is in Houlbrooke 1974:83. Mueller 1988 discussed the publication of *Lamentation*. Cecil's comments are in *Lamentations of a Sinner*, preface p31. James 2008 287–8, Bradford 1936:42–3 and Jordan 1968:366–7 recount William's divorce. *Chronicle of Henry VIII* (pp137–9) claims that Catherine disapproved of the divorce. William Parr to Edward VI, December 1547 (Lemon 1856:5) contains William's petition for a divorce. Francis Bourgoyne to John Calvin, 22 January 1552 (Williams 1967:415) describes Somerset as all but king.

16. THE QUEEN WAS JEALOUS

Thomas and Elizabeth's conduct is taken from Examination of Katherine Ashley on 2 February 1549 and Katherine Ashley's final Handwritten Deposition, late February 1549 (Marcus, Mueller and Rose 2002:25–6 and 29–30) and The Confession of Katherine Ashley (Haynes 1740:99–100). The Life of Jane Dormer (Clifford 1887:86–7) criticises Elizabeth's conduct. Gordon p44 claims that Elizabeth bore Thomas a child. The *Legend of Throckmorton* (Nichols 1874:18) states that Catherine was barren and that her conception was miraculous. Catherine's letter to Lady Wriothesley is in Nichols 1831:14. Elizabeth's comments on Catherine's pregnancy are in Elizabeth to Catherine Parr, 31 July 1548 (Marcus, Mueller and Rose 2002:20). Elizabeth to Catherine Parr (MacLean 1869:55–6) describes the final interview between the queen and her stepdaughter. Elizabeth's letters to the Protector are dated 28 January 1549 and 21 February 1549 (Marcus, Mueller and Rose 2002:24 and 32-33). Elizabeth's letter to Thomas is in Marcus, Mueller and Rose 2002:19.

17. NOT WELL HANDLED

Catherine and Thomas's letters are from MacLean 1869:56 and 57. *APC II*, 17 January 1549 p236 accuses Thomas of being a danger to the realm. John Fowler (Nichols 1862:cxvii) describes Thomas's attempts to ingratiate himself with Edward. *Wriothesley's Chronicle, vol II* 1877:5 records the drought and the plague. Sudeley Castle is described in Dent 1877:164-7. Mary's letter is dated 9 August 1548 (Strickland 1844:110). Somerset to Thomas Seymour, 1 September 1548 (McLean 1869:67) contains his congratulations on the birth of Mary Seymour. Lady Tyrwhitt's Deposition is in Strickland 1844:112-3. Catherine's Will is from Strickland 1844:114. Thomas Seymour to the Marquis of Dorset, 17 September 1548 (Haynes 1740:78) sets out his pain on Catherine's death. Deposition of Sir Richard Cotton (Knighton 1992:84) states that Thomas would mourn for a year. A Brevyate of th'entirement of the lady Katheryn Parre Quene Dowager, late Wiefe to King Henry th'eight, and after wife to Sr Thomas Lord Seymour of Sudeley & highe Admirall of Englond (Dent 1877:174) details Catherine's death and funeral. Catherine's epitaph is quoted from Nash 1789:9. Deposition of Henry Manners, Earl of Rutland (Knighton 1992:86-7) contains his comments on Catherine's death. William Parr's Deposition notes Seymour's attempts to enlist him (Knighton 1992:88). Thomas's letter to Dorset and negotiations over Lady Jane Grey are in Haynes 1740:75-6 and 78. Seymour's treasonous activities are in the charges against him listed in *APC II* (23 February 1549). Van Der Delft to Charles V, 27 January 1549 (*CSP* 9:332) claims that Thomas tried to abduct Edward. Van Der Delft to Charles V, 8 February 1549 (*CSP* 9:340) includes Paget's claims that Thomas was a great rascal. *APC II*, 22 February 1549 and 23 February 1549 records attempts to interrogate Thomas. Thomas's answer is in *APC II*, 24 February 1549. *APC II*, 25 February 1549 notes that Somerset asked to be excused from condemning his brother. Edward VI's desire for justice to be done is noted in *APC II*, 24 February 1549. Seymour's death is described in Strype 1822, vol II pt I p198.

18. HOW MANY HUSBANDS WILL SHE HAVE?

The list of Mary Seymour's belongings is taken from Strype 1822 vol II pt I p201. The Duchess of Suffolk's letter to Cecil is in Strype 1822, vol II pt I p202. *APC II*, 13 March 1550:411 contains the grant for Mary's upkeep. For example, Gordon p54 and Strickland 1844:131 claim that Mary married Sir Edward Bushel. Friend-James 2002:31 claims descent from Mary. Bradford 1936:45 describes the later life of William Parr. The fall of Somerset is in Edward VI's Diary (North 2005) and the *Diary of Henry Machyn* (1848). John Hayward 1993:100 blames the rivalry of their wives for the fall of the Seymour brothers. There are two accounts of the discovery of Catherine's grave, 'Account of Mr Lucas' opening of the Tomb by Julia Bockett (taken from Dent 1877:316) and Nash 1789:2–4.

BIBLIOGRAPHY

PRIMARY SOURCES

Acts of the Privy Council of England, New Series, vols I–II, ed. Dasent, J.R., (London, 1890–1893)

Ascham, R., *The Scholemaster*, Mayor, J.E.B., ed. (London, 1934)

Askew, A., 'The Examinations and Confession of Anne Askew' in *Writings of Edward the Sixth, William Hugh, Queen Catherine Parr, Anne Askew, Lady Jane Grey, Hamilton and Balnaves* (London, 1831)

Bale, J., 'The Examination of Anne Askew' in *Writings of Edward the Sixth, William Hugh, Queen Catherine Parr, Anne Askew, Lady Jane Grey, Hamilton and Balnaves* (London, 1831)

Bray, G. (ed.), *Documents of the English Reformation* (Cambridge, 1994)

Calendar of State Papers, Spanish vols VI-IX, eds., De Gayangos, P., Hume, M.A.S., and Tyler, R. (London,1888–1949)

Clifford, H., *The Life of Jane Dormer Duchess of Feria*, ed. Estcourt, E.E. and Stevenson (London, 1887)

Constantine, G., *Transcript of an Original Manuscript, Containing a Memorial from George Constantyne to Thomas Lord Cromwell*, ed.

Amyot, T. (Archaeologia 23, 1831)

Crawford, A. (ed.), *Letters of the Queens of England* (Stroud, 2002)

Dent, J.M., *Sermons by Hugh Latimer sometime Bishop of Worcester* (London)

Farrer, W. (ed.), *Records Relating to the Barony of Kendale*, vol I (Kendal, 1923)

Foxe, J., *The Acts and Monuments of John Foxe*, vols V and VI (New York, 1965)

Gante, P., de, *Narrative of the Visit of the Duke of Najera to England in the Year 1543–4*, Madden, F., ed. (Archaeologia 23, 1831)

Hall, E., *The Triumphant Reigne of Kyng Henry the VIII*, vol II (London, 1904)

Halliwell, J.O. (ed.), *Letters of the Kings of England, 2 vols* (London, 1848)

Haynes, S. (ed.), *Collection of State Papers Relating to Affairs in the Reigne of King Henry VIII, King Edward VI, Queen Mary and Queen Elizabeth from the year 1542 to 1570 Transcribed from the Original Letters and Other Authentick Memorials left by William Cecil* (London, 1740)

Hayward, J., *The Life and Raigne of King Edward the Sixth*, ed. Beer, B.L. (Kent, 1993)

Historical Manuscripts Commission Calendar of Manuscripts of the Most Hon. The Marquis of Salisbury. Preserved at Hatfield House Part XIII (London, 1915)

Houlbrooke, R.A., *The Letter Book of John Parkhurst* (Norfolk Record Society, 1974)

Hume, M.A.S. (ed.), *Chronicle of King Henry VIII of England* (London, 1889)

Knighton, C.S., (ed.), *Calendar of State Papers Domestic Series of the Reign of Edward VI 1547–1553* (London, 1992)

Latimer, H., *The Sermons of Hugh Latimer*, Watkins, J. (ed.) (London, 1824)

Latymer, W., *Chronickille of Anne Bulleyne*, ed. Dowling, M. (Camden Miscellany XXX, Fourth Series, Vol 39, 1990)

Lemon, R. (ed.), *Calendar of State Papers, Domestic Series, 1547–1580, vol I* (London, 1856)

Letters and Papers, Foreign and Domestic, of the Reign of Henry VIII, vols I–XXI, eds., Brewer, J.S., Gairdner, J., Brodie, R.H. (London, 1876–1932)

Madden, F., (ed.), *Privy Purse Expenses of the Princess Mary* (London, 1831)

Morice, R., 'Anecdotes and Character of Archbishop Cranmer' in Nichols, J.G. (ed.), *Narratives of the Days of the Reformation* (London, 1859)

Nichols, J.G., (ed.), *The Diary of Henry Machyn* (London, 1848)

Nichols, J.G. (ed.), *Narratives of the Days of the Reformation* (London, 1859)

Nichols, J.G. (ed.), *Literary Remains of King Edward the Sixth* (London, 1862)

Nichols, J.G. (ed.), *The Legend of Sir Nicholas Throckmorton* (London, 1874)

Nicholson, C., *The Annals of Kendal* (London, 1861)

North, J. (ed.), *England's Boy King: The Diary of Edward VI, 1547–1553* (Welwyn Garden City, 2005)

Parr, C., 'Prayers, or Meditations', in *Writings of Edward the Sixth, William Hugh, Queen Catherine Parr, Anne Askew, Lady Jane Grey, Hamilton and Balnaves* (London, 1831)

Parr, C. 'The Lamentation or Complaint of a Sinner', in *Writings of Edward the Sixth, William Hugh, Queen Catherine Parr, Anne Askew, Lady Jane Grey, Hamilton and Balnaves* (London, 1831)

Pollard, A.F., (ed.), *Tudor Tracts* (Westminster, 1903)

Robinson, H., (ed.), *Original Letters Relative to the English Reformation*, 2 vols (Cambridge, 1847)

Rose-Troup, F., *Two Book Bills of Katherine Parr* (The Library II, 1911)

Savage, H., (ed.), *The Love Letters of Henry VIII* (London, 1949)

Singer, S.W. (ed.), *The Life of Cardinal Wolsey by William Cavendish* (Chiswick, 1825)

St Clare Byrne, M. (ed.), *The Letters of King Henry VIII* (London, 1936 and 1968)

St Clare Byrne, M. (ed.), *The Lisle Letters*, vol V (Chicago, 1981)

Strype, J., (ed.), *Ecclesiastical Memorials*, vols I–II (1822)

Williams, C.H. (ed.), *English Historical Documents, vol V* (London, 1967)

Wood, M.A.E. (ed.), *Letters of Royal and Illustrious Ladies*, vol II (London, 1846)

Wriothesley, C., *A Chronicle of England During the Reigns of the Tudors*, 2 vols ed. Hamilton, W.D., (London, 1875)

Writings of Edward the Sixth, William Hugh, Queen Catherine Parr, Anne Askew, Lady Jane Grey, Hamilton and Balnaves (London, 1831)

Secondary Sources

Bernard, G.W., *The King's Reformation* (London, 2007)

Bradford, C.A., *Helena Marchioness of Northampton* (London, 1936)

Bush, M.L., *The Government Policy of Protector Somerset* (London, 1975)

Colvin, H.M., *The History of the King's Works*, vol IV (London, 1982)

Complete Peerage, The, vols II and VII (London, 1912 and 1929)

Dent, E., *Annals of Winchcombe and Sudeley* (London, 1877)

Dodds, M.H. and Dodds, R., *The Pilgrimage of Grace, 1536–1537 and the Exeter Conspiracy, 1538, 2 vols* (Cambridge, 1915)

Elton, G.R., *Reform and Reformation* (London, 1977)

Fraser, A., *The Six Wives of Henry VIII* (London, 2002)

Friend-James, B., *Queen Katherine Parr and Friends* (Manchester, 2002)

Gordon, M.A., *Life of Queen Katharine Parr* (Kendal)

Haugaard, W.P., *Katherine Parr: The Religious Convictions of a Renaissance Queen* (Renaissance Quarterly 22, 1969)

Herbert, E., *The History of England under Henry VIII* (London, 1870)

Hume, M., *The Wives of Henry the Eighth* (London)

James, S., *Catherine Parr* (Stroud, 2008)

Jordan, W.K., *Edward VI: The Threshold of Power* (London, 1970)

Kemeys, B. And Raggatt, J., *The Queen who Survived* (London, 1993)

King, J.N., 'Patronage and Piety: The Influence of Catherine Parr, in Hannay M.P. (ed.), *Silent But For The Word* (Ohio, 1985)

Lake, P., and Dowling, M. (eds.), *Protestantism and the National Church in Sixteenth Century England* (London, 1987)

Levin, C., 'John Foxe and the Responsibilities of Queenship' in Rose, M.B. (ed.), *Women in the Middle Ages and the Renaissance* (1986)

Levine, M., *The Last Will and Testament of Henry VIII: A Reappraisal Appraised* (The Historian 26, 1964)

Loades, D., *Henry VIII and his Queens* (Stroud, 1994)

Locke, A.A., *The Seymour Family: History and Romance* (London, 1911)

MacLean, J., *The Life of Sir Thomas Seymour, Knight* (London, 1869)

Marcus, L.S., Mueller, J. and Rose, M.B. (eds.), *Elizabeth I, Collected Works* (Chicago, 2002)

Martienssen, A., *Queen Katherine Parr* (London, 1975)

McConica, J.K., *English Humanists and Reformation Politics* (Oxford, 1965)

Mueller, J., 'A Tudor Queen Finds Her Voice: Katherine Parr's Lamentation of a Sinner' in Dubrow, H. And Strier, R. (eds.), *The Historical Renaissance* (London, 1988)

Nash, T., *Observations on the Time of the Death and Place of Burial of Queen Katharine Parr* (Archaeologia 9, 1789)

Norton, E., *Anne Boleyn, Henry VIII's Obsession* (Stroud, 2008)

Norton, E., *Jane Seymour, Henry VIII's True Love* (Stroud, 2009a)

Norton, E., *Anne of Cleves, Henry VIII's Discarded Bride* (Stroud, 2009b)

Scarisbrick, J.J., *Henry VIII* (Harmondsworth, 1968)

Scott, D., *The Stricklands of Sizergh Castle, Westmorland* (Kendal, 1908)

Seymour, W., *Ordeal by Ambition* (London, 1972)

Smith, L.B., *Henry VIII: The Mask of Royalty* (London, 1971)

Starkey, D., *Six Wives* (London, 2003)

Strickland, A., *Lives of the Queens of England,* vol IV (London, 1844)

Withrow, B.G., *Katherine Parr* (Phillipsburg, 2009)

LIST OF ILLUSTRATIONS

1. Kendal Castle, Cumbria. © Elizabeth Norton.

2. The Parr Chapel in Kendal Church. © Elizabeth Norton.

3. The tomb of Sir William Parr, Catherine's grandfather in the Parr Chapel in Kendal Church. © Elizabeth Norton.

4. Catherine Parr, portrayed as a Protestant heroine. © Jonathan Reeve JR833b53fp484 1500 1550.

5. William Parr, Marquis of Northampton. © Elizabeth Norton.

7. Princess Mary, daughter of Henry VIII and Catherine of Aragon. © Elizabeth Norton.

8. Catherine of Aragon, Henry VIII's first wife. By kind permission of Ripon Cathedral Chapter.

9. Tomb of Thomas, Lord Dacre at Lanercost Priory. © Elizabeth Norton.

10, 11 & 12. Gainsborough Old Hall in Lincolnshire. © Elizabeth Norton.

13 & 14. Interior views of Gainsborough Old Hall. © Elizabeth Norton.

15. A coverlet supposedly embroidered by Catherine during her time at Sizergh Castle. © Elizabeth Norton.

16. Gainsborough Church. © Elizabeth Norton.

17. Sizergh Castle, Cumbria. © Elizabeth Norton.

18. Catherine Howard, Henry VIII's disgraced fifth wife and Catherine's predecessor as queen. © Elizabeth Norton.

19. Thomas Seymour. © Elizabeth Norton.

20. Henry VIII in his prime. By kind permission of Ripon Cathedral Chapter.

21. & 22. Hampton Court. © Elizabeth Norton and © Jonathan Reeve JR1091b20p884 15001550.

23. Anne of Cleves. © Elizabeth Norton.

24. Edward VI. © Jonathan Reeve JR1153b66fp16R 15001550.

25. Catherine's badge in stained glass at Sudeley Castle. © Elizabeth Norton.

26. Catherine's signature during her time as regent of England. © Elizabeth Norton.

27. Princess Elizabeth. © Jonathan Reeve JR998b66fp56 15001600.

28. The Family of Henry VIII. © Jonathan Reeve JR997b66fp40 15001600.

29. Henry VIII reading. © Jonathan Reeve JR1164b4p663 15001550.

30. Catherine Willoughby, Duchess of Suffolk. © Elizabeth Norton.

31. Greenwich Palace. © Jonathan Reeve JR735b46fp186 14501500.

32. Thomas Cranmer, Archbishop of Canterbury, from his memorial in Oxford. © Elizabeth Norton.

33. Whitehall Palace. © Jonathan Reeve JR779b46fp192 14501500.

34. An extract from Henry VIII's Will. © Jonathan Reeve JRCD2 b20p961 15501600.

35, 36 & 37. St George's Chapel, Windsor Castle. 35 and 37,

© Jonathan Reeve B67, 36, © Elizabeth Norton.

38. Thomas Seymour depicted in stained glass at Sudeley Castle. © Elizabeth Norton.

39. Catherine Parr depicted in stained glass at Sudeley Castle. © Elizabeth Norton.

40. Edward Seymour, Duke of Somerset. © Elizabeth Norton.

41. The tomb of Anne Stanhope, Duchess of Somerset, at Westminster Abbey. © Elizabeth Norton.

42. Mary Tudor as queen. By kind permission of Ripon Cathedral Chapter.

43. Lady Jane Grey, depicted in stained glass at Sudeley Castle. © Elizabeth Norton.

44. Sudeley Castle Chapel. © Elizabeth Norton.

45. The Tower of London from a drawing by Anthony van Wyngaerde *c.*1543. © Jonathan Reeve JR1165b4p688 15001550.

46, 47 & 48. Sudeley Castle. © Elizabeth Norton.

49 & 50. The tomb of Catherine Parr at Sudeley. © David Sawtell.

51. Helena, Marchioness of Northampton, as the chief mourner for Elizabeth I. © Elizabeth Norton.

52. Elizabeth I at prayer. © Jonathan Reeve JR1168b4fp747 15501600.

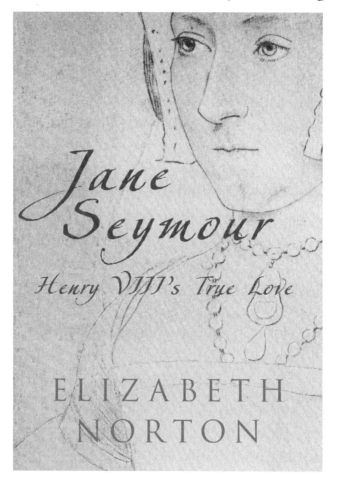

Also available from Amberley Publishing

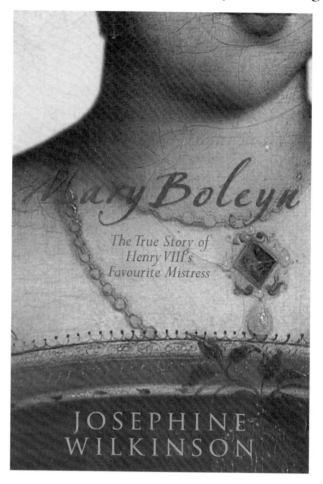

The scandalous true story of Mary Boleyn, infamous sister of Anne, and mistress of Henry VIII

Mary Boleyn, 'the infamous other Boleyn girl', began her court career as the mistress of the king of France. François I of France would later call her 'The Great Prostitute' and the slur stuck. The bête-noir of her family, Mary was married off to a minor courtier but it was not long before she caught the eye of Henry VIII and a new affair began.

Mary would emerge the sole survivor of a family torn apart by lust and ambition, and it is in Mary and her progeny that the Boleyn legacy rests.

£18.99 Hardback
30 colour illustrations
240 pages
978-1-84868-089-0

Also available from Amberley Publishing

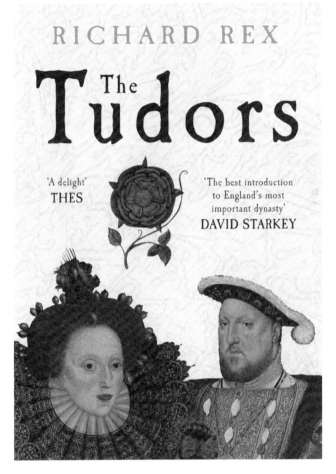

RICHARD REX

The Tudors

'A delight'
THES

'The best introduction
to England's most
important dynasty'
DAVID STARKEY

An intimate history of England's most infamous royal family

'The best introduction to England's most important dynasty' DAVID STARKEY
'A lively overview... Rex is a wry commentator on the game on monarchy' THE GUARDIAN
'Gripping and told with enviable narrative skill. This is a model of popular history... a delight' THES
'Vivid, entertaining and carrying its learning lightly' EAMON DUFFY

The Tudor Age began in August 1485 when Henry Tudor landed with 2000 men at Milford Haven intent on snatching the English throne from Richard III. For more than a hundred years England was to be dominated by the personalities of the five Tudor monarchs, ranging from the brilliance and brutality of Henry VIII to the shrewdness and vanity of the virgin queen, Elizabeth I.

£20.00 Hardback
100 colour illustrations
320 pages
978-1-84868-049-4

Available from all good bookshops or to order direct
please call **01285-760-030**
www.amberley-books.com

INDEX

Index